D1281078

Shakespeare's
Derived Imagery

Shakespeare's Derived Imagery

by

John Erskine Hankins

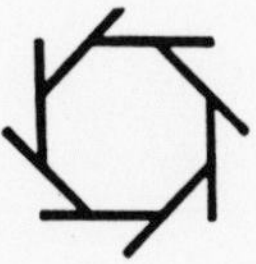

1967
OCTAGON BOOKS, INC.
New York

Reprinted 1967

by special arrangement with the University of Kansas Press

OCTAGON BOOKS, INC.
175 FIFTH AVENUE
NEW YORK, N. Y. 10010

LIBRARY OF CONGRESS CATALOG CARD NUMBER: 67-18767

Printed in U.S.A. by
NOBLE OFFSET PRINTERS, INC.
NEW YORK 3, N. Y.

TO MY WIFE

NELLIE POTTLE HANKINS

THIS BOOK

IS AFFECTIONATELY DEDICATED

Preface

In a study of this kind, involving some hundreds of quoted passages, there is always danger that the main outlines of the work will be obscured by a multiplicity of details. To lighten the reader's burden and the printer's bill, I have adopted the following practices:

1. Passages quoted as parallels to Shakespeare's lines are assigned numbers and letters for quick and easy reference. This will require a good deal of page-turning by the reader, an inconvenience which has seemed unavoidable. The abbreviation "Q." is used with quotation numbers, except in cases where a letter accompanies the number, in order to avoid confusion with page references.

2. I have usually not sought to trace the complete history of critical comments on individual passages but have selected those which seem most pertinent. The reader may wish to compare my suggestions with those in the *Variorum* Shakespeare and other standard editions. References to the older scholarship which I give without assigning a definite source will in most cases be found in the *Variorum* notes.

3. To avoid repeating myself needlessly, I have several times referred the reader to my own earlier book, *The Character of Hamlet and Other Essays,* University of North Carolina Press, 1941.

After completing the first draft of this book, I discovered at the University of Illinois an unpublished Master's thesis by Mr. Charles Byford Garrigus on the parallels between Shakespeare and Palingenius. Mr. Garrigus had noted from the first half of the *Zodiacus Vitae* approximately twenty passages which seemed parallel to certain lines of Shakespeare; of these twenty, fourteen were already included in my text. I finally decided to add nothing from Mr. Garrigus' list of parallels which was not already in my own; but I have gratefully made use of his introductory material on the contemporary reputation of the *Zodiacus Vitae.*

I wish to acknowledge my indebtedness and express my gratitude to the following; to the John Simon Guggenheim Memorial Foundation, for a fellowship that afforded me the leisure in which to write this book; to Harvard University, for admitting my family to a graduate housing unit and extending to me the use of library facilities; to Professors T. W. Baldwin of Illinois, Hardin

Craig of Missouri, and Robert Penn Warren of Yale, for making useful comments; to my colleagues at the University of Kansas, Professors C. K. Hyder, M.D. Clubb, A. C. Edwards, and L. R. Lind, for a meticulous examination of my manuscript; and to a number of others who have read it in more cursory fashion.

J. E. H.

Contents

Chapter 1

On Shakespearean Imagery

In Shakespeare studies, as well as in literary criticism generally, the most exciting discussions of recent years have centered upon the subject of imagery. The term itself has been much broadened from the *imago* of Renaissance rhetoricians and now is often used to include figurative language of almost any kind, description which appeals to the physical senses, and even abstract ideas which are strikingly expressed. To be an "image" it seems enough that a phrase should impart to the reader a mental picture of some kind. The subject has been handled in a variety of ways. The objective analysis of Miss Caroline Spurgeon[1] and the subjective impressionism of G. Wilson Knight[2] have called forth a host of emulators who seek to analyze the quality of an author's poetic imagination by an intensive study of his text. Among recent book-length studies of this kind are Edward Armstrong's *Shakespeare's Imagination* (1946), Robert B. Heilman's *This Great Stage* (1948), Donald A. Stauffer's *Shakespeare's World of Images* (1949), and W. H. Clemen's *The Development of Shakespeare's Imagery* (1951, expanded from the earlier German version). While these books differ widely in method from each other, they are alike in basing their conclusions upon the Shakespearean text without regard to its possible sources. I shall not cite the many shorter pieces which employ the same technique.

Stimulating as this kind of analysis may be, it cannot give a complete picture without some attention to an author's sources. Literary reminiscence differs from personal experience, and this difference should be taken into account when we draw from the text conclusions about Shakespeare's habits, interests, and ways of thinking. If a Shakespearean phrase is demonstrably indebted to a literary original, this fact may well modify the kind of interpreta-

[1] *Shakespeare's Imagery and What It Tells Us*, 1935.

[2] *The Wheel of Fire*, 1930; *The Shakespearean Tempest*, 1932; *The Imperial Theme*, 1939; *The Crown of Life*, 1947.

tion we should give to the phrase. Miss Rosemond Tuve's *Elizabethan and Metaphysical Imagery* (1947) helps us to understand the conventional nature of many images; and Professor T. W. Baldwin's extensive research, which I shall discuss later, shows how essential to accurate literary criticism is some consideration of sources. We should, therefore, not throw aside too readily the efforts of the source-hunters. Unfortunately, the excessive claims of some of these, such as William Theobald of an earlier generation,[3] have brought their method into disrepute. It is too easy to assume that verbal parallels indicate an author's indebtedness to a particular source. Skepticism as to such borrowing often obscures a more important point: that the author is indebted to some source, that our difficulty proceeds from the presence of too many possible sources instead of from the absence of any. To say that an image is conventional is to say that the author did not invent it but borrowed it. In our study of an author's mind the fact of such borrowing is more significant than the particular source from which he borrows, and an error in detecting the latter should not blind us to the borrowing itself.

This book is an attempt to show that much of Shakespeare's imagery was derived from earlier sources, to suggest what some of these sources were, and to trace their influence upon his fund of ideas. If this can be accurately done, it should tell us a good deal about his imaginative processes and his methods of work. At the beginning I should like to introduce and distinguish between two terms, *invention* and *adaptation*. By *invention,* an author perceives some correspondence or analogy to his thought in the world of men, manners, and physical phenomena, and uses this correspondence as the basis of an image to express his meaning. By *adaptation,* an author recalls one or more earlier verbal utterances of his thought and adapts them to his own purposes. Thus, the first lover to compare his lady's teeth to pearls exercised invention, but later poets who recalled and used the image were exercising adaptation.

---

[3] *The Classical Element in the Shakespeare Plays,* 1909. The author should not be confused with Lewis Theobald, the eighteenth century editor of Shakespeare.

At first glance it seems that invention would be highly superior to adaptation as a poetic method, that freshness must be superior to triteness. Invention strikes both the author and the reader with feelings of novelty and surprise, while adaptation presents old truths in a new dress or sometimes in one only slightly altered. Yet it is an open question which method has produced the more memorable literary utterances. Novelty and surprise are not always conducive to the deepest feelings or to the most perfect sense of form. Sometimes a trite image or worn platitude achieves greatness through a more nearly perfect utterance than anyone has given it before. In the finest instances of adaptation, the image may be so transformed as to be hardly traceable to its source, and the author may even be unconscious that it is a derived image, the transformation being the work of his subconscious mind. Such is not usually the case with an invented image, the author of which is likely to be self-conscious as to its content and may therefore not achieve complete spontaneity of utterance.

It is impossible to draw an absolute line of demarcation between invention and adaptation, since both of them are present in varying degrees in the work of all good poets; and in applying them we always mean that a poet is predominantly inventive or predominantly adaptive in his technique, never entirely one or the other. We must also remember that imagery itself is only one of several factors in determining the effect of a poem. John Donne is an excellent example of a poet whose talents for imagery are primarily inventive. His comparison of two lovers to the two arms of a pair of compasses ("A Valediction Forbidding Mourning"), his mingling their bloods in the flea which has sucked from both their veins ("The Flea"), his account of their souls holding converse in the air between them while their voices are silent ("The Ecstasy") are apparent inventions of his own. They may properly be classed among the "curious conceits" of his work, and they show great ingenuity. Yet one of Donne's noblest utterances, his sonnet "Death," is essentially an instance of adaptation. The image of Sleep as the picture of Death was already well known (*infra*, p. 127). His final line, "And death shall be no more; Death, thou shalt die," recalls such biblical phrases as "There shall be no more death" (Rev. 21:4) and St. Paul's triumphant climax to his argument for the existence of a resurrection of the dead, "Death is swallowed up into victory" (I Cor. 15:54). A much closer parallel is La Primaudaye's statement of the theme on the final page of *The French Academie,* Part One (1586; ch. 72):

> 1 Now then, seeing *death is dead* to them that beleeue in him, there is nothing in death which a man ought to feare. . . . So our *death dieth,* and is not able in any sort to hurt vs, if we behold with the eies of faith the death of Jesus Christ. Briefly, it is nothing but an image and shadow of death, and the beginning and entrance vnto true life.

The dominant impression in the images quoted from Donne's other poems—though not necessarily the total effect of the poems—is one of intellectual ingenuity; in the sonnet "Death" it is one of strong emotional conviction. The fact that both author and readers are familiar with the imagery used in the sonnet eliminates any feeling of strangeness and allows us to view it as a profound statement of accepted truth. Instead of surprising us, it confirms by a fresh statement ideas already familiar to our consciousness. This common ground of author and readers makes possible a more immediate emotional response than a completely novel image would call forth. I do not argue that "Death" is a better poem than the others mentioned, but only that the reader's response to it is more spontaneous and immediate. So far as imagery is concerned, its appeal is to familiarity rather than to novelty.

When an author's style seems to have been influenced by adaptation, we are naturally interested in the sources from which his images are derived. Such sources may help us to understand his ideas as well as his phraseology. Frequently no direct source can be ascertained, as when the borrowing derives from a common proverb; yet in a surprising number of cases there are distinguishing characteristics which point to one source rather than another. If we can say what these characteristics are, we shall have a valuable technique of literary investigation; for the development of an author's thought is often largely determined by what he reads, and verbal parallels are frequently the only clue to whether or not he has read a given work.

The correct evaluation of such verbal parallels is one of the hardest tasks known to the student of literature. There can never be complete certainty in his conclusions. His audience's reactions, being necessarily subjective, will vary widely; some readers will be unduly credulous, others entirely impervious, to the significance of verbal parallels. He will face attack on the weaker parallels if he includes them, yet their inclusion is necessary to a complete picture of the evidence. Nor does this exclude the possibility that other uses of a particular phrase or image were also recalled, that the poet's words represent a synthesis or fusion of several sources. Again, one must always consider the possibility that a source is indirect, the image having reached the poet through conversation or other casual reference. None of these circumstances can alter the central fact that the phrase or image is a result of adaptation.

We must emphasize the point that detection of specific sources is not the most important part of scholarly criticism. It is but a means to a greater understanding and appreciation of the works studied. Such works find their genesis in an author's experiences, actual and vicarious. The principal sources of vicarious experience are conversation and reading. Conversation is usually lost to succeeding generations or is preserved only in fragments, but frequently the reading matter remains extant and can help us to interpret an author's mind. First we must know what he read. Such works may be discovered by biographical evidence if we have it, by resemblances to his own writings in the larger elements of plot and theme, and by verbal parallels. These last are clues used in the detective work of literature, for the word can often be traced where the thought is somewhat elusive. The discovery of such parallels is the spadework which must be done, the better to understand an author's vicarious experience.

Here we reach the crux of the source-hunter's problem. How can he judge whether a verbal parallel represents an actual borrowing or not? At best he deals in probabilities and must determine what degree of probability will justify the identification of a particular source. Similarly, the reader must determine by what standards he will accept or reject such identifications when they are made. At present the matter is almost wholly personal, depending upon the individual's credulity or skepticism for the attitude that he will take. There are no generally accepted bases of judgment. Since my work is very largely a study of parallels, I shall try to state briefly some tests that should be applied in determining the validity of an apparent verbal indebtedness to an earlier source.

First the source-hunter should consider questions of external probability. Is the author known to have read the book in question? Was it available to him; e.g., was it in print before his own composition was written? Was it generally popular? Was it a textbook in use when he attended school? Was it read by his friends? Do his known tastes make it likely that he would have desired to read such a book? If it is in a foreign language, could he read that language?

So little is known of Shakespeare's reading habits that we cannot base too much on external evidence. Still, certain inferences can be made. In Hamlet's third soliloquy occurs the phrase, " 'Tis a *consummation* devoutly to be wish'd." Professor Kittredge points out a passage of very similar tenor in Florio's translation of Montaigne, in which the key-word "consummation" is used (*infra,* p. 132). Florio's translation was printed in 1603. The First Quarto of *Hamlet* was printed in 1603 but was registered for publication a year earlier. This Quarto is imperfect, and in it the word "consummation" does not appear. The word does appear in the Second Quarto of 1604, in which the soliloquy is much changed from the earlier version. We are now brought face to face with a vexing problem of Shakespearean scholarship: Is the Second Quarto text a revision of the play from its earlier form, or is the First Quarto a pirated and imperfect version of the play, which existed from the beginning in substantially its present form? Or are both these theories in part correct, the First Quarto being an inaccurate version of Shakespeare's first draft, which he subsequently expanded and revised? If the "consummation" passage is based on Florio's Montaigne—and the resemblance is very close—it would seem to have been added during a revision of the play, for the book was not in print when Shakespeare's *Hamlet* was first registered for publication. The other possibilities are that Shakespeare may have read Florio's translation in manuscript before 1603, or that the verbal resemblance is only a coincidence after all, or that the two passages are both indebted to a common earlier source. Again, if we admit this parallel as a borrowing from Montaigne, we increase the likelihood that other verbal resemblances are echoes of Montaigne, all of whose essays were included in the single volume which Shakespeare probably read. This question illustrates vividly the fact that external probability must be carefully weighed in any study of sources. (Cf. *infra,* pp. 101, 277.)

We may apply the tests of external probability to the question of Shakespeare's classical learning. Long ago it was observed by Richard Grant White that in *Troilus and Cressida,* III. iii. 95-102, Ulysses' quotation from a book he is reading has a resemblance to Plato's *First Alcibiades.* Though the parallel is by no means definite, we may accept it for the purposes of argument. We must then ask in what form Shakespeare could have read the *First Alcibiades.* Since it had not appeared in English, he probably read it in Latin. In scanning the editions of Plato in Latin, we find that most commonly his complete works appeared in one volume, the translation by Marsilio Ficino being the most popular if we judge by the number of editions published. This translation also included Ficino's famous commentary upon the *Symposium,* a document which greatly influenced Renaissance Platonism. There was no separate Latin edition of the *First Alcibiades.* We may conclude that, if Shakespeare read it, he probably read other works of Plato also, for he had them in his hands.

We may ask the same question concerning Shakespeare's use of Aristotle. He twice mentions Aristotle by name, both times in apparent reference to passages in the *Nicomachean Ethics.* Does this suggest that he therefore read other works of Aristotle? Not necessarily, for the *Nicomachean Ethics* was frequently printed separately in Latin translations, and there was one short English compendium based upon it. He may have read other works of Aristotle, but his use of the *Ethics* affords no proof that he did.

External probability must also be considered in studying Shakespeare's use of the Bible. The Authorised Version (1611) appeared later than the composition of nearly all his plays, yet it is natural to use that version for the simple reason that modern concordances are based upon it. Nor is this practice as misleading as it might seem, for the Authorised Version is essentially a revision of earlier English versions, retaining something like 90 per cent of the language used by Tyndale and Coverdale in the first sixteenth century translations. Intervening versions, such as the Genevan (1558) and the Bishops' (1567) represent stages in this revision of the Tyndale-Coverdale text. Still, it is clear that any parallels between Shakespeare's lines and the Authorised Version must be carefully checked with earlier versions that Shakespeare could have used.[4] Several times I have noted in working from the Authorised Version apparent borrowings which find support in none of the earlier English versions, the inference being that what had seemed to be a verbal borrowing by Shakespeare was in fact a coincidence.

This question of coincidence leads us to a second group of tests, which we may call internal tests of probability. When is a verbal parallel an actual borrowing and when is it a coincidence? If coincidence can account for apparent borrowings which external evidence shows to have been impossible, why are not other apparent borrowings examples of coincidence also? Undoubtedly they may be, and some of them are; yet we can be reasonably sure that not all of them are. We may use certain standards by which to judge more accurately the validity of an apparent borrowing, realizing that all

[4] In this volume all quotations from the Psalms are taken from the Prayer Book. Other biblical quotations are taken from Cranmer's Great Bible of 1539 (C), or the Geneva Bible (G), or the Bishops' Bible (B). I have modernized the spelling.

conclusions in this field are necessarily tentative and subject to revision by later evidence.

The first test is one of vocabulary. Where there is an apparent borrowing of a single word, there must be some distinguishing feature in the word itself or in the manner of its use if the parallel is to be held significant. If we could find any earlier use of Jaques' word *ducdame* (*As You Like It,* II. v. 56), we should probably deem it a source, since no earlier use is now known. More common words can be held significant only if their contexts show a parallelism of thought; then such words may be very significant indeed. Such an instance is the key-word "consummation" already cited from Montaigne. We should realize that a similarity of sentiments expressed, without any similarity of wording, is quite inconclusive unless the sentiments themselves are unique. Conversely, a passage of similar sentiments in which several distinctive words recur together is more likely to be a genuine case of indebtedness to a source than if only one word recurs. When such resemblances extend beyond a single sentence into a passage of paragraph length, the indebtedness is more probable still.

Sometimes two verbal reminiscences from the same source will reinforce each other as indications of Shakespeare's borrowing. Even more convincing are those instances in which two images closely associated in the original are likewise closely associated in Shakespeare's text, indicating that he recalled the sense of the whole passage. This test is particularly useful when the images are common to a number of possible sources, for it enables us to fix upon some one as the most probable immediate source.

When the poet has used several sources for a single passage, we may call them all contributory sources. Among these, we should make a distinction between primary and secondary sources. A primary source is that which is most immediately recalled by the poet, not always the earliest one in point of time. A secondary source is any other use of the same image which the poet has read and which has modified or added to his recollection of the primary source.

From my studies of his imagery, I believe that Shakespeare had an extremely retentive and associative mind, with an especial sensitiveness to words. The reading of one striking image was sufficient to recall half a dozen other uses of the same image, if he had read that many. Professor John Livingston Lowes, in *The Road to Xanadu,* showed that Coleridge possessed this retentive and associative power to an eminent degree and demonstrated how varied images coalesced and fused in the "deep well" of his subconscious mind. Professor Lowes had the support of external probability in a manuscript notebook which recorded the books that Coleridge had read or had planned to read. We have no such notebook of Shakespeare's reading, but we can nevertheless trace in his work the same strong power of association. It may thus be inaccurate to speak of *the* source of a Shakespearean image when there were several possible sources. More than likely all of them were recalled together, and it is our task to separate the primary source from the secondary ones. The multiplicity of sources does not alter the fact that Shakespeare has adapted the image and has not invented it.

I have come to believe that Shakespeare's genius was more adaptive and less inventive than has been commonly thought. Certainly he had all the inventive genius that one could desire, but he did not feel the necessity of saying something "new" every time he put pen to paper. His normal practice of borrowing other men's plots suggests that he would not hesitate to borrow their words if such borrowing served his purpose. Yet borrowing is scarcely the term for the process of absorption and transformation by which Shakespeare employed words and images of others. Some of the best passages in his works are a tissue of images derived from earlier sources, yet they are more typical of Shakespeare than some uninspired and perfunctory lines that show not a single verbal reminiscence of earlier works. His reading provided an enrichment rather than an ornamentation of his poetic style. So thoroughly are his derived images absorbed and transformed that they are often difficult of detection; they do not seem artificial but have become his natural medium of utterance.

It is not my intention in this study to deny Shakespeare credit for originality but rather to modify somewhat our conception of that term as applied to literary creation. The verbal parallels which I shall quote, numerous as they are, represent only a fraction of Shakespeare's imagery. The great portion received from his conversation and personal experiences cannot very well be evaluated. Only in his reading can we trace with some degree of accuracy the elements which entered into his thought. One should not imagine that, because the tracing of verbal associations is slow and laborious, the associations themselves were slow and laborious. More likely they were instantaneous sparks struck off at white heat in the fire of poetic creation. This spontaneity of the associative process must be emphasized lest the poet be made to seem pedantic and artificial.

Modern scholarship has begun to explore the extent of Shakespeare's derived imagery. Mr. Richmond Noble's epoch-making book *Shakespeare's Biblical Knowledge* (1935) gives us for the first time a full realization of Shakespeare's extensive debt to the Scriptures. A colleague of mine, Professor James L. Wortham, is working upon Shakespeare's transformations of proverbial material and is finding it a fruitful field. Professor T. W. Baldwin's two massive volumes *William Shakspere's 'Small Latine & Lesse Greeke'* (1944) have reconstructed the probable background of the poet's schooling and incidentally have reviewed his borrowings from classical sources. These and others are increasing our knowledge of Shakespeare's adaptations, both as to extent and as to kind.

In his lists of Latin schoolbooks, Professor Baldwin names two which were usually read in the early years of grammar school, before the students began Cicero, Virgil, and Horace. These two are the *Eclogues* of Baptista Mantuanus and the *Zodiacus Vitae* of Marcellus Palingenius. He further notes that Elizabethan schoolmasters made use of English translations, copies of which sometimes found their way into the hands of students (II. 400-402). These two popular textbooks were early translated into English verse, the *Eclogues* by George Turbervile in 1567, the *Zodiacus*

Vitae by Barnabe Googe, begun in 1560 and completed in 1565 under the title *The Zodiake of Life*. The *Eclogues* are mentioned by Holofernes in *Love's Labour's Lost,* IV. ii. 96, where the opening line is quoted from the Latin. There is no similar quotation from the *Zodiake,* but one reference therein has caused some comment. In a marginal reference Googe has a note: "The world a stage play." Professor Baldwin observes that he had discovered this analogue to Jaques' line in *As You Like It,* "All the world's a stage" (II. vii. 139). He later found that at least three earlier readers had discovered it and had said so in print (I. 652). In a subsequent article, Mrs. Josephine Waters Bennett mentions the passage from the *Zodiake* as a possible Shakespearean source (*infra,* p. 20, n. 4), crediting the suggestion to Miss Rosemond Tuve, who has edited the volume for Scholars' Facsimiles and Reprints, where it is now available. Miss Tuve's introduction to this edition and her earlier article on Palingenius[5] (probably a pseudonym for Pietro Manzoli) give the reader all the biographical and bibliographical evidence that he is likely to need. The *Zodiacus Vitae* is a compendium in verse of astronomical, moral, and philosophic thought, with different points of view put into the mouths of different speakers. Since I shall go further than any previous critic in asserting Shakespeare's indebtedness to Googe's translation of this work, it is well to review briefly the evidence for its popularity in England.

In her Introduction (p. v) Miss Tuve notes that Giordano Bruno praised Palingenius as an astronomer and scientist to be ranked with Cusanus, Copernicus, and Paracelsus; we should remember that Bruno visited England and lectured at Oxford. She further quotes Gabriel Harvey's *Marginalia* in praise of Googe's translation, the original of which Harvey called "a most learned . . . and pregnant introduction into Astronomie, & both philosophies." She gives the admiring comment of Thomas Digges, an eminent English scientist of the time, who declared that he had learned by heart the eleventh book of the *Zodiake* ("Aquarius," on the stars). We may

---

[5] "Spenser and the *Zodiake of Life,*" *JEGP,* XXXIV (1935), 1-19.

add, for whatever it is worth, that Thomas Digges and his family were probably friends of Shakespeare in London.[6] Miss Tuve notes that there were sixty editions of the *Zodiake* in Latin, ten of them printed in England.

The standard work upon the Latin *Zodiacus* is Foster Watson's *The 'Zodiacus Vitae' of Marcellus Palingenius Stellatus: An Old School-Book,* London, 1908. His conclusions, together with other evidence, are presented by Mr. C. B. Garrigus in an unpublished Master's thesis, *A Study of the Parallels between Shakspere and Palingenius,* University of Illinois, 1938. The following evidence is taken from Mr. Garrigus' thesis, though most of it is also available in Professor Baldwin's volumes already cited.

The *Zodiacus Vitae* is listed as a prescribed textbook in the records of St. Saviour's Grammar School (1562), St. Bee's Grammar School (1583), the Durham School (1593), the Aldenham School (1600), and the Camberwell Grammar School (1615). The introduction to the Basle edition of 1574 is addressed to the tutors or *moderatores* of Christian youth, "that beardless boys may first learn pious teachings, and that afterwards they may further read the sweet writings of the poets." When John Marshall, curate of Bishopton, a hamlet of Stratford, died in1607, an inventory of his library included copies of Palingenius, both in Latin and in English (C. C. Stopes, *Shakespeare's Environment,* p. 58). Roger Ascham, in the second part of *The Scholemaster* (1570), writes: "In deede, *Chauser, Th. Norton,* of Bristow, my L. of Surrey, *M. Wiat, Th. Phaer,* and other Ientlemen, in translating *Ouide, Palingenius,* and *Seneca,* haue gonne as farre to their great praise, as the copie they followed could carry them"; but Ascham thinks they would have done even better if they had not used rime in their verse. William Webbe, in *A Discourse of English Poetrie* (1586), discusses the better classical poets and adds: "Onely I will adde two of later times, yet not farre inferiour to the most of them aforesayde, Pallingenius and Bap. Mantuanus; and for a singular gyft in a sweete Heroicall verse,

[6] Leslie Hotson, *"I, William Shakespeare, Do Appoint Thomas Russell, Esquire"* (1938), ch. 6.

match with them Chr. Oclan(d), the author of our Anglorum Proelia." Later Webbe praises Googe's translation of Palingenius. Likewise, Francis Meres, in his *Palladis Tamia* (1598), says that Palingenius has "obtained renown and good place among the ancient Latin poets"; Meres also compliments Googe upon his translation of the work.

To this evidence should be added Professor Baldwin's numerous references to the *Zodiacus Vitae;* since these can be so easily found by consulting the index of his two-volume work, I shall not repeat them here.

The conclusions based upon this evidence would seem to be that the Elizabethans ranked Palingenius high among the minor Latin poets and considered Googe's translation of him to be good if not great verse. Modern readers may not share this judgment, but it is likely that Shakespeare did. After publication of Googe's work in incomplete form in 1560 and 1561, the complete translation appeared in 1565, 1576, and 1588. Miss Tuve observes that the 1576 edition, which she reprints and which I have used for this study, was the first to have marginal notes, and that the 1588 edition was a fairly exact reprint of it. Since the marginal notes show several interesting parallels to Shakespeare's text, including "The world a stage play," I judge that he must have read one of the later editions. If he read it in connection with his study of the Latin *Zodiacus* in school, he must have read the 1576 edition, which appeared when he was twelve years old. At that time he would have had little great English poetry available for a comparison. Except for Chaucer, who offered difficulties of language, his reading of poetry was probably drawn from Wyatt, Surrey, and the other Tottel poets, from Googe, Turbervile, Sackville, Golding, Gascoigne, Phaer, and Elderton. The great renaissance which began with *The Shepheardes Calender* (1579) was yet to come. By comparison with his contemporaries Googe was a good poet, the subject matter of the *Zodiake* is thoughtful but not subtle, and the youthful Shakespeare probably read it at the most impressionable period of his life. That he remembered it well and probably knew much of it by heart, I believe can be assumed from the internal evidence yet to be presented.

The facts thus far listed indicate a strong external probability that Shakespeare read the *Zodiake of Life* either in Latin or in English or in both languages. Certainly it was available to him, and a large proportion of English schoolboys did read it. The parallels of subject matter between his works and the *Zodiake* could be indebted to either the English or the Latin, but the verbal parallels are clearly reminiscent of Googe's lines. Accordingly, this study employs such parallels as a recognition signal and then seeks to show how the thought in the *Zodiake* has affected the thought and imagery of Shakespeare. It is not easy to say how much he may have recalled of the Latin, since he quotes none of the phrases in Latin, but I have observed approximately a dozen instances in which the Latin seems to have supplied him with details that Googe's English version omits. A likely explanation of this circumstance is that he read the two versions together, using Googe's English translation to help him in translating the Latin for himself. Or he may have recalled phrases from the Latin when reading the translation at a later date. His recollection of any particular passage might therefore contain details from both the Latin and the English texts, a fact which would become evident only when the two texts differed from each other.

Many of the images and ideas of the *Zodiake* are acknowledged commonplaces, though they may have seemed less commonplace to Shakespeare than they do to us, since his own use of them has served to popularize them. Their widespread use makes it difficult to say in all cases that the *Zodiake* was Shakespeare's specific source for them. Yet, if my argument concerning the association and fusion of images holds good, the *Zodiake* was probably a contributory source of all these commonplaces, provided we can assume that Shakespeare was familiar with the book. In my judgment, a considerable number of the parallels which I note are unusual enough in themselves or in their combinations of images to show that they were recalled from the *Zodiake* rather than from any other source. Not all readers will agree on the significance of every one of these, but their cumulative effect should make Shakespeare's indebtedness reasonably certain. This indebtedness once acknowledged, it becomes more likely that other verbal parallels represent an indebtedness to the same source. Whether or not they are admitted as actual borrowings, they often indicate parallelisms of thought that help us to understand Shakespeare against the background of his time. For this reason I have admitted a number of verbal resemblances which would be of doubtful significance if forced to stand alone but which contribute to the cumulative impression of the *Zodiake's* influence. They serve to illustrate Shakespeare's method of adaptation and to show his familiarity with the ideas of Palingenius, though he may not have recalled those ideas exclusively from this particular source. Thus, while all of the "borrowings" which I quote could have been drawn from the sources named, not all of them necessarily were. I have tried to indicate my own degrees of belief and doubt by such qualifying words as *certainly, definitely, probably, possibly, may have been*. In some instances I have taken a verbal parallel to the *Zodiake* as a point of departure, tracing the image through its varied uses by Shakespeare in order to show the extent of its influence upon his thought, without implying that all of these uses are immediately derived from the sources under discussion. I have thus sought to accomplish a double purpose: to demonstrate Shakespeare's indebtedness to certain sources, and to study the development of his ideas.

Shakespeare's habit of recalling the same image from several sources is amply shown in the following pages. Except for a few illustrative examples, I have usually omitted reference to parallels suggested by other scholars unless I judged that such parallels represented contributory sources of Shakespeare's imagery. Two works repeatedly demanded my attention, for they constantly presented images which Shakespeare seemed to have recalled in connection with similar images in the *Zodiake*. The first was the Bible, particularly Psalms, Proverbs, and the Book of Job. The second was *The French Academie* of Pierre de la Primaudaye. This prose compendium of scientific, moral, and philosophic knowledge appeared in four parts, which were translated into English in 1586, 1594, 1601, and 1618 respectively.[7] Originally in French, it has much in common with the ideas of Palingenius and may well have drawn some information from his work. The first two parts have been described and used in Professor Hardin Craig's *The Enchanted Glass* (1936), and numerous scholars have explored it with reference to Shakespeare. I had read it before also, but not until I began the study of Palingenius did I perceive the significance of La Primaudaye as a Shakespearean source. His work seems to have supplemented the *Zodiake* in a number of instances.

Since this study of verbal parallels depends upon the cumulative effect of a large number of small points, the reader will do well to reserve his final judgment until he has finished the book. The author cannot expect complete agreement from every reader; but, Gratiano-like, he hopes that even the unfavorable critic will find a few grains of wheat among the bushels of chaff.

---

7 For convenience I quote from the 1618 edition, which includes all four parts. A collation of the text with extensive passages in the earlier editions shows no significant differences. There are slight variants in spelling and punctuation.

Chapter 2

All the World's a Stage

FEW PASSAGES FROM Shakespeare are better known than Jaques' speech on the Seven Ages of Man. Actually, the passage contains two figurative devices skillfully woven together. One is the figure of the world as a stage upon which all human beings are the players. The acts of the stage play are made equivalent to the "ages" or periods of the life of man, thus introducing the second figure of the Seven Ages. While both of these were highly popular figures, they have no inherent connection with each other and do not occur together in most of the parallels which have been quoted as sources. By using a test of internal probability, two significant figures appearing together, we can perhaps determine which was the immediate source used by Shakespeare.

The first important study of possible sources appeared in 1853, John Winter Jones' "Observations on the Origin of the Division of Man's Life into Stages" (*Archaeologia,* XXXV. 167-189). The title is deceptive, for "Stages" here has nothing to do with the theater but is merely the equivalent of Jaques' "Ages," referring to the different periods of life. Jones quotes analogues from Philo Judaeus, Codronchus, Censorinus, Clement of Alexandria, St. Ambrose, Dilherus, and Sir Thomas Browne. He also reproduces three old prints which illustrate these divisions of life. The first two divide life into ten ages. The third, assigned by Jones to the fifteenth century, makes the division into seven ages: Infans, Puericia, Adolescencia, Juventus, Virilitas, Senectus, Decrepitus. The image used in the drawing is not that of a stage, but of a wheel, which starts from the earth with "Generacio" and returns to the same point with "Corrupcio." The figure of a man is stretched upon the wheel, which bears the inscription:

2 Sic ornati nascuntur in hac mortali vita. Est velut aqua labuntur deficiens ita.

Obviously this wheel does not correspond to the stage of the world. It does, however, recall Edmund's dying speech in *King Lear:*

> *Edgar.* My name is Edgar, and thy father's son.
> The gods are just, and of our pleasant vices,
> Make instruments to plague us.
> The dark and vicious place where thee he got
> Cost him his eyes.
>
> *Edmund.* Thou'st spoken right, 'tis true.
> *The wheel is come full circle;* I am here. (V. iii. 169-174)

The "place where thee he got" is the womb of Edmund's mother and suggests "Generacio" as the starting point of life. Edmund's image of the wheel does not suggest the alternate periods of prosperity and adversity on Fortune's wheel (the analogy usually given) so much as it represents the complete revolution of one's fate from birth to death, the Aristotelian cycle of generation and corruption, which in this case has been much accelerated. This may have proceeded from the print reproduced by Jones. It may have been originally suggested to the artist by the "wheel of nativity" *(rota nativitatis)* in the Vulgate reading of James 3:6, a reading not retained in the English translations. The fact that there are seven steps or periods of life represented on the wheel may have called it to Jaques' mind—if we assume with Jones that Shakespeare had seen the print—but the fact that his Seven Ages are associated with a stage and not with a wheel means that the primary source must be sought elsewhere.

Since Jones' study, new analogues have been found for the Seven Ages. Professor Samuel C. Chew's entertaining essay in the J. Q. Adams Memorial Volume (1948) shows the popularity of the theme in Renaissance art. Professor Draper mentions Lemnius, Cuffe, and La Primaudaye, but dismisses them in favor of Stephen Batman.[1] Professor Gilbert revives the claim of Censorinus,[2] already mentioned by Jones. Professor Allen would have Pedro Mexia

[1] John W. Draper, "Jaques' 'Seven Ages' and Bartholomaeus Anglicus," *Mod. Lang. Notes,* LIV (1939), 273-276.

[2] Allen H. Gilbert, "Jacques' 'Seven Ages' and Censorinus," *Mod. Lang. Notes,* LV (1940), 103-105.

be the source.[3] Mrs. Bennett would assign the honor to Julius Pollux and mentions additional analogues from Macrobius and the pseudo-Platonic *Axiochus*.[4] I suggest as an analogue, but not as a source, Thomas Wright's *A Succinct Philosophical declaration of the nature of Clymactericall yeeres, occasioned by the death of Queene Elizabeth,* London, 1604, in which the various ages are described and limited: Infantia, to 7 years; Pueritia, to 14; Adolescentia, to 21; Iuventus, to 28; in Statu Virili, to 49; Senectus, to 63; Decrepita Aetas, to 70 or 77, and thereafter.[5]

The comparison of life or the world to a stage has an even greater antiquity. Professor Kittredge, in his edition of *As You Like It,* cites Suetonius, Petronius, and John of Salisbury, and briefly calls attention to Rudolf Helm's *Lucian und Menipp* (1906). In this work (pp. 45-53) Helm shows that the comparison was a favorite figure with Lucian and cites other analogues from Dio Chrysostom, Ariston of Chios, Maximus of Tyre, Cicero, Seneca, Marcus Aurelius, and Plato (*Philebus,* 50 B, *Republic,* 577 B). To these instances I can add Francesco Piccolomini's *Universa Philosophia de Moribus* (1583). In giving various metaphors for the life of man in this world, he writes:

4 Insuper utimur metaphora a theatro deprompta, in quo Comici partes suas (ut eos decet) explere tenentur. (VIII. xxiii)

I also observe in Florio's Montaigne this sentence, quoting Cicero's *De Finibus:*

5 We may make an Exit from our life which doth not please, as from a stage. (*Essais,* I. xl; p. 210 in Mod. Lib. ed.)

Again Montaigne writes:

6 Most of our vacations are like playes. *Mundus universus exercet histrioniam. All the world doth practise stage-playing.* Wee must play our parts duly, but as the part of a borrowed personage. (*Essais,* III. x; p. 916)

[3] Don Cameron Allen, "Jacques' 'Seven Ages' and Pedro Mexia," *Mod. Lang. Notes,* LVI (1941), 601-603.

[4] Josephine Waters Bennett, "Jaques' Seven Ages," *Shakespeare Association Bulletin,* XVIII (1943), 168-174.

[5] Appended to the second edition of the same author's *The Passions of the Minde in Generall,* 1604. For other analogues, see the Shakespeare *Variorum,* Henry Green's *Shakespeare and the Emblem Writers* (1870), pp. 405-410, and the *Gentleman's Magazine,* May, 1853.

Porter and Clarke, in their "First Folio" edition, cite other parallels from Richard Edwards' *Damon and Pythias* (1571) and Stephen Guazzo's *Civile Conversation* (1586). The image is also used at some length in Erasmus' *Praise of Folly.*

In Sonnet 54 of his *Amoretti,* Spenser writes:

7 Of this worlds theatre in which we stay,
My love, lyke the spectator, ydly sits,
Beholding me, that all the pageants play,
Disguysing diversly my troubled wits.
Sometimes I joy, when glad occasion fits,
And mask in myrth lyke to a comedy:
Soone after, when my joy to sorrow flits,
I waile, and make my woes a tragedy.

Finally, the *Variorum* among other parallels cites the motto of the Globe Theatre, "Totus mundus agit histrionem." Certainly there can be no question of the popularity of this figure of speech.

Among the numerous analogues to the world-stage and to the ages of man, I have observed only three that show them in association with each other. One is a passage from Palingenius' *Zodiake of Life* (p. 99). The *Variorum* quotes Henley as having seen "an old print, entitled, 'The Stage of Man's Life,' divided into seven ages." Again it cites from *The Legend of Orpheus and Eurydice* (1597) these lines:

8 Unhappy man
Whose life a sad continual tragedie,
Himself the actor, in the world, the stage,
While as the acts are measur'd by his age.

This passage, while not specifying the different ages, uses age as the measure of the separate acts in the drama of life and thus introduces the link used by Shakespeare to connect the two images. Since there are five acts in the usual Elizabethan play, and since Palingenius uses only five "ages" in his survey of the life of man, Shakespeare may have felt the resemblance with redoubled force, though in Jaques' speech he changes the number to accord with the more conventional Seven Ages.

Here we may cite from Montaigne yet another passage, which does not refer explicitly to the world-stage but which does refer to the "acts" in the "comedy" of life:

> 9 And if the worst happen, the distribution and varietie of all the *acts of my comedie,* is performed in one yeare. If you have observed the course of my foure seasons; they containe the infancie, the youth, the virilitie, and the old age of the world. He hath *plaied his part:* he knowes no other wilinesse belonging to it, but to begin againe, it will ever be the same, and no other. (*Essais,* I. xix; p. 60)

It is well to refresh our memories briefly on the context of Jaques' metaphor:

> *Duke.* Thou seest we are not all alone unhappy.
> This wide and *universal theatre*
> Presents more woeful pageants than the scene
> Wherein we play in.
> *Jaq.* *All the world's a stage,*
> And all the men and women merely players.
> They have their exits and their entrances,
> And *one man* in his time *plays many parts,*
> His acts being seven ages. (*As You Like It,* II. vii. 136-143)

In Shakespeare's lines we find reminiscences, not only of Googe's note "the world a stage play" (accompanying the passage observed by Professor Baldwin and others), but also of another note on p. 194, "The theater or stage of mans life."[6] This second note accompanies two significant lines of text:

> 10 I then began to note and marke *the partes that men do play,*
> And sundry sorte of liues they leade (As God gaue grace) to way.

Here is a general resemblance to Jaques' line, "And one man in his time plays many parts." The word "theater" in Googe's note has apparently contributed to the Duke's use of "universal theatre" in connection with Jaques' image of the world-stage. Perhaps Shakespeare also recalled two striking phrases from the
[11] Latin, for Palingenius describes the world as a "pulchrum amphitheatrum" adorned with starry gems (VII. 205-206)
[12] and refers to God as "Omnipotens ille astriferi faber amphi-

[6] This phrase also occurs in Arthur Golding's translation of Simon Grynaeus' introduction to the history of Trogus Pompeius (1564). It is quoted in Miss Lily B. Campbell's *Shakespeare's 'Histories'* (1947), p. 38.

theatri" (VIII. 121), phrases which are not rendered into English by Googe.

We now turn to the lines which accompany Googe's note "The world a stage play." The passage is quite long, covering several pages. Here are its first lines:

13 Wherefore if thou dost well discerne, thou shalt behold and see (p. 99)
This mortall lyfe that here you leade, a *Pageant* for to bee.
The *diuers partes* therein declarde, the chaunging world doth showe,
The *maskers* are eche one of them with liuely breath that blowe.
For almost euery man now is disguised from his kinde.
And vnderneth a false pretence they sely soules do blinde.
So moue they Goddes aboue to laugh wyth toyes and trifles vayne,
Which here in *Pageants* fond they passe while they doe life retayne.

The reader will observe that "pageants" has now been added to the number of verbal parallels with Shakespeare's lines.

There intervene twenty-four lines before the author proceeds to the Ages of Man. Googe accompanies the Ages with a marginal note:

14 The misery of man from his byrth to his graue.

Five ages are described. Ten lines describe the helplessness of man in infancy; five lines his childhood, with whippings from parents and masters; eleven lines his lustfulness and riot in youth; ten lines the hard labor and urgent ambition of middle age. These show only general resemblances to Shakespeare's lines. But it is different with the fifth age, which contains every element of Jaques' poignant speech on the final decrepitude of man:

Last scene of all,
That ends this strange eventful history,
Is second childishness and mere oblivion,
Sans teeth, sans eyes, sans taste, sans everything.

Palingenius writes as follows:

15 Then wrinkled age with hoary hayres encrocheth in apace, (p. 101)
The body fades, the strength abates, the beauty of his face
And colour goes, *his senses* fayle, his eares and *eyes* decay,
His *taste* is gone, some sicknesse sore frequenteth him alway,
Scarce chaws his meate his tothless chaps, scarce walks with staff in hand

His croked olde vnweldy limmes, wheron he scarce may stand.
The mind likewise doth feele decay, *now dotes he like a childe,*
And through his weake and aged yeres is *wisdome quite exilde.*

The second childhood, loss of mental powers, and loss of the senses all appear in the *Zodiake's* vivid lines. The form of Jaques' final line is suggestive of a phrase in Florio's Montaigne:

16 Sanse tongues, sanse eyes, and sanse ears.[7]

Jaques' speech is not the only instance in which Shakespeare compared life to a play, the world to a stage. The image fascinated him and recurs in his work many times. Two of these uses are especially important, for they reflect the image of the world-stage and at the same time show a close indebtedness to other images in the same passage here under discussion. When two images appear in conjunction in one possible source and also in conjunction in the later work studied, the probability of a direct borrowing is greatly increased. Here such repeated conjunctions of images occur not once, but twice. Sixteen lines after Q. 13 the following passage appears:

17 *a* Now will I here declare and tell of man the mischieues all, (p. 100)
Assone as he from mothers wombe with bloud embrued doth crall,
He straightway cries, and weeping luck him brings to wretched life,
Forseeing well by nature shewde, the cares and bitter strife
b Wherwith this mortall life abounds. So depe with groning winde
The Merchant sighes, and feares as oft as he doth call to minde
The perils great that ships are in, the force of Pirats hand,
The boystrous winds & raging Seas, with rockes & drenching sand.

These are the opening lines of Palingenius' discussion of the ages of man, in which he begins the portrayal of infancy. The merchant is introduced merely for comparison; as he groans for fear of danger to his ships, so the newborn child cries for fear of the dangers of life. The images are a continuation of the general discussion of the world-stage.

The lines on the merchant may have suggested the opening lines of *The Merchant of Venice*. Antonio is the "Merchant" who

[7] In his "Apologie of Raymond Sebond," p. 474. Cf. *Notes & Queries,* III. xii. 123. Cf. also Halliwell's citation of Garnier's *Henriade:* "Sans pieds, sans mains, sans nez, sans oreilles, Meurtri de touts parts."

sighs and is afflicted with an inexplicable melancholy. When Gratiano rallies him upon it, he says:

> I hold the world but as the world, Gratiano,
> *A stage where every man must play a part,*
> And mine a sad one. (I. i. 77-79)

Here, in addition to the passages on the world-stage already quoted, Antonio recalls another from the *Zodiake:*

18 Some are besides that doo impute, each thing to Destinye, (p. 132)
And iudge that force of fatall lawes, the world is ordered by, (p. 133)
And that with one continuall course (as *pageants* shew to minde)
All things doe moue, and *euery man hath here his parte assignde,*
That he must play, till all be done: a question to be sought
Right profitable fayre and hard, nor to be left vntaught.

Most interesting, however, is the manner in which 17*b,* on the merchant, here closely associated with the world-stage, is likewise associated with it in *The Merchant of Venice.* Antonio's reference to the world-stage is preceded earlier in the scene by Salarino's playful explanation of his sadness: Antonio, as a merchant, must be worried about his ships at sea. In lines 22-36, Salarino ingeniously elaborates and transforms the images, but the perils, winds, raging seas, rocks, and drenching sand are all there; only the pirates are omitted. The pirates have their innings, too, for in the third scene the images reappear, this time in the words of Shylock concerning Antonio's vessels:

> But ships are but boards, sailors but men; there be land-rats and water-rats, water-thieves and land-thieves, I mean *pirates,* and then there is the *peril* of *waters, winds,* and *rocks.* (lines 22-25)

This time the pirates got in and the sand was left out. The same combination of images had already appeared in *Lucrece,* 335-336 (*infra,* p. 55). Shylock's phrase "water-thieves and land-thieves" was apparently suggested by another description of a rich trader in the *Zodiake:*

19 From *theues by land,* from *theues by seas,* full oft he flieth fast. (p.13)

From these instances it should be apparent that the world-stage and the merchant's fears recurred together in Shakespeare's mind, and that this double recurrence was in all probability a result of their close conjunction in the *Zodiake*. This probability approaches certainty when we find the preceding image of Palingenius, that of the child who cries at birth for fear of the world's evils, also repeated by Shakespeare in connection with the world-stage. King Lear in his madness cries out:

> Thou must be patient; we came crying hither.
> Thou know'st, the first time that we smell the air,
> We wawl and cry. . . .
> When we are born, we cry that we are come
> To *this great stage of fools.* (IV. vi. 182-187)

Here the identity of the "great stage" with the world-stage is not expressed but is implicit in Lear's words. It is the same image found in Sonnet 15:

> That *this huge stage* presenteth nought but *shows*
> Whereon the stars in secret influence comment.

In Lear's speech there is again a remarkable concurrence of images. The stage of the world and the child who cries at birth, anticipating earthly ills, are associated in Lear's mind—and therefore in Shakespeare's—the apparent cause being the close conjunction of the same images in the *Zodiake*.

The *Variorum* finds no analogues to this passage in *Lear,* but there are some. Porter and Clarke, in their "First Folio" edition, cite the proem to Bk. VII of Holland's Pliny (1601):

20 Man alone, poor wretch, [nature] hath laid all naked upon the bare earth, even on his birthday to cry and wraule . . . from the very first houre that he is borne into this world.

Seneca expresses a similar sentiment in his *Ad Polybium de Consolatione,* iv. 3. It also occurs in George Pettie's "Tereus and Progne," from *A Petite Pallace of Pettie His Pleasure* (1576). Mr. Noble cites Wisdom 7:3, from the Apocrypha:

21 And when I was born, I received like air as other men, and fell upon the earth which is of like nature, crying and weeping at the first as all other do. (B)

I find the image again in Stephen Batman's *Batman vppon Bartholome* (1582), Bk. VI, ch. 5:

> 22 Then when he commeth out into the aire that is too hot or too colde, he is put to wretchednesse and to woe: that witnesseth openlye his kinde, wretchedly crieing and weeping.

In *The French Academie,* Pt. II, ch. 72, La Primaudaye writes of the newborn child:

> 23 Nowe so soone as it is come into the light it crieth, as if it did prognosticate and foretell of the miseries of that life into which it is entred.

The image is given at some length in Lucretius' *De Rerum Natura,* V. 222-227. Montaigne quotes Lucretius' lines in his "Apologie of Raymond Sebond" (*Essais,* II. xii); I quote them here in Florio's translation:

> 24 An infant, like a shipwracke ship-boy cast from seas,
> Lies naked on the ground and speechlesse, wanting all
> The helpes of vitall spirit, when nature with small ease
> Of throw's, to see first light, from her wombe lets him fall,
> Then, as is meet, with mourn'full cries he fils the place,
> To whom so many ils remaine in his lives race. (p. 403)

The image also occurs in the pseudo-Platonic *Axiochus.* I quote it here from the Elizabethan translation ascribed by Professor Padelford to Edmund Spenser:

> 25 For what parcell . . . of our life is not full of wretchednes? dooth not the babie euen taken from the mothers wombe, powre out plenty of teares, beginning the first step of life with griefe? neither afterward hath it once any breathing or resting time from sorrow. . . .[8]

In the *Axiochus* these lines are the beginning of a discourse on the ages of man, but there is little resemblance to the Seven Ages of Jaques except possibly in the second age, in which "he is yet afflicted with greater griefes, being subiect to the tyranny of the Schoolemaister and Tutor" (p. 47). We remember that the schoolboy is Jaques' example of the second age.

Finally, in Vincent de Beauvais' *Speculum Naturale* (XXXI. 77) we find a whole catalogue of various uses of the image by the church fathers, including St. Augustine, St. Bernard, William of Conch,

[8] Ed. F. M. Padelford, Johns Hopkins University Press, 1934, p. 46.

and Peter Comestor. We receive the interesting information that Zoroaster was the only person ever known who laughed at birth instead of crying. We learn from Comestor that Adam called his wife Eva in allusion to the misery of man and the cries of children. A male child newly born will sound the vowel *A,* while a female child newly born will sound the vowel *E,* in their Latin pronunciations, of course. Hence Adam called his wife "E or A"; that is "E vel A." By abbreviating the conjunction he derived the name EVA, signifying thereby the miseries of all children born of women, miseries which begin in the hour of their birth.

This excursion among analogues shows us how popular was the image of the child crying at birth in fear of future ills. In none of these instances, however, is the crying child associated with the world-stage. This association does exist in the *Zodiake* and also exists in *King Lear*. We can be reasonably sure, therefore, that the *Zodiake* was Shakespeare's primary source, around which recollections of other sources may have clustered. So sensitive was Shakespeare's mind to verbal resemblances, and so keen his memory of them, that quite possibly five or six recollections of the crying-child image were associated in his mind. With this embarrassment of riches, we fall back on our test of internal probability, the repetition of two images in conjunction, to discover the *Zodiake* as the primary source.

It is most interesting to see that the world-stage has become for Lear a "stage of fools." While Palingenius has many denunciations of fools, who he thinks comprise a great part of the human race, their association with the world-stage may spring from the line just before Q. 17:

26 As when vpon the stage a foole comes dreste vp like a King. (p. 99)

This is in such close proximity to the crying-child image that their intimate connection is evident; it is also part of the passage on the world-stage.

It seems to me that this single line may have provided or contributed to a valuable motif for the play. The "fool a king" image is repeatedly stressed. Lear is compared to a court jester, but the term "fool" is applied to him in other senses as well. In the beginning, other people call Lear a fool; in the end he applies the epithet to himself, realizing the folly of his self-willed rashness and calling himself a king only with the most bitter irony. A few quotations will illustrate this progression:

Kent. To plainness honour's bound
When majesty falls to *folly.* (I. i. 150-151)

Goneril. Old *fools* are babes again. (I. iii. 19). Cf. Q. 15.

Lear. Dost thou call me *fool,* boy?
Fool. All thy other titles thou hast given away; that thou wast born with. . . . That such a *king* should play bo-peep,
And go the *fools* among. (I. iv. 162-164, 193-194)

Fool. If thou wert my *Fool,* nuncle. (I. v. 45)

Fool. This cold night will turn us all to *fools* and *madmen.* (III. iv. 81)

Fool. Prithee, nuncle, tell me whether a *madman* be a gentleman or a yeoman?
Lear. A *king!* a *king!* (III. vi. 10-12)

Lear. Ay, every inch a *king!* . . . I am even the natural *fool* of fortune. . . . Come, come; I am a *king.* (IV. vi. 109, 195, 203)

Lear. I am a very *foolish* fond old man. . . . I am *old and foolish.* (IV. vii. 60, 84)

In this last quotation there seems to be also an echo of Ecclesiastes 4:13, as rendered in the Geneva Version:

27 Better is a poor and wise child, than *an old and foolish king,* which will no more be admonished. (G)

Since "admonished" here means "advised," the aptness of the phrase as a description of Lear is self-evident, for he is an old and foolish king who will not take advice. The verbal parallel suggests the scriptural verse as a contributory source.

We can now see how the irony of Palingenius' line may emerge in the character of Lear. He had trodden the stage of the world in the guise of a great king. But was he a king, he came to ask himself. He was dressed as a king and bore the title of a king, but he was really a fool. The world that recognized him as a king must be a world of fools to be so deceived, and the world-stage is a "stage of fools," a place where sham and pretense are mistaken for reality.

In several instances Palingenius names as fools those who devote themselves to pleasure or give way to thoughtless anger. He constantly applies the term to the rich and powerful who devote themselves to earthly affairs instead of to heavenly concerns, thus showing their short-sightedness. Without using the word "fools" he again pictures mankind as hapless victims of destiny, as "simple sheep" whom the butcher Death slaughters as he sees fit (*infra,* Q. 34). All of these meanings seem to be comprehended in Lear's phrase "stage of fools," which includes the entire human race. For instance, when Lear cries above Cordelia's body, "And my poor *fool* is hang'd" (V. iii. 305), he is not speaking cynically of her evil qualities; he is rather expressing pity for a victim of destiny. The same implications seem to apply in his characterization of himself as the "natural fool of fortune" and in Romeo's description of himself as "fortune's fool" (III. i. 141). Hamlet's phrase "we fools of nature" (I. v. 54) carries the same meaning. We are therefore mistaken if we assume that Lear's "stage of fools" involves a cynical condemnation of the human race as villains, such a cynical view as Timon develops, for instance. In Lear's condemnation there is an element of pity, an element not present in Timon. Because of this element, his sufferings broaden and strengthen his character, whereas Timon undergoes no such development but ends his life with a bitter aversion to all mankind. (Cf. *infra,* p. 180.)

This concept of man as the victim of destiny appears in *1 Henry IV,* in Hotspur's dying speech:

> But thought's the slave of life, and *life time's fool.* (V. iv. 81)

This same figure appears in Sonnet 116, "Love's not Time's fool," and in Sonnet 124, where the "fools of Time"—apparently the human race—are called upon to witness the enduring nature of love.

How this complex of images became involved in Shakespeare's mind with the world-stage may be traced in a series of quotations, the words of which supply what Professor Lowes (quoting Coleridge) called "the hooks and eyes of the memory."[9] The "fools of time" are verbally recalled in Prince Hal's remark upon his own folly:

> Well, thus we play the *fools* with the *time,* and *the spirits of the wise sit in the clouds and mock us.* (*2 Henry IV,* II. ii. 154-157)

The second part of this sentence stems from several passages in the *Zodiake.* First we may repeat line 7 of Q. 13, on the actors upon the world-stage:

> 28 So moue they Goddes aboue to laugh wyth toyes and trifles vayne.

The image is given more extensively in another passage:

> 29 And thus vnto my selfe I saide. Is *wisedome* euermore (p. 203)
> In vaine of vs desirde, and praisde? and vainely looked for?
> *And only dealt to saintes aboue?* Then of necessitie,
> Here in this wretched mortall life, *all men must foolishe be,*
> And *laughing stocks,* and *pageants* fonde, *vnto the Gods in sky.*

As the lines from the *Zodiake* show, the world-stage is envisioned as a source of amusement for the heavenly audience, who are so much wiser than the poor puppets or "maskers" that move about on the stage. The phrase "all men must foolish be" shows the sense in which the world-stage is a stage of fools; men have wisdom insufficient for their needs and therefore make ridiculous blunders which convulse with merriment those who are truly wise.

The theme appears again when the poet asks Jove to explain why he allows man to do such foolish things:

> 30 Perhaps thou dost it to that ende our doings [t]o deride, (p. 62)
> And makest *man thy laughing stocke.* For nothing els to be
> The *life of men on earth* doth seeme, then *staged Comedie.*
> And as the Ape that counterfets, to vs doth laughter moue:
> So we likewise doe cause and moue *the Saintes to laugh aboue.*

Here the saints are pictured as the heavenly audience, the gods not being mentioned. This combines with the reference to the saints as the only possessors of wisdom, in the preceding quotation, with the resultant allusion to the "spirits of the wise" as the heavenly audience. The image appears again in *Measure for Measure,* with a definite echo of Q. 30 (*infra,* p. 143).

---

[9] *The Road to Xanadu,* ch. 18.

In *Coriolanus* the gods are pictured as the heavenly audience (as in QQ. 28, 29) laughing at the follies exhibited on the world-stage. Coriolanus says, as he yields to his mother's plea to spare Rome:

> O mother, mother!
> What have you done? Behold, the heavens do ope,
> *The gods look down,* and this unnatural *scene*
> *They laugh at.* (V. iii. 182-185)

He means that the changing of his sworn purpose because of a few maternal tears seems an act of ridiculous folly such as only human beings could commit; hence it excites the laughter of the gods.

Shakespeare constantly envisions human deeds as actions on the stage of the world. No doubt his profession caused him regularly to think of human affairs in terms of stage drama. It is quite possible, though, that Palingenius' image of the world-stage and of life as a great drama had inclined the youthful Shakespeare's thinking in the direction it was to take. It also helps to account for the cosmic proportions which his characters sometimes assume. They are larger than life, not merely trivial people with trivial concerns. The pervasiveness of dramatic imagery in Shakespeare may be shown by a few illustrations; a concordance will supply the rest:

> *Juliet.* My dismal *scene* I needs must *act* alone.
> (*Romeo and Juliet,* IV. iii. 19)
>
> *Bastard.* By heaven, these scroyles of Angiers flout you, kings,
> And stand securely on their battlements
> *As in a theatre,* whence they gape and point
> At your industrious *scenes* and *acts* of death.
> (*King John,* II. i. 373-376)
>
> *Abbot.* A woeful *pageant* have we here beheld.
> (*Richard II,* IV. i. 321)
>
> *Richard.* Thus *play* I in one person many people.
> (*Richard II,* V. v. 31)
>
> *Hamlet.* You that look pale and trembling at this chance,
> That are but mutes or *audience* to this *act.*
> (*Hamlet,* V. ii. 345-346)
>
> *Ross.* Thou seest the heavens, as troubled with man's *act,*
> Threaten his bloody *stage.* (*Macbeth,* II. iv. 5-6)

To these we may add a longer passage which employs the world-stage in a context of disillusionment and despair. In *2 Henry IV,* when Northumberland hears of his son Harry's death, he cries out:

> Let heaven kiss earth! Now let not nature's hand
> Keep the wild flood confin'd! *Let order die!*
> And let *this world* no longer be *a stage*
> To feed contention in a ling'ring *act;*
> But let one spirit of the first-born Cain
> Reign in all bosoms, that, each heart being set
> On bloody courses, the rude *scene* may end,
> And *darkness* be the burier of the dead! (I. i. 153-160)

Here the world-stage is truly cosmic. The author seems to envision a return to ancient chaos, in which all "order" shall disappear, overwhelmed by the "wild flood" of primal matter. This wreckage of the physical universe is to accompany the breaking down of the moral order among men, when every man's hand is turned against his fellow, as Cain's was against Abel. The speech involves two themes which we find frequently in Shakespeare. One I shall call Cosmic Despair, in which an individual under the stress of great emotion attributes to the universe about him a similar agitation. In Shakespeare, this most commonly is occasioned by the death of a loved one. Montaigne recognizes the tendency to see one's own troubles reflected in the universe and derides it as a narrow point of view:

31 If the frost chance to nip the vines about my village, my Priest doth presently argue, that the wrath of God hangs over our head, and threatneth all mankind: and judgeth that the Pippe is alreadie falne upon the Canibals.

In viewing these intestine and civill broiles of ours, who doth not exclaime, that the worlds vast-frame is neere unto a dissolution, and that the day of judgement is ready to fall on us? . . . He on whose head it haileth, thinks all the Hemisphere besides to be in a storme and tempest.

(*Essais,* I. xxv: "On the Education of Children," pp. 119-120)

Here may be a hint for Northumberland's outburst and possibly for Lear's ravings in the storm scene, since the characters do have just such a reaction as Montaigne describes. We must remember, of course, that *2 Henry IV* (1600) appeared before Florio's translation of Montaigne was printed, but it is not impossible that Shakespeare had read the French or had seen Florio's manuscript. He does not share Montaigne's derision of this point of view. It is used with telling effect to make the struggles in his tragedies more than the clash of individual persons; in a larger sense they seem to represent the conflicting forces of good and evil in nature itself.

This theme of man's "sympathy" with the universe in turn involves another theme much used by Shakespeare, that of the microcosm, or little world, and the macrocosm, or great world. The topic has been discussed by numerous modern scholars and needs only brief presentation here. Man himself is a "little world" (*King Lear,* III. i. 10) and is in all respects a pattern or copy of the "great world" of the physical universe. His soul corresponds to the World-Soul, his body to the World's body. His veins are rivers, his bones are rocks, etc.; the reader may find an extended sample of such imagery in Phineas Fletcher's *The Purple Island* (1633). There is a sympathy of feeling between the two worlds, great moral upheavals in the world of men being reflected in great physical upheavals of nature.

Northumberland's words, "Let order die . . . And darkness be the burier of the dead," show an apparent verbal indebtedness to Job's account of the land of the dead:

> 32 Before I go and shall not return, even to the *land of darkness* and shadow of *death;*
> Into a land, I say, dark as darkness itself, and into the shadow of death, *where is none order,* but the light is there as darkness.
> (10:21-22) (G)

The first phrase also suggests Hamlet's "undiscover'd country" (*infra,* p. 134) and immediately follows other phrases echoed in Shakespeare (*infra,* p. 45). The combination of these parallels makes the passage a probable Shakespearean source.

While Northumberland's Cosmic Despair has literary precedent, its combination with the world-stage is Shakespeare's own device. The image borrowed from the *Zodiake* has broadened into the conception of all human life as a mighty drama reflecting an even mightier drama of unseen forces moving through the earth, the heavens, and the stars. The actor is man, the stage is the world, the backdrop is the universe.

Chapter 3

Dusty Death

THE IMAGERY OF the world-stage reaches its climax in a passage expressive of despair, spoken by Macbeth upon hearing of his wife's death. Perhaps nowhere else in all literature is there better evidence that adaptation can result in passages of the highest poetic power. The images of Macbeth's speech are largely derived images drawn from two principal sources, the Bible and *The Zodiake of Life*. His lines are these:

She should have died hereafter;
There would have been a time for such a word.
Tomorrow, and tomorrow, and tomorrow
Creeps in this petty pace from day to day
To the last syllable of recorded time;
And all our yesterdays have lighted fools
The way to dusty death. Out, out, brief candle!
Life's but a walking shadow, a poor player
That struts and frets his hour upon the stage
And then is heard no more. It is a tale
Told by an idiot, full of sound and fury,
Signifying nothing. (V. v. 17-28)

The player is life, the stage is the world, trodden by the "fools" who are daily lighted to their deaths. These images are easily perceived as a continuation of those mentioned in the preceding chapter. We shall now consider their context:

She should have *died* hereafter;
There would have been *a time for such a word.*

As Mr. Noble has observed, these lines are reminiscent of Ecclesiastes 3:1-8:

33 To all things *there is* an appointed time, and *a time* to every purpose under the heaven. A time to be born, and *a time to die*. . . . a time to weep, and a time to laugh, a time to mourn, and a time to dance. . . . a time to keep silence, and *a time to speak:* a time to love, and a time to hate: a time of war, and a time of peace. (G)

The next significant phrase reads:

Tomorrow, and tomorrow, and tomorrow.

The context of this line suggests an indebtedness to the *Zodiake,* where we find a passage of similar tenor:

34 *a* O fading life that subject art to thousande casualties, (p. 235)
O to to shorte and doubtfull state, that smokelike from vs flies,
b Now this, now that man drops away, and thou this present day,
To morrowe I: thus at the last we all do passe away,
None otherwise than simple sheepe, that Butcher hath preparde
In folde to kill, now these now those, with knife he striketh harde.
To morrowe other *the next day* moe, thus all in time they dye,
Till that by this his slaughters great, the folde doth emptye lye.
c This fading lyfe therfore despise, which first beginning takes
With teares, his middest is toile & griefe, and death conclusion makes.

In 34*c* we again find the "crying child" image, which furnishes a link to associate this passage with 17*a* and the world-stage. It therefore seems likely that Macbeth's threefold "tomorrow" may reflect Palingenius' "To morrowe. . . . To morrowe. . . . the next day." This seems even more probable from the Latin, in which "tomorrow" is repeated all three times: "Cras . . . cras . . . post cras." Here is an instance in which Shakespeare apparently recalled the Latin and the English together. In the Latin, Q. 34 reads as follows:

35 O fragilis nimium, innumerisque obnoxia vita
Casibus, o nimium brevis atque incerta, recedens
Fumi instar! Nunc hic moritur, nunc ille: hodie tu,
Cras ego: sic demum paulatim extinguimur omnes,
Non secus ac pecudes, lanius quas servat ovili
Mactandas; nunc has ferro, nunc percutit illas,
Cras alias, *post cras* alias: sic denique cunctas
Dilaniat: donec caulae reddantur inanes.
Hanc igitur fragilem vitam contemnite, cuius
Principium est fletus, medium labor et dolor, et mors
Finis. (XII. 312-322)

The passage gains more significance from its context. On the preceding page (234) Palingenius warns "Fooles and beastly people" not to concentrate their attention upon perishable treasures of earth but to think of a future life. He then proceeds to his figure of Death the butcher as given in the quoted passage. His lines thus suggest "fools" as thoughtless materialists and as hapless victims of destiny; in either or both senses they may correspond to Macbeth's "fools" who proceed inevitably to death.

All our yesterdays.

Life's but a walking shadow.

A tale told.

These phrases represent an interesting complex of images from the Book of Job and the Psalter:

36 For we are but of *yesterday,* and are ignorant: for *our days* upon earth are *but a shadow.* (Job 8:9) (G)

37 Thou turnest man to destruction. . . . For a thousand years in thy sight are but as *yesterday,* seeing that is past as a watch in the night. As soon as thou scatterest them they are even as a sleep; and fade away suddenly like the grass. . . . For when thou art angry, *all our days* are gone: we bring our years to an end, as it were *a tale that is told.* (Psalms 90:3-6, 9)

38 For man *walketh* in a vain *shadow,* and disquieteth himself in vain. (Psalms 39:7)

Here it seems highly probable that "yesterday," "our days," and "all our days" have been recalled together to produce Macbeth's "all our yesterdays." The similar phrasing in the two scriptural passages would cause the attentive reader to associate them with each other. Likewise, the comparison of life to a shadow, which is the intent though not the exact phrasing of the first and third passages above, would cause them to be recalled together. Professor Kittredge points out the indebtedness of Macbeth's "walking shadow" to Psalms 39:7 in the Prayer Book Version (G and B have the same reading). The reading which I have given from Job is that of most sixteenth century versions but not of the Authorised, which omits the word "but" in the phrase "but a shadow." The earlier inclusion of the word is significant for verbal reminiscence, since "our days upon earth" is a close equivalent for "Life" as Macbeth uses the term and Job's line amounts to a statement that "life is but a shadow." It becomes a "walking shadow" because of the association of the image with Psalms 39:7, "man walketh in a vain shadow." It is even possible that "struts and frets" was suggested by "disquieteth himself in vain," for the mental pictures evoked by the two phrases are somewhat similar, though the words are entirely different and would have no significant resemblance except for their contexts.

Edmund Malone cited Psalms 90:9, "a tale that is told," as a probable source of *King John,* III. iv. 108: "Life is as tedious as a twice-told tale" (*Variorum,* p. 271). Mr. Noble suggests as a
[39] source for the line Wisdom 2:1, "Our life is short and tedious." (Cf. Q. 154.) Here the two biblical phrases seem to have combined in Shakespeare's mind to produce the line quoted. The "tale told" appears again in the same play, this time combined with the world-stage: "This *act* is as an ancient *tale* new *told*" (IV. ii. 18). Here "act" suggests a theatrical performance. We are not surprised to find the same association of images reappearing in Macbeth's lines, where life is first a poor player upon the stage and then "*a tale told* by an idiot."

Shakespeare's "sound and fury" resists any precise attribution of sources, but some lines from his reading may have contributed to the formation of his phrase. Palingenius uses "fury" to describe conditions in time of war, when laws are overridden and all restraints are cast aside:

40 In time of battaile Lawes do ceasse, and ouerthrowne do lye, (p. 189)
Then *fury* raines, and vice doth rage, abrode at libertie. . . .
To tosse the blades mad men do loue. . . .

This condition is sure to follow when a wicked prince ascends the throne:

41 Then commes the yron world againe, and Mars approcheth neare, (p. 170)
Then *fury* conquers lawes and right, then lawfull is it found
For vice to liue vnpunished, then vertue lies a ground.

A third description of war emphasizes the loud sounds of battle and the fact that only "idiotes" desire it:

42 But[1] *idiotes,* none do enuy peace, and couet Martial ground. . . . (p. 52)
All things doth Discorde vile disturbe, wyth raged motion mad:
And filles and *feareth* euery place, wyth *broyling tumult* sad.
Nowe fierce we forced are to be, & lawes wyth sworde to slake:
The *furies* all of hel they swarme, a thousand brondes they shake.

[1] *But.* Except.

While the "furies" here are the Erinyes of Greek mythology, the word adds a verbal link with the other two passages; all three emphasize the madness of war and the overthrow of law. The comment on the wicked prince in Q. 41, and the "broyling tumult" with which Discord "feareth" or terrorizes every place, recall Job's description of the tyrant fearful of his destruction:

> 43 The ungodly sorroweth all the days of his life . . . and the number of a *tyrant's* years is unknown. A *fearful sound* is in his ears, and when it is peace, yet feareth he destruction. He believeth never to be delivered out of darkness, for the sword is always before his eyes. . . . Sorrow and carefulness will make him afraid, and compass him round about, like as it were *a king with his host ready to the battle.* For he hath stretched out his hand against God, and armed himself against the Almighty. (Job 15:20-25) (C)

In this explanation of "sound and fury" the chain of evidence is clearly incomplete. I suspect that somewhere in Shakespeare's reading such a phrase as "furious sound" occurred in a suitable context and acted as a catalyst to bring together in his mind the passages I have quoted. I cite them, from works with which he was familiar, as possible contributory sources of his phrase because they agree with Macbeth's situation and with the mood of his speech in the final act. In this phrase Shakespeare suggests the unthinking violence and comfortless despair of those who can see no purpose in life. He expresses in one vigorous image what Matthew Arnold later said more quietly in the final lines of *Dover Beach:*

> For we are here as on a darkling plain,
> Swept with confused alarms of struggle and flight,
> Where ignorant armies clash by night.

Or, as Palingenius sums it up in a single line descriptive of this our life:

> 44 Here daily warres, and darknesse blind, and euery kinde of paine. (p. 218)

We now return to what is perhaps the most memorable image of Macbeth's speech, "dusty death." No other phrase conveys quite so strong a connotation of the evanescence and futility of earthly existence. It has a double significance, suggesting the dust within the grave and also the dust to which the body shall be changed after entering the grave. J. P. Collier pointed out that the precise form of the phrase occurs in Anthony Copley's *A Fig for Fortune* (1596) and that Shakespeare may be echoing it (*Variorum,* p. 334). This is quite probable, yet it is not a sufficient explanation of the images in the background of Shakespeare's mind. Some attention to these is necessary if we are to comprehend the tremendous emotional power which the phrase conveys in Macbeth's speech. Our principal difficulty is an embarrassment of riches, for the phrase or its substance had become a thoroughly conventional image.

The ultimate source of the image is apparently God's condemnation of mankind after the Fall:

45 Dust thou art, and into dust shalt thou be turned again.
(Gen. 3:19) (B)

This phrase anticipates other biblical passages using the same image and also the "dust to dust" in the Burial Service. Shakespeare's remembrance of this usage is indicated by several passages. Hamlet calls man "this quintessence of dust" (II. ii. 320). The Duke in *Measure for Measure* says: "For thou exist'st on many a thousand grains That issue out of dust" (III. i. 20-21). The dirge for Fidele in *Cymbeline* uses "must . . . come to dust" as its effective refrain (IV. ii. 258-281). Other biblical statements to the same effect are found in Job 34:15, Psalms 103:14, and Ecclesiastes 3:20. The last of these occurs in a context of pessimistic disillusionment and may have had some effect on the mood of Macbeth's speech.

In this juncture we may fall back upon our tests of internal evidence, seeking to discover when the dust-image occurs in conjunction with other images used by Shakespeare. By this test we can be quite certain of one indebtedness to the Bible, again from the Book of Job:

46 My flesh is clothed with worms and *dust of the earth*. . . . My days pass over more speedily than *a weaver's shuttle,* and are spent without hope. . . . The cloud is consumed and vanished away: so he that goeth down to the grave shall come no more up. . . . When I say, My bed shall comfort me, . . . then fearest thou me with dreams, and makest me so afraid through visions, that my soul wisheth rather to

> perish and die, than my bones to remain. . . . Behold, now must I *sleep in the dust,* and if thou seekest me *tomorrow* in the morning, I shall not be. (7:5-21) (B)

The "weaver's shuttle" clearly appears in Falstaff's lines:

> I fear not Goliath with a weaver's beam; because I know also life is a shuttle. (*Merry Wives of Windsor,* V. i. 23-24)

Here Falstaff himself is made to illustrate Shakespeare's mental habit of associating similar images occurring in different sources.

He recalls from I Samuel 17:7 that the shaft of Goliath's
[47] spear "was like a weaver's beam" (B), and from Job 7:6 that
one's days pass like "a weaver's shuttle." The presence of "weaver" in both passages has caused their instant association in his mind, resulting in a truly confused reference to the Bible. Shakespeare has achieved a comic effect by having Falstaff use clumsily a technique which he himself used constantly and well.

Since we can be sure of Shakespeare's acquaintance with this passage, it is highly probable that the dust-images from it were in his mind during his composition of Macbeth's speech. This also lends significance to Job's account of his terrifying dreams, which are so bad that they make him prefer death to life. Here may be a very definite hint for Macbeth's earlier lines:

> But let the frame of things disjoint, both the worlds suffer,
> Ere we will eat our meal in fear and sleep
> In the affliction of these terrible dreams
> That shake us nightly. Better be with the dead
> Whom we, to gain our peace, have sent to peace,
> Than on the torture of the mind to lie
> In restless ecstasy. (III. ii. 16-22)

The first line of the quotation stamps this as another instance of Cosmic Despair. The similar accounts of terrifying dreams illustrate another point which I believe to be true of Shakespeare. His use of such recollected sources is not limited to mere verbal reminiscences but is sometimes worked out at length in character-revealing thoughts and actions. We shall see later that Macbeth's "terrible dreams" have drawn some hints from the *Zodiake* (*infra,* p. 92).

We also have reason to believe that Shakespeare's dust-image is indebted to the *Zodiake,* where it occurs four times, each time in conjunction with other images used by Shakespeare. Three of these uses will be discussed later (*infra,* pp. 132, 140, 145). Most significant of all is a line on p. 68, where in the midst of a passage on God's greatness there is a parenthetical admonition to man:

48 (O *candle* set before the windes, O subiect *dust* to graue).

Here is the exact combination found in Macbeth's line: "The way to dusty death. Out, out, brief candle!" In both passages the candle is the life of man, the dust is that of man's body in the grave. Shakespeare has reversed the order in which the images are given by Googe but gives the same order as that appearing in the Latin original:

49 (O mortale lutum, ventisque obiecta lucerna). (V. 284)

The proximity of the two images in a single line of the *Zodiake* may account for their proximity in a single line of Macbeth's speech.

As is here demonstrated, Macbeth's lines show to an eminent degree the technique of adaptation. The recollection and transmutation of familiar images may produce poetic utterances of a high order. Their familiarity may produce a favorable impression on both author and reader, who will find in them no sense of strangeness and may regard them as the fresh utterance of an accepted truth. The passage further illustrates the process of enrichment which Shakespeare's images draw from the various sources in the background of his mind. His most memorable phrases are likely to be a crystallization, as it were, of the essential thought in several sources, caught in a few unforgettable words.

Chapter 4

Brief Candle

BRIEF CANDLE," the second image in Macbeth's memorable line, likewise is traceable to the Scriptures; but, through its association with other sources in Shakespeare's mind, it comes to have a significance far beyond that of mere verbal reminiscence. It has a definite symbolic value, for Macbeth clearly means the candle to represent the life of man. This usage is biblical:

50 The *candle* of the wicked shall be put out. (Prov. 13:9) (G)

51 The *candle* of the ungodly shall be put out. (Prov. 24:20) (B)

52 How oft shall the *candle* of the wicked be put out. . . . They shall be as stubble *before the wind,* and as chaff that the storm carrieth away. (Job 21:17-18) (G)

The final instance here quoted has the verbal links to associate it with Palingenius' description of life quoted in the preceding chapter: "O candle set before the windes"; and our knowledge of Shakespeare's methods makes it seem likely that he did associate the two passages with each other. Still other uses of the light-symbol occur in the Scriptures:

53 The *lantern* of the Lord is the breath of man. (Prov. 20:27) (B)

54 He that curseth his father or his mother, his *light* shall be put out in obscure darkness. (Prov. 20:20) (G)

55 Yea, the *light* of the ungodly shall be put out, and the spark of his fire shall not shine. The *light* shall be dark in his dwelling, and his *candle* shall be put out with him. (Job 18:5-6) (B)

These examples are sufficient to show the probable ultimate sources of the light-symbol in Shakespeare when used as an equivalent for life, though the symbol appears elsewhere also; e.g., in Lucretius' *De Rerum Natura,* V. 989. While it is dangerous to press Shakespeare's use of symbolism too far, it is well to recognize his adoption of a symbol so common as this, one which would be readily understood by his audience. His particular interpretation of the symbol was seriously modified by his reading of the *Zodiake* and *The French Academie*. In the former we read:

56 *a* Now let vs seeke to know (p. 122)
How liuing things doe waxe so great, what causeth them to grow:
b And why at certeine time they cease. A *fiery spirit* doth raine,
Which quickneth euery liuing thing, in world which doth remaine.
This heate doth liuely moisture feede, as *flame of Candle* bright,
(When Sunne withdrawes himself from vs) the *Oile* preserues in sight. . . .
c At length it makes an end and stayes, when spent is all the heate, (p. 123)
Which fading, body fades: as shewes in them whose yeares are great,
For wasted they like pined Ghostes, their aged lymmes doe crooke,
And stouping low with hollowed eyes vpon the earth doe looke.
d For fyre is gone, and *liuely heate,* and moysture doth decay,
Without the which no lyfe remaines: as *Lampes* no longer may
Giue out their *light* than *oyle* doth serue, but dies and darknesse brings.

In this passage the "fiery spirit" (56*b*) recalls Virgil's
[57] "spiritus . . . igneus vigor" which springs from celestial
seeds and animates all living things (*Aeneid,* VI. 724-732). The speculations concerning man's growth and decline are reflected in one of Shakespeare's sonnets (*infra,* p. 253). It is to be noticed that the light, lamp, and candle all appear in Palingenius' lines, with the added explanation of the way in which "liuely heate" is fed by the moisture of the body. This process is made even more explicit by several passages in *The French Academie:*

58 Now the vital spirit is as it were a most bright & liuely flame, like to the celestiall nature, which carrieth heat & life to the whole body, and is the instrument of the chiefe actions & works therof. (Pt. II, ch. 38)

59 For as we haue already touched, our life is much like to a flame in a lamp, that receiueth food from the oile put into the lamp, euen so the vital spirit, which is as a flame within vs, draweth & taketh nourishment from the veins. (Pt. II, ch. 63)

60 For we haue already heard, how after the liuing body is growne vp to his full vigor and strength, it beginneth then little and little to faile, and to tend vnto death, whereby in the end it falleth away altogether. For according vnto that comparison and similitude, which hath beene already propounded vnto vs of a lamp, the flame whereof cannot be ioyned still with the weake [wick] except there bee some cleauing moisture to knit the parts together: so there is in a liuing body a certaine humiditie that holdeth of the nature of the aire, which moisture

is very good, & is dispersed throughout the whole body, hauing his propagation of the seede, and ioyning together all the parts of the body. This is commonly called the *Radicall humour,* because it is as it were the roote of life, and hath the celestiall and quickening heate brought immediatly and directly vnto it: so that when this moisture is extinguished, the heate also vanisheth, & fadeth away. And looke as the heate drinketh vp and consumeth by little and little this humidity so doth the heate it selfe diminish and languish away because his food faileth that is in the moisture: euen as the flame, lesseneth and loseth his vigor, as the oyle, or tallow, or wax faileth in a lamp, or in a candle. (Pt. II, ch. 69)

In these passages the flame of life nourished by its "oil" or radical humor is an analogy consciously employed to explain the waxing and waning of human strength and energy. Shakespeare is fully cognizant of this physiological explanation. He uses the eyes as the windows through which this flame of life shines, perhaps recalling Matt. 6:22, "The light of the body is the eye." (G)

In *1 Henry VI,* Mortimer's dying speech draws upon Palingenius for the extinguished lamp and for other images as well:

These eyes, *like lamps whose wasting oil is spent,*
Wax dim, as drawing to their exigent;
Weak shoulders, overborne with burdening grief,
And pithless arms, like to a withered vine
That droops his sapless branches to the ground.
Yet are these feet, whose strengthless stay is numb,
(Unable to support this *lump of clay*)
Swift-winged with *desire to get a grave,*
As witting I no other *comfort* have. (II. v. 8-16)

Here the eyes are compared to the lamps without oil, but it is clear that these represent the fading of the lamp of life. They are perhaps the "hollowed eyes" of Palingenius' lines. The weak shoulders, arms, and feet may stem from his "aged limmes." The phrase "lump of clay" as a synonym for the human body probably comes from the *Zodiake* also, where it is used in combination with the dust-image (*infra,* p. 132).

The two final lines of Mortimer's speech reflect the phraseology of Job 10:18-20:

61 O that I had perished, and that no eye had seen me! And that I were as though I had not been, but brought from the womb *to the grave.*

> Are not my days few? Let him then leave off from me, and let me alone, that I may *comfort* myself a little. (B)

The verses immediately following refer to "the land of darkness . . . where is none order," already quoted (*supra,* p. 34), and the two borrowings reinforce each other as a probable source of Shakespeare's lines.

The image of the eyes as "wasting lamps" which show the fading flame of life appears again in Aegeus' speech from *The Comedy of Errors:*

> Though now this grained face of mine be hid
> In *sap-consuming* winter's drizzled snow,
> And all the conduits of my blood froze up,
> Yet hath my night of life some memory,
> My *wasting lamps* some *fading* glimmer left,
> My dull deaf ears a little use to hear. (V. i. 311-316)

The "sap" is the "radicall humor" which is gradually consumed as old age comes on.

In *Richard II,* John of Gaunt employs both the lamp and the candle to describe his state after Bolingbroke's exile:

> My *oil-dri'd lamp* and *time-bewasted light*
> Shall be extinct with age and endless night;
> My inch of *taper* will be burnt and done,
> And blindfold Death not let me see my son. (I. iii. 221-224)

Here "age" and "endless night" may owe something to the description of age and "darknesse" of death in Palingenius' lines (56*c, d*). "Blindfold Death" is probably a reference to Atropos, the third Fate, whose shears cut the thread of life (cf. *King John,* IV. ii. 91, *Pericles,* I. ii. 108).

A similar reference to the flame of life appears in *All's Well* in the King's words concerning Bertram's father:

> 'Let me not live,' quoth he,
> 'After *my flame lacks oil.*' (I. ii. 58-59)

These lines express a wish for death before one reaches the feebleness of extreme senility.

The candle, used alone in the image, appears in *3 Henry VI,* in Clifford's dying speech on the battlefield:

> Here *burns my candle out,* ay, here it dies,
> Which, while it lasted, gave King Henry light. (II. vi. 1-2)

Sometimes the flame of life appears as a torch, essentially the same image, since Shakespeare's "waxen torch" (*Lucrece,* 178) is apparently a large candle. At Mortimer's death, in the scene already cited from *1 Henry VI,* Plantagenet observes:

> Here dies the dusky *torch* of Mortimer. (II. v. 122)

In *Measure for Measure* the Duke observes to Angelo:

> Heaven doth with us as we with *torches* do,
> Not light them for themselves. (I. i. 33-34)

He is urging Angelo not to be self-centered. The same idea in a different context is associated with the oil-dried lamp in Venus' amorous plea to Adonis:

> Be prodigal: the *lamp* that burns by night
> *Dries up his oil* to lend the world his light. (755-756)

She expresses essentially the same meaning as our proverbial phrase, "to burn the candle at both ends."

The image of the flame of life is used to convey intense emotion in *Antony and Cleopatra.* Believing that Cleopatra is dead, Antony says:

> I will o'ertake thee, Cleopatra, and
> Weep for my pardon. So it must be, for now
> All length is torture; since *the torch is out,*
> Lie down, and stray no farther. (IV. xiv. 44-47)

Here the torch refers to Cleopatra's life, which Antony pictures as necessary to his own existence. Later, as Cleopatra sits by the dying Antony, she says:

> Ah, women, women, look,
> *Our lamp is spent, it's out. . . .* Come, away;
> This case of that huge *spirit* now is cold. (IV. xv. 84-89)

In this instance the "lamp" refers to Antony's life or spirit, which Cleopatra pictures as the light of her existence.

The images of the flame of life darkened by death reach a climax in Othello's soliloquy by Desdemona's bedside. Here the transforming power of imagination is working at its highest pitch:

> It is the cause, it is the cause, my soul,—
> Let me not name it to you, you chaste stars!—
> It is the cause. Yet I'll not shed her blood,
> Nor scar that whiter skin of hers than snow,
> And smooth as monumental alabaster.
> Yet she must die, else she'll betray more men.
> Put out the light, and then put out the light.
> If I quench thee, thou flaming minister,
> I can again thy former light restore,
> Should I repent me; but once put out thy light,
> Thou cunning'st pattern of excelling nature,
> I know not where is that Promethean heat
> That can thy light relume. When I have pluck'd the rose,
> I cannot give it vital growth again,
> It needs must wither. I'll smell it on the tree. (V. ii. 1-15)

It is obvious that the "flaming minister" is a lamp, candle, or torch in Desdemona's bedchamber, here used for a direct comparison with the flame of life. The adjective "flaming" may have been recollected from La Primaudaye, who defines the vital spirit as a flame (Q. 58). The phrase "flaming minister" is verbally reminiscent of Hebrews 1:7:

62 Who maketh his angels spirits, and his *ministers* a *flame* of fire. (B)

The phrase "Promethean heat" recalls Palingenius' "liuely heate" (56*d*), which means life-giving heat and thus is an exact equivalent of Othello's phrase. Shakespeare probably remembered Ovid's *Metamorphoses* (I. 76-86), which states that Prometheus fashioned man from moist soil retaining some portion of celestial aether (often identified with fire) remaining after the separation of the four elements, and that this provided the vital spark of life to the man so formed. Arthur Golding, in the prefatory *Epistle* to his translation of Ovid, explains that the fire stolen by Prometheus from heaven represents the spark of life which animates our bodies of clay, and he identifies Prometheus with Christ the divine Word. Prometheus' creation of man symbolically represents the creation of Adam in or near the Garden of Eden (*Epistle,* 421-454).

In Othello's speech, the image of the flame of life appears in a framework of other images, also derivative for the most part. His thrice-repeated exclamation, "It is the cause," is elusive in meaning.

It seems to imply a cause or case at law, which Othello has tried in his own mind, with a verdict of guilty. It is a cause which should not be named to the *chaste* stars, presumably because it concerns unchastity. The threefold repetition of "cause" suggests that Shakespeare may have been peculiarly sensitive to the sound of this word. It is used again with the same refrain-like quality in Cordelia's reply to Lear:

> *Lear.* You have some cause, they have not.
> *Cordelia.* No cause, no cause. (IV. vii. 75)

I suggest that his interest in the word may stem from Psalm 35 and that the sound-image may have impressed him from his hearing it read or chanted in church:

63 Plead thou *my cause,* O Lord, with them that strive with me, and fight thou against them that fight against me. . . . For they have *privily laid their net* to destroy me *without a cause;* yea, even *without a cause* have they made a pit for my soul. . . . that hate me *without a cause.* . . . Awake and stand up to judge my quarrel; avenge thou *my cause.* (vv. 1, 7, 19, 23)

This is the Prayer Book reading. In the Bishops' Bible, Psalms 35:7 reads:

64 For without a cause they have *privily laid for me a pit full of their nets:* without a cause they have made a digging unto my soul.

It should be observed that the psalm uses "cause" in two senses. "My cause" refers to the right to demand or exact justice, just such a cause as Othello mistakenly thinks he has. The word is echoed in Desdemona's "I never gave him cause" (III. iv. 158) and in Cassio's "I never gave you cause" (V. ii. 299). Again, the Psalmist's phrase "without a cause" suggests Iago's motiveless hate toward Othello, which has no real cause proportionate to its vehemence. Without cause he has "privily laid his net" for Othello's soul. He speaks of this "net":

> And out of her own goodness make the *net*
> That shall *enmesh* them all. (II. iii. 367-368)

Othello refers to this net, and his puzzlement at Iago's malignity again suggests the phrase "without a cause":

> Will you, I pray, demand that demi-devil
> Why he hath thus *ensnar'd* my soul and body? (V. ii. 301-302)

Here the "net" of Psalm 35 may have become a snare from the association of the two words in Job:

65 For his feet are taken as it were in the *net,* and he walketh upon the *snares.* . . . The *snare* is laid for him in the ground, and a pitfall in the way. (18:8, 10) (B)

The combined use of "net" and "pitfall" (C, B, but not G) could readily have recalled the "nets" and "pit" of Psalms 35:7 and have identified them with the "snares" of Job 18. (Q. 55 comes from the same chapter of Job.)

The word "alablaster," to give it the Elizabethan spelling, is used by Palingenius to describe the beauty of a woman's skin (p. 44), and this may be Shakespeare's source, though the usage is not uncommon. Shakespeare had used it before in *Lucrece,* 419. The phrase "whiter skin than snow" involves an interesting complex of biblical
images. It recalls Psalms 51:7, the *Miserere*: "Thou shalt
[66] wash me and I shall be *whiter than snow.*" The implication
is that Desdemona looks innocent and pure, as one wholly without sin. But "white as snow" is also the biblical phrase used to describe the skin of a leper (2 Kings 5:27). Therefore, the use of the phrase in connection with the word "skin" may also suggest impurity, such as that of Cressida, who was unchaste and ultimately succumbed to leprosy (cf. Henryson's *Testament of Cresseid*). Perhaps this double meaning is in Othello's mind, with some such connotation as "whited sepulchre" conveys to us, for he stresses Desdemona's viciousness in line 6, immediately following.

Othello also uses the rose as a symbol for life. His own words "vital growth" indicate that the rose is the life of Desdemona. The rose as a symbol for life probably stems from the *Zodiake,* where it appears in close conjunction with other images borrowed by Shakespeare (163*f, infra*). We may also ask what is the tree on which the rose grows. While Desdemona lives, the rose is still attached to the tree; her death will separate it from the tree. Her breath, which

Othello smells as he kisses her, is the fragrance given off by the rose. This may reflect the double meaning of the Latin *anima,* which means both "breath" and "soul" or animating force; it is not limited to the rational soul but includes the whole life-force within the individual. Such was the "breath of life" which God breathed into Adam after forming his body of earth (Gen. 2:7).

The "tree" is hardly comparable to the body of Desdemona, from which her life is to be separated, for the body will be a dead thing, while the tree will continue to live. Perhaps Shakespeare is recalling the Tree of Life, in the Garden of Eden, figuratively presenting it as a central tree of existence of which individual lives are the separate blossoms and fruits. Desdemona, dying young, is pictured as a blossom rather than as a fruit. Such a figurative use of
a Tree of Existence is found in Marsilio Ficino's *Commen-*
[67] *tary on Plotinus,* which states that "underlying the individ-
ual lives of living things there exists from the World-Soul a power of growth common to them all and waking all things everywhere in the World-Tree."[1] While there is no evidence that Shakespeare had read this passage, the figure could well have come to him indirectly from this or some other source.

We know that in *Othello* Shakespeare does have in mind the Garden of Eden, for he has made Iago analogous to the Serpent. In denouncing the unknown villain who has slandered Desdemona, Emilia invokes "the serpent's curse" upon him (IV. ii. 16). This is the curse which God spoke to the Serpent after the Fall:

> 69 And the Lord God said unto the serpent, Because thou hast done this, thou art cursed above all cattle, and above every beast of the field: upon thy belly shalt thou go, and dust shalt thou eat all the days of thy life. (Gen. 3:14) (B)

In several other instances Iago is compared to the devil with something more than mere objurgation (II. iii. 357, V. ii. 287, 301). It seems that Shakespeare is thinking of the original temptation as a prototype of that in his play. We may therefore suggest that, since

[1] "Semper vero memento, praeter vitas animantium proprias, subesse cunctis communem vim ex mundi anima vegetalem in *arbore mundana* totam ubique vigentem." (Annead IV, bk. III: *De Dubiis Animae,* cap. 8, in *Opera Omnia,* Basle, 1576, p. 1736)

Adam and Eve sinned through trying to be like gods, Othello's real
fault consists in his readiness to usurp the function of God:
[70] "Vengeance belongeth unto me . . . saith the Lord" (Heb.
10:30—G; cf. Deut. 32:35, Psalms 94:1).

Two other biblical reminiscences should be mentioned before we leave this scene. When Othello says, "I would not kill thy soul" (line 32), he is echoing Christ's words in Matt. 10:28, a verse which is also echoed in *Richard III,* I. ii. 46-48, and in *Hamlet,* I. iv. 64-67. The verse reads as follows:

> 71 And fear ye not them which kill the body, but are not able to *kill the soul:* but rather fear him which is able *to destroy both soul and body in hell.* (G, B)

Our knowledge that Christ's words were moving in the background of Shakespeare's mind tells us something of his intent in this scene. Desdemona has nothing to fear, though she is to die; the fate of her body is a small matter compared with the fate of her soul. Othello has great cause to fear, though he does not yet know it. He is in danger of losing both soul and body; he is in danger of hell. This fearful realization emerges in his lines:

> When we shall meet at compt,
> This look of thine will hurl my soul from heaven,
> And fiends will snatch at it. . . .
> Whip me, ye devils. . . .
> Blow me about in winds! roast me in sulphur!
> Wash me in steep-down gulfs of liquid fire! (V. ii. 273-280)

In his self-condemnation he does not think that he should be forgiven and even desires the pains of hell as the utmost expiation that he can make. In theological terms, the agony of his repentance should give sufficient satisfaction for his crime and for the salvation of his soul. Even his suicide is part of his expiation and perhaps should not be regarded with the usual attitude toward self-murder. We need not accept his gloomy view of his own future fate.[2]

---

[2] For additional discussion, see *The Character of Hamlet:* "Suicide in Shakespeare."

Chapter 5

The External Symbol

IN THE SCENE AT Desdemona's bedside, Shakespeare has introduced an actual light—a candle or lamp or torch—to reinforce his symbolic image of the light of life, to which Othello also clearly refers. This intentional introduction of an external symbol suggests that we examine his other works for possible uses of the same symbol. We do find lights introduced into many scenes, as they naturally would be when the supposed time of action is at night. They do not all have symbolic value, but I think that some of them do. The most interesting example occurs in *Lucrece,* where the symbolic presence of a torch foreshadows similar uses in his later works.

In *Lucrece* the torch is constantly emphasized. After Tarquin springs from his bed, he strikes fire from his flint with a sword and lights a waxen torch to show his way to Lucrece's room. The light seems to burn unwillingly. Tarquin says:

> As from this cold flint I *enforc'd this fire,*
> So Lucrece must I force to my desire. (181-182)

He then hesitates and reasons with himself:

> Fair torch, burn out thy light, and lend it not
> To darken her whose light excelleth thine. (190-191)

He reasons that he is foolish who "sells eternity to get a toy" (214). But his lust drives him on. He holds debate " 'tween frozen conscience and hot, burning will" (247). "Burning" might suggest that the torch represents the will, but such is not the case, for the will compels the torch to burn. As he forces his way through the doors from room to room, the wind puts out the torch and blows the smoke into his face as though trying to delay him, but his scorching desire causes him to blow on the torch till its spark kindles into life again (311-315). When he draws the curtain of Lucrece's bed, he is dazzled as though by a light greater than his own, and for the moment his hot desires are quelled (372-378). But they revive. He touches Lucrece, who opens her eyes,

> Who, peeping forth this tumult to behold,
> Are by his flaming torch dimm'd and controll'd. (447-448)

After their lengthy debate, he declares that he is more determined than ever, since

> Small lights are soon blown out, huge fires abide,
> And with the winds in greater fury fret. (647-648)

Finally, he will hear no more words.

> This said, he sets his foot upon the light,
> For light and lust are deadly enemies;
> Shame folded up in blind concealing night. (673-675)

The deed done, he is filled with revulsion for his conduct and rushes away, leaving her behind.

> He in his speed looks for the morning light;
> She prays she never may behold the day. (745-746)

Apparently these lines involve more than mere objective description. The light is an external symbol, but its symbolism is difficult to come by. It is made to serve Tarquin's lust by guiding him to Lucrece, yet it is a deadly enemy of lust and is crushed under foot just before lust's consummation. In his admonition to his torch not to darken Lucrece's superior light, he clearly seems to symbolize some personal quality, such as virtue, in which Lucrece excels himself. Before trying to find a consistent explanation, we may examine a passage from one of Shakespeare's favorite sources. Remembering that Tarquin planned murder as well as adultery, we read these lines from Job 24: 13-17:

72 These are they that abhor the light; they know not the ways thereof, nor continue in the paths thereof. The murderer riseth early and killeth the poor and the needy: and in the night he is as a thief. The eye also of the adulterer waiteth for the twilight, and saith, None eye shall see me: and disguiseth his face. They dig through houses in the dark, which they marked for themselves in the day: they know not the light. But the morning is even to them as the shadow of death: if one know them, they are in the terrors of the shadow of death. (G)

Mr. Noble suggests this passage as a source of *Richard II,* III. ii. 36-46.

The passage contains several suggestive parallels to *Lucrece.* It concerns a murderer and an adulterer, both of which Tarquin had intended to be. In the night the murderer is "as a thief"; after his crime Tarquin creeps away "like a thievish dog" (736). The digging through houses in the dark suggests Tarquin's difficulties in breaking through the doors of the intervening rooms. The abhorrence of the light may be reflected in Tarquin's setting his foot upon his light. The "terrors of the shadow of death" which come with the morning remind us that Tarquin's soul is made a thrall to "living death" by the commission of his crime (726). The darkness and the phrase "No eye shall see me" may have suggested this descriptive stanza:

> Now stole upon the time the dead of night,
> When heavy sleep had clos'd up mortal eyes.
> No comfortable star did lend his light,
> No noise but owls' and wolves' death-boding cries;
> Now serves the season that they may surprise
> The silly lambs. Pure thoughts are dead and still,
> While *lust* and *murder* wakes to stain and kill. (162-168)

Here, as in Job, adultery and murder are listed as crimes which seek the darkness of night for their performance.

A reminiscence from the *Zodiake* also appears in *Lucrece.* We have already observed in 17*b* the source of passages in *The Merchant of Venice.* The same images from the same source appear in *Lucrece* when Tarquin is making light of the heaven-sent obstacles that delay his crime:

> Huge *rocks,* high *winds,* strong *pirates,* shelves and *sands,*
> *The merchant fears,* ere rich at home he lands. (335-336)

The images occur here because 17*b* has recalled to Shakespeare a similar passage which compares the merchant to a violent lover:

73 For as the Marchaunt bolde (p. 49)
> That vnderneth vnhappy starre with wares his ship doth freight,
> And cuts the fearefull foming seas, is often spoild of weight
> By losse of ship, or Pirats fierce: so he that flames wyth loue,

The starres, & luck agaynst hym both: doth seeke the rockes to moue.
An euil name, and cruel wound, receyueth he agayne.
And efte his loue to get, doth he the losse of lyfe sustayne.

Here the merchant's loss of ships to the sea or to pirates would immediately recall the similar imagery of 17*b,* and from that passage Shakespeare borrowed the images; but the analogy in the above lines is the one applicable to Tarquin's situation. He "flames wyth loue," as shown in his "hot burning will" (247) and "huge fires" (647). Luck is against his love in that Lucrece is married and is not open to honorable proposals (241). He seeks to overcome all obstacles—"rockes to moue"—in order to enjoy his love (cf. *infra,* p. 261). The "euil name" and "cruel wound" appear in these lines:

That through the length of times *he stands disgraced.* (718)

Bearing away the *wound* that nothing healeth,
The *scar that will, despite of cure, remain.* (731-732)

These lines also have a verbal indebtedness to La Primaudaye's anecdote of Medius' advice to the flatterers in the court of Alexander the Great:

74 This fellow taught, that they should not spare to nip boldly, and to bite with store of slanders. For (quoth he) *although he* that is bitten *should bee cured of the wound,* yet *the skar* at the least *will* still *remaine.* (Pt. I, ch. 43)

In the same paragraph, five sentences earlier, occurs the statement:

75 For seeing good fame and credite is more precious than any treasure, a man hath no lesse iniurie offered him when his *good name* is taken away, than when he is spoiled of his substance.

This sentiment recalls Prov. 22:1:

76 A *good name* is more to be desired than great riches. (B)

These passages have been recalled and expanded in Iago's speech to Othello:

Good name in man and woman, dear my lord,
Is the immediate jewel of their souls.
Who steals my purse steals trash; 'tis something, nothing;
'Twas mine, 'tis his, and has been slave to thousands;
But he that filches from me my *good name*
Robs me of that which not enriches him,
And makes me poor indeed. (III. iii. 155-161)

We return to our attempt to find a consistent symbolism for Tarquin's torch. A clue is found in his words, already quoted:

> Small lights are soon blown out, huge fires abide,
> And with the winds in greater fury fret.

These lines suggest that there are two fires involved. The "small light" is the flame of Tarquin's torch which had been blown out once by the wind and which is eventually crushed under foot. The "huge fire" is the flame of his "hot heart" which had forced the torch to resume its burning (314). It is also the flame of his "hot burning will" which is opposed by Conscience (247). We should observe that in the sixteenth century "will" was sometimes used as a synonym for "lust." It is this hot flame of lust that causes his hand, "*smoking* with pride," to caress Lucrece's naked breast (438). We therefore find that, by implication at least, the torch is associated with conscience, the fire of lust with will. This double fire may possibly be reminiscent of La Primaudaye's statement that each man bears in himself the material of two fires, the one celestial and divine, the other infernal and diabolic, and that he can decide which of these is to be lighted within him (Pt. II, ch. 96).[1]

To understand the opposing forces in Tarquin's internal struggle, we should observe that they are reason and the affections. "Affection is my captain," he exclaims (271) and again declares:

> But nothing can affection's course control,
> Or stop the headlong fury of his speed. (500-501)

We must remember that the Elizabethans used "affections" much as we use "passions," applying the term to all the emotional impulses of human nature. It is emotional inclination of the mind that develops into passion if it is not checked. Thus Shylock calls affec-

[1] Here and later in this chapter, external probability must be considered, for Part II of *The French Academie* did not appear in English translation until 1594, the same year in which *The Rape of Lucrece* was published. Part I had appeared eight years earlier. While I use Part II to illustrate lines from *Lucrece,* I do not insist upon it as an actual source, though it could have appeared some months before the final draft of *Lucrece* was written. *Lucrece* was not entered in the Stationers' Register for publication until May 9, 1594. Part II of *The French Academie* was entered on June 4, 1589, and thus had existed in manuscript or was in process of translation for five years before it was published. It was available in French before that.

tion "master of passion" which guides passion according to its own inclinations (*Merchant of Venice,* IV. i. 50-52). And Brutus says of Caesar:

> I have not known when his affections sway'd
> More than his reason. (II. i. 20-21)

These lines show that affection is considered the force in the soul that opposes the regimen of reason.

The war between reason and the affections leads us to the *Zodiake,* where a lengthy account of it is given in a discussion of free
will and predestination. It cannot be that man is predestined
[77] to commit wicked deeds, "for Euill deedes doe harme the
Soule," which God created (p. 141), and it is not reasonable to assume that he would have created it for wicked purposes. The free will may be misguided by sickness, madness, the impotence of extreme youth or extreme age. But more often it is obscured in those

> 78 whose filthy minde doth vices foule aray, (p. 142)
> And fonde Affections makes to faint, withdrawing it with strife,
> From Reason farre, and from the path of Right, and Vertuous life.

But the will is free only so long as it obeys reason and is not captured by the affections. The two natures of man are thus described:

> 79 *a* A certeine *Part diuine* in vs that Minde and Reason hight (p. 143)
> There is, which Nature in the head hath plaste aloft in sight,
> And seruants vnto it appoints the senses, that there bee,
> By meanes whereof the Skies and Earth and al things it may see.
> *b* *Another fading force* there is within the breast inclosde,
> By meanes whereof we moue, and growe with helpe of heate disposde.
> (Thus hath it pleased God) this straynes, molests, & grieues the minde,
> And to this part a number great of seruaunts is assignde,
> As Fond delight, Wrath, and Feare, with great Desire to gayne,
> *c* Ambition hauty harmfull thing, with fumes that vex the brayne.
> With these his lusty souldiours he giues battayle to the minde. . . .
> [These are like the giants that fought against Jove.]
> With wor[l]dly thoughtes hie heapt they vexe, the Part diuine aboue,
> *d* Except that *grace from Heauen* hye lyke Lightning them remoue:
> *e* As when the raynes are once let lose, the Chariot *headlong* driues,
> And swiftly runnes, to stay the course in vaine the Carter striues,
> *f* The first Beginnings must be stopt, while sparke but kindled lies.
> •When Fyre hath caught the lofty partes, and flames approch the skyes
> Especially when Boreas blastes from Northerne pole doth fall,

And rageth fierce, in vaine, alas, for water then they call.
g As when from top of hawty rocke, *some waighty stone* down trowles
What force can it of course restraine? al things with it it *rowles,*
Asunder crackes the mighty Trees, that on the mountaine springs,
Which at the first might well be stayed, with force of smallest things.
h Euen so the *Affections* of the minde, if that with all their sway,
The minde opprest they do inuade, them scarce, can Reason stay,
And helme and al forsaken quite, with streame *dame Reason* driues.
In raging windes, and yeldes to foe a captiue kept in gyues. . . .
i But if the assault be now begonne, and siege the foe doth lay,
And shakes with *battrey* great the *walles*: except (beleue me wel,)
Some God with better grace defend, Reason doth byd farewell,
And cannot byde so sore a brunt.

The imagery of this passage greatly affected Shakespeare's thinking. The image of the fire from the unquenched spark (79*f*) occurs in *Venus and Adonis,* where it foreshadows the climactic scene of *Lucrece:*

Affection is a coal that must be cool'd,
Else, suffer'd, it will set the heart on fire. . . .

Who sees his true-love in her naked bed,
Teaching the sheets a whiter hue than white,
But, when his glutton eye so full hath fed,
His other agents aim at like delight?
Who is so faint that dare not be so bold
To touch the fire, the weather being cold? (387-388, 397-402)

Here the fire of affection is associated with the lover standing by his lady's bed. The same situation and similar imagery are worked out carefully in the description of Tarquin's feelings. His "hot heart" (314) was set on fire by his failure to check the spark of affection in the beginning. His image of affection as a huge fire driven into greater fury by the wind (647-648) is apparently borrowed from the like image in the *Zodiake* (79*f*). The "headlong fury of his speed" in reference to affection comes from the image of the "headlong" runaway chariot (79*e*). The assault of the affections against the "Part diuine," or Reason, is given in the analysis of Tarquin's feelings after the crime:

Besides, his soul's fair temple is defaced;
To whose weak ruins muster troops of cares,
To ask the spotted princess how she fares.

She says, her subjects with foul insurrection
Have batter'd down her consecrated wall,
And by their mortal fault brought in subjection
Her immortality, and made her thrall
To living death and pain perpetual;
Which in her prescience she controlled still,
But her foresight could not forestall their will. (719-728)

The "princess" is the Dame Reason of Palingenius' lines (79*h*); her title may have been recalled from a sentence in *The French Academie:*

80 For God hath lodged the vnderstanding & reason in the braine of man, as it were in a high towre, in which it ought to raigne as a Queene and *Princesse,* and guide vnder her lawes al the affections & actions of men, as eyes guide all the members of the body. (Pt. II, ch. 11)

There may also be a recollection of Princess Alma in *The Faerie Queene* (II. xi), whose castle was attacked by the affections, under Maleger. In Tarquin's case the attack was successful; the affections temporarily overcame reason and smirched his soul with crime. "Batter'd . . . wall" seems to reflect the "battrey" and "walles" of 79*i*.

The phrase "mortal fault" refers to the Church's official designation of mortal sin as a particular crime so heinous as to damn the soul irrevocably unless repentance and atonement can be successfully made. The Church included murder, adultery, and witchcraft among such crimes. Until full repentance could bring a fresh infusion of God's grace, a person guilty of such a crime lived in a state of damnation, his soul a "thrall To living death and pain perpetual."

These stanzas accordingly tell us what Tarquin did when he set his foot upon the torch, marking his final decision to consummate his crime. He crushed the light of his immortal soul. He did not blow it out but crushed it violently, as a man might stamp a cigarette stub under foot. If it were blown out, a spark might remain, as it did earlier when he blew it again into life. So he tried to extinguish it utterly, to consummate his crime in spiritual as well as physical darkness.

This leads us to ask just what is the "light" of man's soul. After the crime Tarquin still has his reason or rational faculty. He is not injured in body, though Shakespeare speaks of his "wound that nothing healeth." It seems that he may have lost his "Part diuine"; but Palingenius defines this as reason, which Tarquin has not lost. We seem to be involved in contradictions.

The answer lies in the several connotations of the word "reason" or rational faculty. Since man is the only earthly being capable of logical thought, this capability is his distinguishing characteristic, making him superior to beasts and plants. It makes him capable of understanding and loving God,[2] as no beast or plant could, no matter how virtuous their lives. This capability, or rational soul, is bound up with the two lower souls which control bodily functions and sensory perception, the whole constituting the "soul" of man. The "flame of life" may refer to continued physical existence, as in many of the instances already quoted, but the "light of life" has frequently a different connotation. It is the bond between man and God. It refers to that "godlike reason" which makes us capable of desiring union with God. But that reason may be misdirected by an error of the will and may be turned against God. In such a case, the reason is a candle or torch which no longer shines and cannot until man's will is once more in harmony with God's.

Some connotation of this kind is definitely found in biblical uses of "light." The references to the wicked who "walk in darkness" (Ps. 82:5) and "abhor the light" (Job 24:13—G) are not references to those lacking reason but to those whose wills are not in harmony with God's will. Christians are saved "from the power of darkness" (Col. 1:13—G). In false teachers there is no light (Isa. 8:20—B). Christ is the light of the world, and those that follow him shall have the "light of life" (John 8:12—C, G). Figuratively speaking, "life" consists in harmony with God and "death" in alienation from God, without reference to the extinction of the vital or mental powers.

There is something in the spirit of man which resents the suppression of its light and struggles to revive it when suppressed. The

[2] Cf. Thomas Aquinas, *Summa Theologica,* Pt. I, Q. XII, AA. 1, 7, 12.

natural state of the rational faculty is harmony with God. Though it may succumb to the will perverted by affections, it never succumbs willingly but waits an opportunity to reassert its claims when the affections are satiated or otherwise weakened. It clamors to be revived. The assertion of this claim accounts for the tortures of conscience, and the awakening of conscience is symbolized by the desire for light. Thus, almost in the moment his desire is accomplished, Tarquin feels the revulsion of conscience which prevents him from carrying out his plans to murder Lucrece:

> He thence departs a heavy convertite . . .
> He in his speed looks for the morning light. (743-745)

To desire the light is not to achieve it but constitutes the first step thereto. Tarquin may achieve the difficult task of repentance, or he may continue in a state of comfortless despair; but either state is preferable in the sight of God to callous indifference. The most
terrible state of all is that of the man who can experience no
[81] remorse, whose conscience is "seared with an hot iron" and
can feel no more (I Tim. 4:2—B).

Is this symbolism consistent with the earlier uses of the torch in *Lucrece*? I think that it is. We may recall Hamlet's reference to "this capability and godlike reason" which distinguishes men from beasts (IV. iv. 38). It is this capability of rational thought which makes man like God. But this capability can be turned against God if the will which controls it is perverted. Rational thought can be directed toward wrong ends. Reason is the natural guide and adviser of the will, but if the will chooses a different path reason can be forced to follow it and lend aid, albeit unwillingly. This psychology is clearly set forth by both Palingenius and La Primaudaye. The former writes:

82 But some by reason rather led, doe walke as she doth shew, (p. 121)
And onely are by vertue drawne: but such are very few.
For fleshly fond *affections,* oft the minde doe ouerrunne,
None otherwise then mists do darke the cleere and shining Sunne.
Loe, this the cause why bodie moues. The *mouing force of minde*
(Whom moued *will doth still commaund*) *obeyes* as is assignde.

La Primaudaye's explanation is even more definite:

> 83 Now although we said before, that reason held the soueraignty amongst the powers, vertues and offices of the soule, yet wee must know, that reason reigneth not ouer will as Lady and Princesse, but onely as Mistresse to teach and shew it, what it ought to follow & what to flie from. For the will hath no light of it selfe, but is lightned by the minde, that is to say, by reason and iudgement, which are ioyned with it, not to gouerne and turne it from one side to another by commandement and authority, either by force or violence, as a Prince or Magistrate, but as a counsellor or director, to admonish and conduct it.
> (Pt. II, ch. 34)

Though La Primaudaye elsewhere calls the mind a princess (Q. 80), he here makes clear the sense in which the word is used. The will actually makes the decisions as to what a person will do. Its adviser is reason, but at times it may choose not to follow reason, because other strong forces, the affections, seek to guide it in a different direction. Palingenius makes it clear that in such a case the will can command reason. Just before his image of the oil-dried lamp in Q. 56, he has the following lines:

> 84 For Will her selfe of proper force, is altogether blinde, (p. 122)
> And cannot any thing desire, without the light of minde.
> By whom if she be not informde, she takes the vntoward way,
> And with the shew of good beguilde, her vertue doth decay.

For our purpose, the significance of these lines is greatly enhanced by Googe's accompanying marginal note:

> 85 The minde of man is the *candle* of his will.

Here is the clue to the symbolism of Tarquin's waxen torch. His will debates against conscience (247). Lucrece implores, "From a pure heart command thy rebel will" (625). His rational soul, the "spotted princess," says she foresaw the danger arising from the revolt of the affections, "But her foresight could not forestall their will" (728). It is thus clear that Tarquin's will impelled him to commit the crime, against the advice of his mind, and that the will was nevertheless able to command the assistance of the mind in carrying out its nefarious purpose. The mind is the "candle" of the will and must serve when the will has use for it. Such an interpretation explains its use as a symbol in the description of Tarquin.

Tarquin, "madly toss'd between desire and dread" (171), is not exercising reason at all. But when his will, conquered by lust, is bent toward the violation of Lucrece, there are practical difficulties in the way which can only be overcome by the use of the rational faculty. There are unfamiliar passages and locked doors to be traversed, the household must not be awakened by excessive noise, and Lucrece must not be warned of his approach. Accordingly, his will forces his reluctant reason to give aid, symbolized by his lighting the torch. He "forces" the spark from the "cold" flint, just as later his "burning will" overcomes his "frozen conscience." These images of cold express the rational faculty's reluctance to be so employed. It almost wins out when Tarquin says:

> Fair torch, burn out thy light, and lend it not
> To darken her whose light excelleth thine.

But in spite of Conscience's pleadings, the speech ends, "My will is strong, past reason's weak removing" (243). He concentrates on keeping the torch burning, that is, on keeping his rational faculty alert in the midst of his growing excitement. The wind blowing out the torch symbolizes a momentary mental confusion from the violence of his emotions, but he forces the torch to revive and his mind to concentrate on opening the remaining doors. When he draws the curtain of Lucrece's bed, he is dazzled as though by a greater light than his own, that is, by her superior goodness. In their long dialogue, though he declares his intent, he is actually still debating with himself. There is still hope that her words may reinforce his light of reason and move him from his purpose. With his final decision he no longer needs his light nor can endure it. He sets his foot upon it.

It should be clear from this discussion that Shakespeare thinks of the rational faculty as both a skillful planner and a moral arbiter. In its first capacity it unwillingly assists Tarquin to find his way to Lucrece's bed; in its second it violently opposes his action but is overcome by the will. The moment his lust is satiated and his affections thus weakened, it reasserts its control over the will and causes Tarquin to forego the rest of his crime; he rushes away instead to seek for light. This double function of the rational soul is implicit in most of our thinking about it and helps us to understand the double symbolism of the torch, which represents both mental ingenuity and the divine "light of life" which burns brightly only while man's will is in harmony with God's. Such is Lucrece's light which dims Tarquin's, the light of a goodness and virtue possible only to rational beings. And it is in this sense that we should interpret Tarquin's light when he treads it under foot.

The nature of this divine light in man is explicitly described by La Primaudaye in a passage so significant that I shall quote it at length:

> 86 The wicked may flatter themselues, and labour as much as they list to rocke themselues asleepe in their impieties and horrible vices, yet they cannot preuaile so much, but they haue continually a warning peece ringing in their eare, and an Apparitour rapping at their doore without ceasing, so that they cannot alwayes sleepe at their ease. . . .
>
> We are then to know, that although sin hath gretly troubled the mind which God hath giuen vs, by the darknesse of error and ignorance wherewith it is filled, yet it could not so wholy blind it, but stil there remained in it *some sparkles of that light of the knowledge of God,* and of good & euill, which is naturally in men & which is borne with them. This remnant that yet remaineth is commonly called by the Diuines Sinteresis: which is taken from a Greek word, that signifieth as much as if we should say, Preseruation, whereby that remnant of the *light* and law of nature that remaineth in vs, is still preserued and kept in our soule after sin. And so this word Sinteresis signifieth that knowledge of the Law which is borne with vs: and it is so called because it alwaies keepeth in man, yea in the most wicked that can be, an aduertisement or instruction, which telleth him what is right and iust, and that there is a iudgement of God. Some distinguish betweene Synteresis and Conscience, others take them both for one and the same thing, calling this Synteresis, the very conscience it selfe: whereas others say it is the naturall iudgement, and some *the light of our minde and spirit.* . . . Now by what name soeuer *this light of our minde,* and this naturall censure is called, by which we iudge what is right and iust, or otherwise, sure it is, that of it owne nature it is alwaies carried to that which is true and good. . . . But as it cannot otherwise bee, but that they who haue eyes see the light, although they will not see it, or say they do not see it: so it cannot be but that the eies of the minde beholdeth *the naturall light that is in it,* & those things that are discouered vnto it thereby seeing it proceedeth from God, who is the fountaine of all light, and who will neuer suffer it to be so cleane ex-

> tinguished in man, but that still there remaineth sufficient to condemne him withall. . . . So that although the wicked and vniust, oftentimes escape the iudgement of man, yet they can neuer saue themselues from their owne iudgement, which their conscience alwaies executeth after the perfection of their processe. (Pt. II, ch. 97)

The continuation of this passage has more to say concerning the tortures of conscience (*infra,* p. 87), but here we are concerned with the symbolism of the light. As in *Lucrece,* it is associated with conscience. It is variously called conscience, natural judgment, light of the mind and spirit. It is that divine element in man which will not let him forget the difference between good and evil, however hard he may try. Tarquin may stamp his foot upon his light and the light will seem to go out, but some faint spark or ember will always remain to make him conscious of wrongdoing and of alienation from God. This is the divine element of man's rational nature, which may be obscured but never lost. It is combined with the ingenious cleverness of intellectual power; and, though such power may be forced to serve the cause of evil, it does so unwillingly because of its natural alliance with that which is good.

In *Lucrece* we find the germs of Shakespeare's technique of tragedy. He is fascinated by the mental processes that precede and follow the accomplishment of a crime. It is no accident that he quotes from himself in Macbeth's soliloquy before the murder of Duncan:

> Now o'er the one half world
> Nature seems dead, and wicked dreams abuse
> The curtain'd sleep . . . and wither'd Murder,
> Alarum'd by his sentinel, the wolf,
> Whose howl's his watch, thus with his stealthy pace,
> With Tarquin's ravishing strides, towards his design
> Moves like a ghost. (II. i. 49-56)

With these lines, compare a stanza from *Lucrece,* already quoted:

> Now stole upon the time the dead of night,
> When heavy sleep had clos'd up mortal eyes.
> No comfortable star did lend his light,
> No noise but owls' and wolves' death-boding cries;
> Now serves the season that they may surprise

> The silly lambs. Pure thoughts are dead and still,
> While lust and murder wakes to stain and kill.

Here the several correspondences are immediately recognizable. Wicked dreams may have been suggested by "Pure thoughts are dead." The wolf's death-boding cry gets into Macbeth's speech, but the owls have to wait a few moments, until Lady Macbeth says, "It was the owl that shriek'd" (II. ii. 3), and again, "I heard the owl scream and the cricket cry" (II. ii. 16). The absence of starlight is also repeated in Macbeth's scene, where a few moments before Banquo observes: "There's husbandry in heaven; Their candles all are out." In other words, no stars are shining, nor is the moon shining either (II. i. 2, 5). Shakespeare thus suggests his image of the extinguished stars in *Lucrece:* the heavenly lights are put out before the commission of a black crime. The extinction of the heavenly candles may prefigure the suppression of the light in Macbeth's soul. He had used the same image earlier, when the thought of murder first occurred to him:

> Stars, hide your fires;
> Let not light see my black and deep desires. (I. iv. 50-51)

This repetition of phraseology accompanies a repetition of criminal psychology. Macbeth undergoes the same hesitation and struggles with his conscience as does Tarquin and experiences the same revulsion of conscience immediately after the crime. This violent revulsion and inner agitation may be externally symbolized by the loud ringing of the alarum-bell and by the knocking at the gate, as in De Quincey's interpretation. It is not impossible that these dramatic devices were suggested by the first paragraph of Q. 86, "a warning peece ringing in their eare, and an Apparitour rapping at their door without ceasing." These are torments of conscience which will not allow the wicked to sleep, perhaps suggesting the voice that cried, "Sleep no more. Macbeth shall sleep no more." Like Tarquin's soul, which "sells *eternity* to get a toy" (214), Macbeth's soul has lost its immortal life, its "*eternal* jewel" (III. i. 68). Lady Macbeth is used to illustrate the craving of the guilty conscience for "light," for after the crime she will never allow the candle by her bed to be extinguished (V. i. 26). This repeats Tarquin's craving for light as he leaves Lucrece's room.

Tarquin's name appears again in Iachimo's speech in Imogen's bedchamber. The use of his name indicates that Iachimo is tempted to repeat his crime. The symbol of the flaming torch is again present in the taper which burns beside Imogen's bed:

> The crickets sing, and man's o'er-labour'd sense
> Repairs itself by rest. Our Tarquin thus
> Did softly press the rushes ere he waken'd
> The chastity he wounded. Cytherea!
> How bravely thou becom'st thy bed, fresh lily,
> And whiter than the sheets! That I might touch!
> But kiss one kiss! Rubies unparagon'd,
> How dearly they do't! 'Tis her breathing that
> Perfumes the chamber thus. The flame o' th' taper
> Bows toward her, and would under-peep her lids
> To see th' enclosed lights, now canopied
> Under these windows white and azure, lac'd
> With blue of heaven's own tinct. . . .
> Swift, swift, you dragons of the night, that dawning
> May bare the raven's eye! I lodge in fear;
> Though this a heavenly angel, hell is here.
>
> (*Cymbeline,* II. ii. 11-23, 48-50)

As in *Lucrece,* the torch here probably has a symbolic significance. Iachimo's own words indicate that he is in the same position and subject to the same temptation as Tarquin. But where Tarquin's reason loses the battle with his affections, Iachimo's reason wins and restrains him from the crime to which he is tempted. Tarquin's stamping upon the light symbolizes the eclipse of his own divine "light"; conversely, Iachimo's failure to put out the light may symbolize the preservation of his own divine "light." We must not sentimentalize such a knave as Iachimo, but in his own eyes the trick which he is playing upon Posthumus is scarcely a sin, certainly not a mortal sin, such as the violation of Imogen would be. He fears that he may commit such a sin, as shown in the final lines; "hell is here" means that he would condemn himself to hell by such a crime. He desires the swift approach of dawn that the trunk may be removed from her chamber and himself no longer subjected to this temptation. His "fear" is the same as that "honest fear" and "heedful fear" which failed to dissuade Tarquin (173, 281), a fear of hell as the consequence of wicked actions rather than a fear of external dangers. We should observe that, when he thinks his trick has had tragic consequences for Imogen, he shows sincere repentance and regret (V. v. 141-160). We may doubt that Iachimo should be considered so great a villain as he is frequently thought to be.

The craving for light which accompanies the awakening of conscience is dramatically illustrated in *Hamlet.* King Claudius, at the play, can bear the rehearsal of his crime no longer. Rising, he cries, "Give me some light!" (III. ii. 280). Here the external scene is perfectly accommodated to the internal mood, the semi-darkness of the hall corresponding to the uneasy state of Claudius' conscience, which has been only half asleep (III. i. 50-54). The cry for light expresses the full awakening of his conscience, the protest of "godlike reason," which demands the reviving of its light.

The use of light is somewhat different in *Richard III.* Awakening from his dream of the ghosts, Richard says:

> O coward conscience, how dost thou afflict me!
> *The lights burn blue.* It is now dead midnight.
> Cold fearful drops stand on my trembling flesh.
> What! do I fear myself? (V. iii. 179-182)

Blue lights were supposed to signalize the presence of a ghost. Since they accompany the awakening of conscience and serve as an external warning, they may also symbolize Richard's internal "light" which torments him with demands that it be revived.

When Tarquin's torch is first blown out by the wind, Shakespeare intimates that even inanimate objects abhor unnatural crimes. Along with the needle which pricks Tarquin's finger, the torch's reluctance to be relighted and the smoke which blows in his face are "poor forbiddings" which seek to prevent his crime and to give him warning, but he thinks of them as mere accidents. The sympathy of the torch's flame for human woes suggests a later passage in *Richard II,* in the king's farewell to his wife:

In winter's tedious nights sit by the fire . . .
Tell thou the lamentable tale of me
And send the hearers weeping to their beds.
For why, the senseless brands will sympathize
The heavy accent of thy moving tongue,
And in compassion weep the fire out;
And some will mourn in ashes, some coal-black,
For the deposing of a rightful king. (V. i. 40-50)

It is possible that this aspect of the fire was originally suggested to Shakespeare by a passage in Seneca's *Thyestes,* in which Atreus prepares the horrible banquet by cooking the flesh of Thyestes' own sons for him. Since Shakespeare has borrowed the device of such a banquet in *Titus Andronicus,* we may assume his knowledge of the passage involved. The Messenger says:

87 He puts the severed limbs
Upon the spits and roasts them by slow fire;
The other parts into the glowing pot
He throws to boil them. From the food the fire
Leaps back, is twice, yea thrice, replaced and forced
At last reluctantly to do its work.
The liver on the spit emits shrill cries,
I cannot tell whether the flesh or flame
Most deeply groaned. The troubled fire smoked,
The smoke itself, a dark and heavy cloud,
Rose not in air nor scattered readily;
The ugly cloud obscured the household gods.
(IV. i. 163-174, tr. Harris)

The fire's unwillingness to aid in a crime appears most notably in *King John,* when Hubert prepares to put out Arthur's eyes. Hubert has brought with him a red-hot iron and the fire-pot wherein it was heated:

Art. O, spare mine eyes,
Though to no use but still to look on you!
Lo, by my troth, the instrument is cold
And would not harm me.
Hub. I can heat it, boy.
Art. No, in good sooth; the fire is dead with grief,
Being create for comfort, to be us'd
In undeserv'd extremes. See else yourself;
There is no malice in this burning coal;
The breath of heaven has blown his spirit out
And strew'd repentant ashes on his head.

Hub. But with my breath I can revive it, boy.
Art. And if you do, you will but make it blush
And glow with shame of your proceedings, Hubert.
Nay, it perchance will sparkle in your eyes,
And, like a dog that is compell'd to fight,
Snatch at his master that doth tarre him on.
All things that you should use to do me wrong
Deny their office; only you do lack
The mercy which fierce fire and iron extends,
Creatures of note for mercy-lacking uses.
Hub. Well, see to live; I will not touch thine eyes
For all the treasure that thine uncle owes. (IV. i. 102-123)

Here the meaning is even clearer than in *Lucrece.* The wind that blows out the flame is the "breath of heaven" and constitutes a divine forewarning to Hubert. His "breath" that can revive the flame is the determination of his perverted will that can force his rational nature to do evil services. Perhaps the flame that may "sparkle" or cast sparks into his eyes if forced to burn may symbolize his own "light" that will torture him with pangs of conscience if forced to assist in carrying out the crime. We need not press the analogy too closely, but there is certainly a general repetition of the theme found in *Lucrece.*

The association of the flame or "light" with the putting out of eyes leads us to wonder whether the same association may have been at all in Shakespeare's mind in *King Lear,* III. vii, when Cornwall puts out Gloucester's eyes. Another bit of action from *Lucrece* seems to be repeated here, for Cornwall stamps Gloucester's eyes under foot after gouging them out (line 68) in the same violent manner with which Tarquin stamped upon his torch in order to put out its light. Perhaps we may assume that here also the symbolism of *Lucrece* is repeated and that Cornwall is figuratively stamping out the "light" of his own soul. Such is the thought of the First Servant, who tries to stop Cornwall's violence:

Hold your hand, my lord!
I have serv'd you ever since I was a child;
But better service have I never done you
Than now to bid you hold.

His "service" is to save Cornwall's soul from the consequences of completing the crime; for Cornwall has already done enough to merit the physical vengeance of Gloucester's friends. By failing to heed the warning, he not only endangers his soul but loses his life.

Another possible use of the light as an external symbol occurs in *Macbeth* at the death of Banquo. He and Fleance enter with a torch, which is put out as the murderers set upon them and slay Banquo. Then follow the words:

> *3 Mur.* Who did strike out the light?
> *1 Mur.* Was't not the way? (III. iii. 18)

Here the torch seems to symbolize the physical life of Banquo, as it had been used in *Othello* to symbolize the physical life of Desdemona.

We return briefly to the scene at Desdemona's bedside. From Othello's words, we know that the burning candle or lamp symbolizes the physical life of Desdemona. But these same words, "Put out the light, and then put out the light," indicate what the stage action is to be: he will first extinguish the candle, then strangle Desdemona. Whether he actually does extinguish the candle is questionable, since no later reference is made to it, but his intent to do so repeats the motivation of Tarquin, who put out the light before accomplishing his crime of violence. It thus may be that in Shakespeare's mind the candle was also symbolic of Othello's inner "light" which is in danger of being suppressed by his approaching crime.

If it seems difficult to accept this double symbolism of the external light, we should remember that Othello uses the Neo-Platonic fancy that the heart and soul of the lover dwell in the body of his beloved (cf. *infra,* p. 156). Othello says of Desdemona:

> But there, where I have garner'd up my heart,
> Where either I must live or bear no life;
> The fountain from the which my current runs
> Or else dries up. (IV. ii. 57-60)

Here the "life" of his heart and soul—not his physical life—is pictured as dwelling within Desdemona, whose physical existence provides the abode of his spiritual existence. It therefore becomes easier for both these existences to be symbolized by the same external light.

We find an echo of *Lucrece* in Desdemona's artless inquiries to Emilia about wives who commit adultery. The climactic lines of *Lucrece* are:

> This said, he sets his foot upon the light,
> For light and lust are deadly enemies;
> Shame folded up in blind concealing night. (673-675)

These lines are reflected in the following passage:

> *Des.* Wouldst thou do such a deed for all the world?
> *Emi.* Why, would not you?
> *Des.* No, by this heavenly light.
> *Emi.* Nor I neither by this heavenly light;
> I might do't as well i' th' dark. (IV. iii. 64-67)

Emilia's jesting remark asserts the enmity between light and lust found in the earlier lines, a repetition of the theme of *Lucrece*. Also reminiscent of Lucrece's "light" of goodness and virtue is the use of the phrase "heavenly light" to characterize Desdemona. She uses it again when she kneels to Iago:

> What shall I do to win my lord again?
> Good friend, go to him; for, by this *light of heaven,*
> I know not how I lost him. (IV. ii. 149-151)

The power of this scene is tremendous if it is rightly understood. She is kneeling to her persecutor; she does not know it, but he does. To Iago it is the critical moment, the crisis of his immortal soul. If anything could move him, this should. No crime has yet been committed, and he can stay the course of events by a few well-placed words. But if he feels remorse he gives no sign beyond a certain impatience to reassure Desdemona and thus end the scene. The fact that Iago's soul is really at stake had been stressed by Othello in an earlier speech:

> If thou dost slander her and torture me,
> Never pray more; abandon all remorse;
> On horror's head horrors accumulate;
> Do deeds to make heaven weep, all earth amaz'd;
> For nothing canst thou to damnation add
> Greater than that. (III. iii. 368-373)

It is difficult to know what Iago feels, because he makes a point of iron self-control (I. i. 61-65). That he may experience some qualms is shown in the street where he has set Roderigo to waylay Cassio. He debates with himself the necessity of their deaths. Roderigo may call him to account for the jewels he has received; "it must not be." Cassio excels him in personal merit and might seek revenge if Othello should ever reveal their plot; "No, he must die" (V. i. 18, 22). Yet Iago concludes this almost regretfully, and it is significant that up to that moment he had not completely made up his mind. His scruples are not strong, but they exist.

The use of light in the succeeding lines is worthy of note. The attempted murder of Cassio has been performed in darkness, the proper time for such a crime (*Lucrece,* 168). Presently Iago re-enters with a light and in his nightgown, as though he had just arisen from sleep. This repeats the action of Tarquin in rising from bed and taking a light in order to commit his crime. As Iago stabs Roderigo, his torch seems to be put out, for he almost immediately fails to recognize Lodovico, who is well known to him. As he bends over Cassio's leg, he calls out: "Light, gentlemen!" A few moments later, as he bends over Roderigo, he says: "Lend me a light." This repetition of the light-image may have symbolic significance, stressing Iago's need for a revival of his inward "light" which has been suppressed with the completion of his crime. The interpretation seems doubtful but can be justified by Shakespeare's practice elsewhere. Iago cannot have been deeply stirred, for he is busily engaged in making a show of innocence and in throwing suspicion upon Bianca. Yet, remembering La Primaudaye's dictum that no man at all can completely extinguish his inward light, we may assume the possibility that the light-images here symbolize faint stirrings of conscience. Subtle villain that Iago is, he is not entirely outside the bounds of humanity.

In an age of allegory, it was not surprising that Shakespeare should use light as an external symbol, as he has done in *Lucrece.* Nor is it surprising that the same symbol should be repeated in his plays. It strengthens them, even though the audience may not have fully comprehended the symbolism, for he never allows it to obscure or delay the action of the drama; instead it reinforces and makes meaningful that action. His "brief candle" is the life of man, which inevitably must go out. The candle which is the mind of man, the rational "light" which binds him to God, need not and should not go out; its suppression is the great and oft-repeated tragedy of mankind. Nowhere is the theme better stated than by the Fool in *King Lear,* I. iv. 237: "So, out went the candle, and we were left darkling."

Chapter 6

The Internal Struggle

We have seen how extensively the war between reason and the affections is developed in the portrayal of Tarquin's character. It also has many other repercussions in Shakespeare's lines. The images from Q. 79 appear several times over. The spark fanned to a raging fire (79*f*) appears in *2 Henry VI,* III. i. 302-303:

> Nay, then, this spark will prove a raging fire,
> If wind and fuel be brought to feed it with.

The rolling stone (79*g*) appears in *Henry VIII,* V. iii. 103-105:

> I told ye all,
> When we first put this dangerous stone a-rolling,
> 'Twould fall upon ourselves.

Here the image from the *Zodiake* has probably combined with one cited by Mr. Noble, from Prov. 26:27:

88 He that rolleth up a stone, it will return upon him. (B)

The war of reason against the affections is the central theme of *Love's Labour's Lost,* as stated by the King at the beginning of the play:

> Therefore, brave conquerors,—for so you are,
> That war against your own affections
> And the huge army of the world's desires. (I. i. 8-10)

Their intent is to subdue all such affections by force of reason alone, that they may devote their lives to study. Biron, though he consents to make the experiment, prophesies its failure:

> Necessity will make us all forsworn
> Three thousand times within this three years' space;
> For every man with his affects is born,
> Not by might mast'red, but by special grace. (I. i. 150-153)

Here he refers to the Christian doctrine that only the grace of God can enable man to overcome and discipline the affections, to resist their temptations. He may recall Palingenius' statement to this effect in 79*d, i.* Part of it reads:

89 With worldly thoughtes hie heapt they vexe, the Part diuine aboue,
Except that grace from Heauen hye lyke Lightning them remoue.

This reference to the lightning-like suddenness with which heavenly grace can strike down the affections which war against reason may well have influenced the handling of Leontes' character in *The Winter's Tale.* He is moved by the affection of jealousy, which has a small beginning when Polixenes kisses Hermione. He himself analyzes the awakening of jealousy in his address to "Affection," which develops the suspicion in his mind (I. ii. 138). Unchecked, his jealousy reaches such proportions that he cannot hear reason and at last profanely denies the truth of Apollo's oracle. At this moment the death of his son is announced. The stunning suddenness of this stroke and Leontes' change of heart remind us of the lines above, for the stroke obviously stems from divine interposition.

Angelo, in *Measure for Measure,* recognizes the war of the affections within himself and in its early stages argues with himself as Tarquin had done:

Shall we desire to raze the sanctuary
And pitch our evils there? O, fie, fie, fie! . . .
O cunning enemy, that to catch a saint,
With saints doth bait thy hook! (II. ii. 171-2, 180-1)

The "enemy" is of course the devil, who is "fishing" for Angelo's soul. Though Angelo recognizes this, his affections conquer his reason. When he tells Isabel that her brother can live only by the surrender of her chastity, he says:

I have begun,
And now I give my sensual race the rein;
Fit thy consent to my sharp appetite . . .
Or, by the *affection* that now guides me most,
I'll prove a tyrant to him. (II. iv. 159-61, 168-9)

"My sensual race the rein" suggests the image of the runaway chariot in 79*e*. Affection has taken control from reason.

In *The Tempest,* Prospero refers to the war of the affections within himself when he says of his former enemies:

> Though with their high wrongs I am struck to th' quick,
> Yet with my nobler *reason* 'gainst my *fury*
> Do I take part. The rarer action is
> In virtue than in vengeance. (V. i. 25-28)

Macbeth uses the same frame of reference to explain his killing of Duncan's grooms:

> The expedition of my violent love
> Outrun the pauser, reason. (II. iii. 116--117)

In *Troilus and Cressida,* Hector refers to affection's conquest of the will in his argument for returning Helen to Menelaus:

> Nature craves
> All dues be rend'red to their owners: now,
> What nearer debt in all humanity
> Than wife is to the husband? If this law
> Of nature be corrupted through *affection,*
> And that great *minds,* of partial indulgence
> To their *benumbed wills,* resist the same,
> There is a law in each well-ord'red nation
> To curb those raging appetites that are
> Most disobedient and refractory. (II. ii. 173-182)

In 79*h* Palingenius has briefly expressed the war of the affections against reason in terms of a storm at sea. This image is developed much more extensively in *The French Academie:*

90 For if we would bee contented with enough, it would not put vs to that torment, which we daily suffer. But nothing sufficeth vs: and therefore the *affections* are in our soule, as the windes vpon the sea. For some windes are very small, and mooue the water but a little: others are more vehement, & rayse vp certaine waues: and some againe are so tempestuous, and make such horrible storms and gustes, whereby the Sea is so mooued, that sea and sand and fish and all seeme to bee turned topsie turuie.

The like may bee sayde of the motions of the soule. For some are so light, that they seeme to be nothing else but smal beginnings of moouing. There are others stronger, which moue it somewhat more. And some also are so violent, that they altogether trouble the soule, euen in such a vehement manner, that they driue her from the seate of iudgement. Therefore these two first kindes of motions are properly called *affections,* and the other that are so violent are termed *Commotions* and *Perturbations*. For they bring a kind of blindnesse with them, which is the cause that iudgement and reason see neuer a whit. Whereupon it followeth, seeing neither Reason nor Iudgement beare any more rule, that the Soule is as if shee had no more power ouer her selfe, but were subiect to the iurisdiction of some other. The Grecians terme such affections with a word that signifieth as much as if wee should say passions.

And in deede we commonly say, that a man is passionate, when he is tormented by such violent affections. For as the whole body suffereth when it is mooued, or thrust too and fro, and stricken on euery side: so is it with the Soule being violently mooued euery way. And as the moouing is more or lesse moderate, so she suffereth more or lesse: and if the motion be very violent, confusion followeth thereupon.

(Pt. II, ch. 42)

La Primaudaye carries the image into the next chapter, referring to the winds, whirlwinds, and tempests on the sea which are comparable to the various affections of the soul. He urges that reason be used to stop these in their first beginnings lest the soul come to shipwreck by allowing the storm of passions to reach their full fury. He then compares such a storm to a civil war within a state:

91 To bee short, these sundry motions of affections are like to stormy waues and billowes, which beeing driuen one of another, doe either augment, or diminish, or wholy oppresse one another. Wherefore the like happeneth in the motion of our affections, that commeth to passe in a sedition and ciuill dissention, in which no man considereth who is the worthyer person to obey and follow him, but who is the stronger and most mighty. So in the fight of the affections there is no respect had to that which is most iust, but onely to that which is strongest and most violent, and which hath gotten such power ouer the soule that it hath wholy subdued her to it selfe: which thing we ought to stand in great feare of. (Pt. II, ch. 43)

In the following chapter, he briefly notices the place of will between reason and the affections:

92 Will beeing corrupted of it selfe through sinne, letteth loose the bridle against the iudgement of reason, and so suffereth her selfe to bee carried headlong by her euill affections, in following some false shewe of good. (Pt. II, ch. 44)

La Primaudaye calls the most violent affections "commotions" and "perturbations." This usage is reflected in the conversation of Norfolk with Henry VIII concerning Cardinal Wolsey:

Nor. My lord, we have
Stood here observing him. Some strange *commotion*
Is in his brain. . . .
King. It may well be;
There is a *mutiny* in 's mind. (III. ii. 111-120)

This does not mean that he thinks Wolsey contemplates leading a revolt against the crown, but rather that his mind is at war within itself. Here occur together the "commotion" of the excited mind and the "sedition and ciuill dissention" to which La Primaudaye compares it; Shakespeare is expressing the same idea by the use of "mutiny" in the mind. The same combination serves to explain a difficult line in *Troilus and Cressida:*

> Imagin'd worth
> Holds in his blood such swoln and hot discourse
> That 'twixt his mental and his active parts
> *Kingdom'd* Achilles in *commotion* rages
> And batters down himself. (II. iii. 182-186)

Here "commotion" expresses the violence of Achilles' feelings, which are so strong as to do injury to himself. "Kingdom'd" is not a reference to Achilles' rank; it expresses the analogy between Achilles' excited mind and a state torn by civil war. Shakespeare is recalling his own earlier use of the same term for Brutus' mind before he determines to murder Caesar:

> Between the acting of a dreadful thing
> And the first motion, all the interim is
> Like a phantasma or a hideous dream.
> The Genius and the mortal instruments
> Are then in council; and the *state* of a man
> Like to a little *kingdom,* suffers then
> The nature of an insurrection. (II. i. 63-69)

Here is the same conjunction of images, though the word "commotion" is not used. It is clear, however, that Brutus experiences the same violent excitement as Wolsey and Achilles, and the image of mutiny in a state is more clearly applied than in either of the other two instances. (For similar uses of "perturbation," see *infra,* p. 113.)

A similar internal struggle is pictured in Tybalt's words when Capulet commands him to ignore Romeo's presence at the ball:

> Patience perforce with wilful choler meeting
> Makes my flesh tremble in their different greeting. (I. v. 91-92)

Tybalt's will wishes to give free sway to choleric anger, but his reason forces him to obey Capulet's command. This enforced patience causes an internal conflict so violent that his flesh trembles, revealing externally the commotion within his mind.

We have already traced in *Lucrece* the psychology of "rebel will" (625) and have observed its power to make reason serve its own purposes. This imagery appears elsewhere in Shakespeare. Antony is blamed for making "his will lord of his reason" in his infatuation for Cleopatra (III. xiii. 3). Hamlet, analyzing his mother's love for Claudius, declares that "reason panders will" (III. iv. 88). Iago, in an acute analysis, makes it clear that the real authority or impelling force of man's actions is the will, which can follow either reason or the affections:

> *Our bodies are our gardens,* to the which our wills are gardeners; so that if we will plant nettles or sow lettuce, set hyssop and weed up thyme, supply it with one gender of herbs or distract it with many, either to have it sterile with idleness or *manured* with industry, why, the power and corrigible authority of this lies in our wills. If the *balance* of our lives had not one scale of reason to poise another of sensuality, the blood and baseness of our natures would conduct us to most preposterous conclusions; but we have reason to cool our raging motions, our *carnal* stings, our *unbitted* lusts, whereof I take this that you call love to be a sect or scion. . . . It is merely a lust of the blood and a permission of the will. (I. iii. 323-39)

This passage recalls Palingenius' statement in Q. 82 that will can force reason to obey, and that the real contest is between reason and "fleshly fond affections" for the guidance of the will. Iago's phrase "unbitted lusts" recalls the image of "unbridled" affections used several times in the *Zodiake* (pp. 35, 144) but is more nearly indebted to a passage in *The French Academie,* which also seems to have supplied Iago's figurative description of man's nature as a pair of balances, with reason poised against sensuality. La Primaudaye writes:

93 The nature of man is like to *a paire of ballance.* For if it be not guided with knowledge and reason vnto the better part, of it selfe it is carried to the worse. And although a man be well borne, yet if he haue not his iudgement fined, and the discoursing part of his minde purged with the reasons of Philosophy, it will fall often into grosse faults, and such as beseeme not a prudent man. For in those men that are not endued with vertue ruled by certaine knowledge, nature bringeth forth such fruits as naturally come from the ground without the *manuring* and

> helping-hand of man. That which commonly causeth men to will euill rather than good, proceedeth chiefly of this, that they haue no knowledge or experience thereof. . . . But here we must acknowledge the first corruption of our nature, whereby it is inclined to pleasure, and to eschew labour, which are the wel-springs of vices, and of infinite euils. And if our nature should be suffered to runne with the *bridle* at liberty, whither soeuer it is driuen by *carnall* desires, hauing none of them cut off by wise admonitions and liuely perswasions, there is no beast so vntamed or sauage, that would not be milder than man. (Pt. I, ch. 16)

The resemblance to Iago's figure of the balance is obvious. The lines on bringing forth fruits have combined with a later passage on gardens to suggest the image of the body as a garden (*infra,* p. 189). Iago's phrase "manured with industry"—i.e., tilled with industry—seems to stem from the "manuring and helping-hand of man" without which man's will is likely to bring forth evil fruits; the listing of idleness as the "wel-springs of vices" may have suggested to Iago that "industry" is the source of virtue in the tillage of the garden of man.

The image of the garden in connection with the will occurs also in *Romeo and Juliet,* in Friar Laurence's meditation upon plants that can serve either as a poison or as a medicine, according to the manner of their use:

> Two such opposed kings encamp them still
> In man as well as herbs, *grace* and *rude will;*
> And where the worser is predominant,
> Full soon the canker death eats up that plant. (II. iii. 27-30)

Here the image of the body as a garden is implied by the Friar's words and by the location of the scene in a garden. The word "death" is used in two senses: physical death of the plant, and spiritual death of man's soul. The opposing forces are "rude will," unguided by reason, and the grace of God, which seeks to restore the rational nature to its rightful place. This contest is reminiscent of 79*d,* where God's grace is named as the only salvation for the mind overcome by the affections. The error of the will is explained by Palingenius in another brief passage:

94 • Vnhappy is he whom will doth leade, vnmindfull of the thing (p. 21)
That is to come, but like to beastes regardes the thing in sight.

In other words, the will always follows that which seems good. In following the affections, it takes the short view of what is good; in following reason, it takes the longer view. Sometimes the two views agree. When they do not agree, an internal struggle ensues. We may recall again *Lucrece,* 727-728, where the rational soul of Tarquin had foreseen the penalties of the crime of the affections, "but her foresight could not forestall their will." (Cf. Q. 92.) The proper relation of will and reason is stated by Lysander in *A Midsummer Night's Dream:*

> The will of man is by his reason sway'd. . . .
> Reason becomes the marshal to my will. (II. ii. 115, 120)

The image of satiate desire and quick revulsion of the will that follows the accomplishment of lust is developed at length in Sonnet 129, where the author has repeated the imagery of *Lucrece,* 688-714:

> Th' expense of spirit in a waste of shame
> Is lust in action; and, till action, lust
> Is perjur'd, murd'rous, bloody, full of blame,
> Savage, extreme, rude, cruel, not to trust,
> Enjoy'd no sooner but despised straight,
> Past reason hunted, and no sooner had
> Past reason hated, as a swallow'd bait
> On purpose laid to make the taker mad;
> Mad in pursuit and in possession so;
> Had, having, and in quest to have, extreme;
> A bliss in proof, and prov'd, a very woe;
> Before, a joy propos'd; behind, a dream.
> All this the world well knows; yet none knows well
> To shun the heaven that leads men to this hell.

Bertram's seduction of the Florentine maid is also reminiscent of *Lucrece:*

> He hath perverted a young gentlewoman . . . of a most *chaste* renown, and this night he *fleshes his will* in the spoil of her honour.
> (*All's Well,* IV. iii. 16-18)

A figurative use of the will occurs in Richard's description of his father, York, in battle:

> My noble father,
> Three times to-day I holp him to his horse,
> Three times bestrid him; thrice I led him off,

> Persuaded him from any further act:
> But still, where danger was, still there I met him;
> And like *rich hangings* in a homely house,
> So was his *will* in his old feeble body. (*2 Henry VI*, V. iii. 7-13)

Here Shakespeare seems to have recalled an image used by Palingenius for a different purpose. Palingenius denies that fame, praise, and glory are of surpassing worth and uses several similes to show that fair appearances may conceal bitter realities:

95 Doe not the *gorgeous Hangings* hyde the dusty mouldred Wall, (p. 98)
Where gaping Riftes vnsemely syt and Wormes consuming crall?

In another context, this passage is associated with one which uses the "wall" as the exterior of the human body (*infra*, Q. 259). It reminds us of Shakespeare's "wall of flesh" (*King John*, III. iii. 20, *Richard II*, III. ii. 167). In the comparison of York's "old feeble body" to a "homely house" there may also be a reminiscence
[96] of La Primaudaye's description of man's body as "an old
ruinous house" which he should be content to leave at death (Pt. I, ch. 72), while its "rich hangings" stem from the "gorgeous Hangings" of Palingenius' "Wall." The two images seem to have combined in Richard's speech. The "mouldred wall" or ruinous house becomes a figure for York's body, while the rich hangings that were a figure for fame and glory become a figure for York's will that urges him on to seek fame and glory.

The "gaping Riftes" in the wall of flesh have a parallel in the final illness of Henry IV:

> The incessant care and labour of his mind
> Hath wrought the *mure* that should confine it in
> So *thin* that life looks through and will break out.
> (*2 Henry IV*, IV. iv. 118-120)

The will becomes the subject of a major debate between Hector and Troilus on the question of returning Helen to the Greeks. We have already quoted a few lines of this debate (*supra*, p. 78). The two brothers take opposite points of view:

> *Hec.* But value dwells not in particular will . . .
> And the will dotes that is inclineable

To what infectiously itself affects,
Without some image of th' affected merit.
Tro. I take today a wife, and my election
Is led on in the conduct of my will,
My will enkindled by mine eyes and ears,
Two traded pilots 'twixt the dangerous shores
Of will and judgement: how may I avoid,
Although my will distaste what it elected,
The wife I chose? There can be no evasion
To blench from this and to stand firm by honour.
(*Troilus and Cressida,* II. ii. 53-68)

Hector thinks that the will should be guided by some objective rational standard of value instead of by imagined values resulting from its own affections. In other words, Paris may feel that Helen is worth the destruction of a kingdom, but she is not worth it by an impartial standard of value. Troilus argues that the Trojans in general and Paris in particular had freely accepted Helen, and not at all against their own wills. To send her back now would imply fickleness of will, a repudiation of their former acceptance of her. Since the motive for this might seem to be fear, honor will not allow them to send her back.

In *Hamlet,* Polonius uses the relation of the will and the affections in commenting upon Hamlet's visit to Ophelia:

This is the very ecstasy of love,
Whose violent property fordoes itself
And *leads the will to desperate undertakings*
As oft as any passion under heaven
That does afflict our natures. (II. i. 102-106)

In the repentance scenes of Claudius and Gertrude (III. iii, iv) the will again appears and enters the realm of formal theology. Since I have discussed these scenes fully elsewhere, I shall not repeat the discussion here.[1]

[1] See *The Character of Hamlet:* "Religion in *Hamlet*: Repentance."

Chapter 7

Mental Sickness

IN THE WAR OF the affections against reason, it frequently happens that the former will triumph and will lead the soul into crime. At such a time the rational soul is overcome and the state of the whole soul is turned from its normal condition. With surprising insight, Palingenius describes the change as a sickness of the soul. The criminal is sick, just as much as though his body were diseased. As physical illness proceeds most often from some malady of the heart or of the brain, so soul-sickness results when the mind and the will are harmed with vice. His account follows:

97 *a* First this it nedefull is to knowe, what Vice or Crime is here, (p. 152)
Is *of the minde a sicknesse sore:* nor men are onely sick
In body here, but minde aye feeles hir wounde and greuous prick,
b No lesse in force, than body doth. Thus *euery euill wight*
Is sick, bicause his will is sick, and iudgement is not right:
c Whereby the wretch the harmefull things, more worth than good esteemes
And sweter aye the filthyest factes[1] to him than honest seemes:
Which if his minde & will were sounde coulde neuer wicked bee,
But iust and vertuous should be found: in this they disagree.
d And as the body all is yll, when any of these twaine
Diseased is with maladie, the Heart, or else the Braine:
So so, alas, the whole estate of Soule is euer ill,
When as these two with vice are harmde the Minde and eke the Will.
e As pleasaunt meate to stomack sick doth seme vnpleasant ay,
And profites nothing vnto him that sicknesse doth assay:
f So *(sick the Soule)* no good thing can, the wicked man come by,
Nor nothing profites him at all: which true I thus will try.

The imagery of this passage is frequently echoed in Shakespeare. In *Measure for Measure,* Isabella begs that the time of her brother Claudio's death be arranged so "that his soul sicken not" (II. iv. 41). Both the Duke and the Provost hesitate to execute the drunken Barnardine in his state of impenitence or soul-sickness (IV. ii. 152, iii. 72). In *2 Henry IV,* Poins jestingly says of Falstaff: "Marry, the immortal part needs a physician; but that moves not him. Though

[1] *factes.* Deeds.

that be sick, it dies not" (II. ii. 112). In *Julius Caesar,* Portia attributes Brutus' restlessness to "some sick offence within your mind" (II. i. 268). Henry VIII describes his conscience as "full sick" and himself adrift on "the wild sea of my conscience" (II. iv. 200-204). Sickness of soul proceeding from a guilty conscience again appears in Hamlet's mother:

> To my *sick soul,* as sin's true nature is,
> Each toy seems prologue to some great amiss;
> So full of artless jealousy is guilt,
> It spills itself in fearing to be spilt. (IV. v. 17-20)

From these quotations, it is evident that soul-sickness may exist both before and after the performance of a crime. It appears before the crime when the affections gain dominance over reason. After the crime reason, acting through conscience, may reassert its claim, but the injury already done to the soul cannot be remedied until repentance and atonement are successfully made. Queen Gertrude's soul-sickness is of this kind.

La Primaudaye explains the terrors of the sin-sick soul in the same chapter that discusses man's "light" (Q. 86):

98 For although nature were so put out and smothered in them, that no sparkle of naturall light to rectifie their iudgement, appeared in them, nor yet any flame of Gods wrath, which burneth the heart that is turned aside from him, yet hee hath other meanes to kindle the same againe, and to set it on flaming, euen after such a manner, that it amazeth them, as if it *thunder* downe vpon them. . . . Hereof it is that none liue in greater feare, then the greatest contemners of God, that are most giuen ouer to all kinds of vice and wickednes, and who declare most euidently by their works, that no fere of God or of his iudgements holdeth them in. For they liue as if they carried death alwaies in their bosome, how good a face soeuer they set vpon the matter outwardly. And because they cast all feare of God farre from them, hee vouchsafe[th] them not the honour to giue them a hart to feare him as they ought, but he beateth down their pride in such sort, that hee causeth them to stand in feare not onely of men, of *tempests,* of *thunders* and of *lightnings,* but he terrifieth them also by dreames, and maketh them to tremble at their owne fancies, yea they quake oftentimes at flies, and mice, and such contemptible thinges: but yet so as this feare commeth from a higher cause. . . . As if nature testified vnto them, that there is some diuine prouidence and vengeance which watcheth ouer offences, and discloseth them how secret soeuer they are, and causeth them to be punished. As experience teacheth in many, whose secret

> crimes haue been discouered by wonderfull & incredible means so that all men are astonished at it, and are constrained to confesse, that there is a diuine iustice, which will not suffer horrible facts to remaine alwaies hid & vnpunished. Therfore how secret and close soeuer they carry the matter, this diuine iustice rappeth continually at the doore of their conscience, as it were an Apparitor or sergeant, calling them to iudgement: so that whether they will or no they must alwaies liue in feare. (Pt. II, ch. 97)

We have already noticed the knocking at the door of one's conscience and its probable significance in *Macbeth* (*supra,* p. 67). The divine use of thunder and lightning to inspire fear and self-revelation of crimes appears again in the *Zodiake:*

99 Contrarywise, the wicked man defamed feares to be, (p. 3)
And *when the lightnings thunder rores, then gilty trembleth he.*
If men doe chaunce in eares to rounde, or whisper when they walke,
Alas then cries he to himselfe, of mee these men do talke,
What shal I do? the Iudge or King doth call, and shall I goe,
Or rather flie the perils great of wretched life? now Loe
By fyxed law of God, doth feare the wicked men torment.

A similar use of the thunder appears in Lucretius' *De Rerum Natura,* V. 1218-1225, which may be the ultimate source of the image.

These passages give point to King Lear's words on the heath in the midst of the violent thunderstorm:

Let the great gods,
That keep this dreadful pudder o'er our heads,
Find out their enemies now. *Tremble, thou wretch*
That hast within thee undivulged crimes,
Unwhipp'd of justice. . . . Close pent-up guilts,
Rive your concealing continents, and cry
These dreadful *summoners* grace. (III. ii. 49-59)

The theme of sickness of the mind is developed most extensively in Macbeth. Throughout the play there is suggested an interrelation between mental and physical illness. With Macbeth the exciting force is mental. Twice during his first scene with the witches Banquo describes him as "rapt" in a trancelike condition (I. iii. 57, 142). The first thought of murdering Duncan "shakes so my single state of man that function Is smother'd in surmise" (140-141). Just before the murder he attributes his vision of the dagger to the "heat-oppressed brain" (II. i. 39). Lady Macbeth calls him "brainsickly" because of his imaginings (II. ii. 46). His "terrible dreams" and "torture of the mind" keep him in "restless ecstacy," or near-madness (III. ii. 18-22). His mind is "full of scorpions" (36). In the scene with Banquo's ghost, he refers to his trancelike condition as his "strange infirmity" (III. iv. 86). Lady Macbeth refers to it as a "fit" which he has often had (55). In the later scene with the Weird Sisters he "stands amazedly" (IV. i. 126). Near the end of the play he is "sick at heart" (V. iii. 19). These various references suggest Palingenius' analogy between bodily sickness of heart and brain, and soul sickness of mind and will (*97d*). They also suggest that Macbeth's sickness of the mind existed before the murder as well as afterwards, and possibly that his physical condition was a contributory cause of the crime. This would accord with Palingenius' observation:

100 For as the bodies seeme to be, so minde and will doe take . . . (p. 120)
The Obiect therefore not alone, nor things our eies behold,
But state of body oftentimes (as witnesse writers olde)
Doth cause vs diuers things to wyll, and moues vs to and froe: (p. 121)
Who marks some Pageants plaid on earth, shall plainly finde it so.

The interrelation of mental and physical sickness is again illustrated in Lady Macbeth. The physician in attendance, after the sleepwalking scene, comments:

Unnatural deeds
Do breed unnatural troubles; infected minds
To their deaf pillows will discharge their secrets.
More needs she the divine than the physician. (V. i. 79-82)

The unnatural trouble is the "great perturbation in nature" that causes sleepwalking (V. i. 9). He reports of her to Macbeth:

Not so sick, my lord,
As she is troubled with thick-coming fancies
That keep her from her rest. (V. iii. 37-39)

Macbeth replies:

Canst thou not minister to a mind diseas'd,
Pluck from the memory a rooted sorrow,
Raze out the written troubles of the brain,
And with some sweet oblivious antidote

Cleanse the stuff'd bosom of that perilous stuff
Which weighs upon the heart? (40-45)

The "perilous stuff" is presumably adust melancholy, or burnt humor. Any of the four humors, when burned by the extreme heat accompanying fiery passion, was called adust melancholy. This sediment or residue could not be absorbed by the body and tended to choke up the veins. It was a principal cause of madness and could, if not purged, ultimately destroy life itself. Here Macbeth expresses hope that a physical purgation can so relieve the body as
to cure mental illness. This may draw a hint from Googe's
[101] marginal note, "An herbe that purgeth madnesse" (p. 4),
accompanying a discussion of hellebore as a purgative for melancholy. The Doctor entertains no such hope, since he knows that Lady Macbeth's illness proceeds from a sick conscience, not from the excess of any natural humor, and cannot therefore be cured by physical means. He replies to Macbeth:

Therein the patient
Must minister to himself. (45-46)

Professor Baldwin (*op. cit.,* I. 705) notes a probable source for this idea in Cicero's *Tusculan Disputations,* III:

102 Corpora curari possunt, animorum nulla medicina est.

He observes that this was quoted in a popular collection of *sententiae* and may have come to Shakespeare's attention in that way.[2]

The sleepwalking of Lady Macbeth is itself indebted to the *Zodiake.* Palingenius gives a discussion of sleepwalking in continuing his account of the will and of the mind. He seeks to determine the means by which the mind can impart its commands to the body and how it can be affected by the body (p. 121):

104 *a* But those in heauy sleepes that lye, how should they mouing make?
As *some doe in their sleepes arise,* and weapon vp do take,
Some in the stable takes his horse, *some writes* as many say,
And some hath earst bene seene, a sleepe vpon the Lute to play.
b It must be knowne that of the thing the Image doth remaine
In vs, of all that we doe see, or Senses can retaine.

[103] [2] Cf. Seneca, *Hercules Furens,* 1268-9: "Nemo polluto queat animo mederi" (Cunliffe's note).

This makes vs think we see the face that late we gased on,
And that we seeme to heare the words were vtred longe agon.
c These formes within the secret celles inclosed in the braine,
A *vapour* moues, which to ascende the stomack doth constraine,
And minde deluded so doth moue, the body styres[3] thereby,
If the Resemblance be of force, that in thy head doth ly.
d But tayle of Lysard, or of Snake, that cut in two doth sprall,
Doth will it moue? Or force of minde, that Greekes do *Fancie* call?
As they whom rage of madnesse moues, or to much drink arayes?
Or *dreadful dreames doe cause to shake?* or happens other wayes?

Beside the lines on sleepwalking, Googe has a marginal note:

105 Vis phantasiae, quam sit in somno efficax: Imagination how mightely it preuaileth in Sleep.

Palingenius' phrase "some writes" (104*a*) gives the cue for Lady Macbeth's conduct. Her attendant says:

> I have seen her rise from her bed, throw her nightgown upon her, unlock her closet, take forth paper, fold it, write upon't, read it, afterwards seal it, and again return to bed; yet all this while in a most fast sleep. (V. i. 4-9)

The statement that all images from our sensory experience are secretly preserved in the brain (104*b*) is an excellent description of the subconscious mind and its powers. Here two of Googe's lines achieve real poignance:

106 This makes vs think we see the face that late we gased on,
And that we seeme to heare the words were vtred longe agon.

Shakespeare captures and intensifies this poignance in Lady Macbeth's recollections, her "thick coming fancies," as the Doctor calls them. These images, preserved in the "secrete celles" (104*c*), are the "written troubles of the brain" of which Macbeth wishes her cured. They are stirred up by a "vapour" ascending from the stomach to vex the brain. If the remembered images strike the mind with sufficient force, it will cause the body to stir from its bed.

The involuntary recollection and association of images is not confined to sleep, though especially potent when the conscious reason has relaxed its control. It is the product of the *vis phantasiae,* or

[3] *styres.* Stirs.

Phantasy, which Googe translates in the margin as Imagination and in the text as Fancie. It is this power which afflicts those whom "dreadful dreames doe cause to shake," a phrase recalled in Macbeth's "terrible dreams That shake us nightly" (III. ii. 18-19). Macbeth's phantasy, or image-making power, is so strong as to overset reason even during his waking hours. His trancelike states, his visions of the dagger and the ghost, the voice that cried "Sleep no more," all are instances of this power. His later murders result largely from a desperate effort to banish these horrid images, to escape the persecution of his own imagination. It is this element of his character which excites pity for Macbeth, even while we shudder with horror at his crimes. His own words, "Present fears are less than horrible imaginings" (I. iii. 138), give us perhaps the best clue to his character.

Googe's use of Fancy and Phantasy as equivalents of Imagination is in accord with the fact that Shakespeare at times makes no distinction between these terms. He uses them constantly. This is not the place for an extended presentation of Scholastic psychology, with its division of the mental functions into Common Sense, Phantasy, Imagination, Judgment, and Memory. It seems likely that Shakespeare received some of his information from La Primaudaye, who devotes several chapters to the subject (Pt. II, chs. 23-29). Here we find repeated references to the "discourse of reason" or power of logical analysis (cf. *Hamlet,* I. ii. 150, IV. iv. 36); this is the same as the "discursio rationis" of the Schoolmen. Considerable discussion is devoted to Phantasy and Imagination. Most interesting is his description of Memory, the servant of Reason, who sits as a judge:

107 Besides, it hath neere vnto it Memory, which is in place of a Notary and Secretary, and as it were a Register booke, in which is entred whatsoeuer is ordayned and decreed by reason. . . . Secondly, forasmuch as the memory is as it were the Register & Chancery Court of all the other senses, the images of all things brought and committed vnto it by them, are to be imprinted therein, as the image and signe of a ring or seale is imprinted and set in wax that is sealed. . . . Therefore must the minde turne ouer all the leaues of this Booke or Register of Memory. (Pt. II, ch. 26)

This image of memory as a book or surface on which all mental images are preserved may account for Macbeth's lines:

> Pluck from the *memory* a rooted sorrow,
> Raze out the *written troubles of the brain.*

It may also explain Hamlet's reply to his father's Ghost:

> Remember thee!
> Ay, thou poor ghost, while memory holds a seat
> In this distracted globe. Remember thee!
> Yea, from the *table of my memory*
> I'll wipe away all trivial fond records,
> All saws of books, all forms, all pressures past,
> That youth and observation copied there,
> And thy commandment all alone shall live
> Within the *book and volume of my brain,*
> Unmix'd with baser matter. (I. v. 95-104)

My colleague, Professor M. D. Clubb, suggests that La Primaudaye's comparison of the memory to a Chancery Court may be reflected in Sonnet 30:

> When to the *sessions* of sweet silent thought
> I *summon* up remembrance of things past.

Since the action of the sonnet takes place in the poet's memory, it seems quite possible that the legal phrases are reminiscences of La Primaudaye's metaphor.

Returning to the theme of soul-sickness, we may note the analogy employed by Palingenius between the erroneous choices of the sin-sick soul and the perverted taste of a person physically ill (97*e*). The same theme occurs again in the *Zodiake:*

> 108 What profits it vnto the sicke to offer deynty meate, (p. 19)
> Whose tast away hath quite bereft the feruent feuers heate?

In *A Midsummer Night's Dream,* Demetrius explains how he now loves Helena, whom formerly he shunned:

> But like a sickness did I loathe this food;
> But, as in health, come to my natural taste,
> Now I do wish it, love it, long for it. (IV. i. 177-179)

In *Twelfth Night,* Olivia says:

> You are sick of self-love, Malvolio, and taste with a distemper'd appetite. (I. v. 97)

Coriolanus thus addresses the Roman populace:

> Your *affections* are
> *A sick man's appetite,* who desires most that
> Which would increase his evil. (I. i. 181-183)

While the alteration of taste by sickness was proverbial, the manner of its use here suggests an indebtedness to Palingenius.

In Q. 97 we find not only sickness of soul and of mind, but also sickness of the will (*97b*). This sickness is combined with erring judgment and results in a person's preferring those things which are filthy and harmful to those which are good and helpful. This concept is particularly evident in Iago's triumphant hypocrisy which deceives Othello. He has already announced his intention of putting Othello "into a jealousy so strong That judgement cannot cure" (II. i. 311). To prepare the ground for this jealousy, he daringly suggests that Desdemona has a perverted judgment and a sick will, the evidence of which is her love for Othello. It is natural for a girl to love one of her own color and rank; it is "unnatural" for her to choose a suitor of a different color and background. Her doing so indicates an appetite for novelty, a desire to be thrilled by the unusual, feelings which endure but temporarily, after which one may expect her to return to the preferences natural for one of her color and class. Commentators have given far too little attention to this speech:

> *Oth.* And yet, how nature erring from itself—
> *Iago.* Ay, there's the point; as—to be bold with you—
> Not to affect many proposed matches
> Of her own clime, complexion, and degree,
> Whereto we see in all things nature tends—
> Foh! One may smell in such, *a will most rank,*
> Foul disproportions, thoughts unnatural.
> But pardon me; I do not in position
> Distinctly speak of her; though I may fear
> Her *will,* recoiling to her better *judgement,*
> May fall to match you with her country forms,
> And happily[4] repent. (III. iii. 227-238)

Here the final three lines picture the will as re-accepting the advice of reason after the appetite which led it astray has been satiated.

[4] *happily.* Haply.

This repeats the psychology of man as set forth in the last two chapters. In the earlier phrase "a will most rank," the will carries also the associated meaning of lust exceeding the normal bounds of desire. This state of mind may be equated with the sickness of the will which has succumbed to appetite. In the light of Palingenius' account, we can see what Iago means. A white woman cannot love a "black" man unless something is wrong with her moral sense; her will is perverted; she is naturally prone to unnatural lusts; when her reason reasserts control over her will, she is likely to prefer a white man. Iago's pose of blunt honesty causes Othello to accept these remarks so derogatory to himself, and Iago puts the argument as a general proposition, not "distinctly" applying it to Desdemona, yet suggesting that she may not be immune from the general rule that would apply in such cases. He is stating a social attitude which must have been fairly common then, as it is now, and which received earlier expression in Brabantio's insistence that his daughter could not love a black man unless seduced by witchcraft. Othello himself cannot help being influenced by this attitude and half believing it. He says of Iago a few moments later:

> This fellow's of exceeding honesty,
> And knows all qualities, with a learn'd spirit,
> Of human dealings. . . . Haply, for I am black
> And have not those soft parts of conversation
> That chamberers have, or for I am declin'd
> Into the vale of years, — yet that's not much —
> She's gone. I am abus'd; and my relief
> Must be to loathe her. (III. iii. 258-268)

Iago is an expert on human nature, says Othello, and doubtless has hit the truth of the matter. This denotes Othello's acceptance of the suggestion that Desdemona's love for a "black" man implies sickness or "rankness" of the will and a proneness to unnatural lust, which may turn her mind to adultery as formerly they turned it to misalliance.

In modern terms, Iago suggests to Othello that Desdemona's love proves her to be a psychiatric case. In terms of the lines from the *Zodiake,* sickness of will and error of judgment indicate a native wickedness of mind. Othello is prepared to attribute such a native wickedness to Desdemona before she is accused of any actual misdeed. His belief that her love for him constitutes unnatural lust makes him ready to believe that she will lust after others; and he is easily persuaded that the wish has become the deed. Though he demands ocular proof, he is already persuaded. The "dangerous conceit" burns in his blood "like the mines of sulphur," its whole course from the first suspicion to the full flame taking only a few minutes. Iago supplied the spark; Othello's mind was ready for the flame.

In the final scene, before crushing out the life of the dearest object to him in all the world, he says: "Yet she must die, else she'll betray more men." This suggests that he might have pardoned her supposed amour with Cassio if that were all; but he is convinced that by her very nature she is incurably lustful. Her marriage to him had been her first aberration, her amour with Cassio her second, and there would be more. This conviction is not based on any suspicion of premarital misconduct, but upon the "rankness" of will shown by Desdemona in her love for himself. It is her innate disposition, which she cannot help if she would. He does not hate her, but it is his duty to kill her and forestall future injuries to others. There may be a thematic significance in his words to her:

> *Oth.* Think on thy sins.
> *Des.* They are loves I bear to you.
> *Oth.* Ay, and for that thou diest. (V. ii. 40-41)

He is speaking the literal truth. To his agonized mind, her love for him has become distorted into the primary evidence of her faithlessness.

In Othello's terrible agony when he learns the truth, there is yet a kind of triumph. His own preconceptions, prompted by Iago and the world's opinion, had been false. Virtuous love of white and "black" was possible and had existed in his own marriage all the time. He had not sufficiently believed it and had thrown his happiness away, but the possibility had been there and the rightness of his marriage is vindicated. He is able to die upon the corpse of his true and loyal wife, realizing that her love for him had never failed.

The conception of an innate nature which gives to particular individuals a disposition toward wickedness receives its classic statement in Hamlet's lines:

> So, oft it chances in particular men,
> That for some vicious mole of nature in them,
> As, in their birth — wherein they are not guilty,
> Since nature cannot choose his origin —
> By their o'ergrowth of some complexion
> Oft breaking down the pales and forts of reason,
> Or by some habit that too much o'er-leavens
> The form of plausive manners, that these men,
> Carrying, I say, the stamp of one defect,
> Being nature's livery, or fortune's star, —
> Their virtues else—be they as pure as grace,
> As infinite as man may undergo —
> Shall in the general censure take corruption
> From that particular fault. (I. iv. 23-36)

Here are listed three kinds of faults which may damn a man in the "general censure" or public opinion: 1) an innate viciousness or defect proceeding from his birth; 2) the predominance or "o'ergrowth" of some physical humor, such as melancholy, which may drive a person into insanity or something near it; 3) a habit that violates accepted standards of good manners; e.g., the Danish habit of excessive drinking at banquets.

Here we are primarily concerned with the first, the "vicious mole of nature" which is born in a man and which he cannot help, but which nevertheless determines the opinions of others concerning him. We may first observe how Shakespeare has come to use the mole as symbolic of this innate vice or defect. That the mole is physically a "stamp of nature" is shown by the identification of Guiderius in *Cymbeline:*

> Guiderius had
> Upon his neck a mole, a sanguine star;
> It was a mark of wonder. —
> This is he,
> Who hath upon him still that *natural stamp.*
> It was wise nature's end in the donation,
> To be his evidence now. (V. v. 363-368)

The mole as a physical blemish, along with other birthmarks, is determined at conception or at birth by Nature. In *A Midsummer Night's Dream* Oberon attributes this power to the fairies as servants of Nature. Calling on his elves to attend at the beds of the newly married couples, he sings:

And the blots of Nature's hand
Shall not in their issue stand;
Never mole, harelip, nor scar,
Nor mark prodigious, such as are
Despised in nativity,
Shall upon their children be. (V. i. 416-421)

That such an external blemish may be indicative of an inborn disposition to wickedness is shown by Queen Margaret's contemptuous words concerning Richard III's deformity:

Thou *elvish-mark'd,* abortive, rooting hog!
Thou that wast *seal'd in thy nativity*
The *slave of nature* and the son of hell! (I. iii. 228-230)

In *King John,* Hubert evidently has some such blemish, for John says of him:

A fellow *by the hand of nature mark'd,*
Quoted, and sign'd to do a deed of shame. (IV. ii. 221-222)

Hamlet's insistence that men cannot be held morally guilty for such blemishes of nature has a precedent in Tarquin's words to Lucrece, when he urges her to yield to him willingly in order to avoid public disgrace:

Then, for thy husband and thy children's sake,
Tender my suit; bequeath not to their lot
The shame that from them no device can take,
The blemish that will never be forgot,
Worse than a *slavish wipe* or *birth-hour's blot;*
For marks descri'd in men's nativity
Are nature's faults, not their own infamy. (533-539)

In one sense Hamlet's speech may mean no more than that ugliness of countenance causes unfavorable opinions in those who see it and may offset goodness of character in the general judgment. Yet his word "vicious" suggests the further meaning of a natural defect of character. This conception is probably derived, in part at least, from an account in the *Zodiake,* discussing the soul's purgation:

109 *a* To euery man hath *nature* delt, some crime or *vicious kinde,* (p. 237)
And nothing is on earth so faire, but fault therin we finde.
Yet are there certaine sinnes so small, and to such trifling end,
That in a manner nought at all, the eyes of God offend,
Wherwith he is not greeued much: no sores are these nor staines,
But as the litle *freckles* that in body faire remaines,
Which easely the Lorde forgiues, since well perceiueth hee,
How weake and fraile the nature is, of such as mortall bee.
b But great and haynous crimes doe much offende the mighty state,
And wicked men he alwaies doth, abhorre, despise and hate.
Nor will he once their praiers heare, except they clense before,
And *washe away their sinnes with teares,* and white for black restore:
Requiring pardon for their faults, with voice of mourning minde,
Obtaining once againe the pathes of vertue for to finde,
c And *casting* of his canckred skinne. As in the pleasant spring,
The Serpent vseth all his skinne, of olde away to fling:
Who, thus *renewed,* departes & leaues, his *slough* in stones behinde,
And casting vp his head aloft, with prone and stately minde,
His dreadfull hissing doubleth oft, with toung of triple kinde.

In the first line of this quotation, we should realize that "kinde" means "nature" and that the phrase means "vicious nature." The line means that Nature has dealt to every man some fault or vicious internal disposition. Palingenius then explains that these faults or dispositions vary in seriousness. He uses the Church's formal distinction between venial and mortal sins. Venial sins are like the "litle freckles" in a fair body, scarcely impairing its beauty; so God takes slight notice of venial sins and easily forgives them. But mortal sins or "great and haynous crimes" are more serious and must be deeply repented. Googe employs "freckles" as an analogy for venial sins and trivial faults, but the word which he thus translates is *naevi,* meaning "moles" (XII. 393). If Shakespeare recalled the Latin and English texts together, we can readily see how the "vicious kinde" dealt to a man by Nature came to be represented as a "vicious mole of nature." Undoubtedly, current superstitions concerning the birthmark also played a part in Shakespeare's various references to it, but Palingenius' lines seem to have contributed to the formation of Hamlet's phrase.

This seems even more probable when we observe that Q. 109 has other echoes in Shakespeare. The image of the serpent's cast-off slough (*c*) appears in *Henry V:*

'Tis good for men to love their present pains
Upon example; so the spirit is eas'd;
And when the mind is quick'ned, out of doubt,
The organs, though defunct and dead before,
Break up their drowsy grave and newly move,
With *casted slough* and fresh legerity. (IV. i. 18-23)

Without mentioning the serpent, Shakespeare seems to have recalled its cast-off slough and renewed quickness of movement as an analogy for the quickening of mind and spirit in man, though without the religious emphasis given the image by Palingenius.

The requirement that wicked men must cleanse themselves of sin before God will hear their prayers recalls Claudius' vain attempt at repentance in *Hamlet,* III. iii. The image of "washing" in this speech is by "rain from heaven," but in the First Quarto version (1603) the cleansing is done by tears:

O that this *wet* that falles vpon my face
Would *wash* the crime cleere from my conscience! . . .
Why say thy *sinnes* were *blacker* than is ieat [jet]
Yet may contrition make them *white as snowe.* (1411-19)

Palingenius' words are:

110 And *washe* away their *sinnes* with *teares,* and *white* for *black* restore.

In both passages the washing is obviously associated with
[111] Psalms 51:7, "Thou shalt wash me, and I shall be whiter than
snow." The washing with tears is recalled from Luke 7:37-48, where the woman washed Christ's feet with her tears and was forgiven her sins. In the *Zodiake* the foot-washing is omitted and the figurative use of the tears is stated directly: they wash away sin. The First Quarto uses it in just this way. Furthermore, both Palingenius and Shakespeare describe sins as black, the opposite of white; while the description of sins as black was certainly common enough, the biblical contrast is between scarlet and white:

112 Though your sins be as red as scarlet, they shall be as white as snow.
(Isaiah 1:18) (B)

These variants suggest a possible reminiscence of the *Zodiake* in the First Quarto version.

It is interesting to note that in the Second Quarto the washing has changed its character, the washing with tears having been discarded in favor of another biblical image:

> Is there not *rain* enough in the sweet *heavens*
> To *wash it white as snow?* Whereto serves *mercy*
> But to confront the visage of offence? (III. iii. 45-47)

In this version the author gives greater stress to the quality of divine mercy and therefore recalls his own description of mercy in Portia's words to Shylock:

> It droppeth as the gentle *rain from heaven*
> Upon the place beneath. (*Merchant of Venice,* IV. i. 185)

Mr. Noble has observed that this image is indebted to Ecclesiasticus 35:19:

113 O how fair a thing is *mercy* in the time of anguish and trouble? It is like a *cloud of rain* that cometh in the time of drouth. (B)

The exact form of Portia's phrase may be an echo of *The French Academie*, where it occurs in connection with the garden of the world (cf. *infra,* p. 189):

114 Let vs then imagine before vs a garden wherein is infinite variety of trees and plants of all sorts, and that this garden is watred either by *raine from heauen,* or by pipes & conduites wherby the water is brought thither and dispersed in all places thereof. (Pt. II, ch. 64)

The two versions of the "washing" in the two quartos of *Hamlet* raise an interesting textual question: was the change the result of conscious revision? I do not wish to discuss at length the controversial problem of the relations between the First and Second Quartos of *Hamlet.* Professor A. A. Raven's *Hamlet-Bibliography and Reference Guide*[5] shows how enormous is the literature on the subject. I merely record my opinion that such changes as the one shown above are planned changes, not accidental ones. It may well be that the text of the First Quarto was imperfectly pirated in shorthand or

[5] University of Chicago Press, 1936, items 684-895.

imperfectly recalled by an actor, but the play thus pirated or recalled was not the text of the Second Quarto. In another study[6] I have sought to show that the changes and additions in the Second Quarto follow a pattern and seem designed to secure certain definite effects. If they are not haphazard but follow a definite plan, they are sure evidence of a revision, before the Second Quarto, of the text on which the First Quarto is based. The two theories of pirating and revision are not mutually exclusive; they may both be true.

In *King John* we find another reference to the moles which are associated with evil and with the world's ill opinion. Constance describes her son Arthur as he is not:

> If thou that bid'st me be content wert grim,
> Ugly and sland'rous to thy mother's womb,
> Full of unpleasing blots and sightless stains,
> Lame, foolish, crooked, swart, prodigious,
> Patch'd with *foul moles* and eye-offending marks,
> I would not care, I then would be content;
> For then I should not love thee, no, nor thou
> Become thy great birth nor deserve a crown. (III. i. 43-50)

The "foul moles" correspond to the blemishes already noted as signs of vicious character. Here is a mother's statement that she could not love a deformed and ugly son, though his defects were Nature's fault and not his own.

Constance's speech is the statement of a theme which Shakespeare had worked out with great care in the character of Richard III. Part of Richard's resolute villainy proceeds from his consciousness of physical ugliness. Margaret's contemptuous reference to his "elvish-mark'd" body is typical of the slurs which he has known all his life. Nor had he experienced much love from his own mother. She thus addresses him:

> Thou cam'st on earth to make the earth my hell.
> A grievous burden was thy birth to me;
> Tetchy and wayward was thy infancy;
> Thy school-days frightful, desp'rate, wild, and furious,
> Thy prime of manhood daring, bold, and venturous. . . .
> Therefore take with thee my most grievous curse. (IV. iv. 166-187)

[6] "Notes on the Structure of *Hamlet*," in *The Character of Hamlet*.

While one can pardon the Duchess' anger at the crimes of Richard the man, this passage suggests that she did not love him when he was a child. Nor has he ever had very much love from anyone. His wife Anne marries him only for ambition's sake. His own wooings are marked by a cynical contempt, as in his remark concerning Elizabeth: "To her go I, a jolly thriving wooer" (IV. iii. 43). Yet his great need of love appears in his attack of conscience after his vision of the ghosts:

> There is no creature loves me,
> And if I die no soul shall pity me. (V. iii. 200-201)

Richard's self-contempt, his belief that his ugliness would prevent any woman from loving him, is the decisive feature of his character. His ruthless ambition proceeds from repeated humiliation. Shakespeare makes this abundantly clear:

> Why, love forswore me in my mother's womb;
> And, for I should not deal in her soft laws,
> She did corrupt frail nature with some bribe . . .
> To disproportion me in every part,
> Like to a chaos, or an unlick'd bear-whelp
> That carries no impression like the dam. (*3 Henry VI*, III. ii. 153-162)

> Then, since the heavens have shap'd my body so,
> Let hell make crook'd my mind to answer it.
> (*3 Henry VI*, V. vi. 78-79)

> I, that am curtail'd of this fair proportion,
> Cheated of feature by dissembling nature,
> Deform'd, unfinish'd, sent before my time
> Into this breathing world, scarce half made up,
> And that so lamely and unfashionable
> That dogs bark at me as I halt by them. . . .
> And therefore, since I cannot prove a lover. . .
> I am determined to prove a villain. (*Richard III*, I. i. 18-30)

Perhaps, like Cyrano de Bergerac, Richard feels that he could have been a great lover except for his physical ugliness. His hatred for the world that so scorns him is manifested in a determination to rule that world without regard to the means used. He is an outstanding instance of the innate defects which obscure great capabilities of virtue.

Yet even Richard, villain though he is, is subject to the pangs of conscience, as shown in its violent awakening after his dream of the ghosts (V. iii). This was anticipated in Queen Margaret's earlier exclamation:

> The worm of conscience still begnaw thy soul. (I. iii. 222)

The "worm of conscience" was probably proverbial, since it occurs in Chaucer's *Phisiciens Tale,* line 280. Its "gnawing" may well have been recalled from La Primaudaye's discussion of the guilty soul afflicted by conscience:

115 For from the very instant, wherein wickednesse is committed, she frameth for, and of her selfe her owne torment, and beginneth to suffer the paine of her mischieuous deed, through the remorse thereof. This is that *worme that continually gnaweth the conscience* of a malefactor, and accompanieth his miserable life with shame and confusion, with frights, perturbations, anguish, and continuall disquietnesse, *euen to his very dreames,* so that all his life time hee is destitute of all tranquility and rest of spirit, wherein onely human felicity consisteth. . . . This is that, which the Scripture teacheth vs in Leuiticus [26:36], saying, That the wicked shall tremble at the fall of the leafe of a tree, and that they shall be as if their life hung by a thread. . . . This is that *worme* whereof Esay speaketh [Isaiah 66:24], which dyeth not, but gnaweth and deuoureth them without ceasing. (Pt. I, ch. 6)

La Primaudaye also identifies the avenging Furies of Greek mythology as symbols for the pangs of conscience. Richard had pretended indifference to conscience and had sought to shut his mind to its admonitions, but it triumphs in his dreams. His line, "O coward conscience, how dost thou afflict me" (V. iii. 179), envisions conscience as a persecutor of guilt, in much the same way that La Primaudaye portrays it.

The quality implanted by nature may be a disposition toward crime, but it will not necessarily result in actual crime. One can largely overcome this natural disposition by good instruction, and by the development of good habits. As repetition of a vice may dull one's perception of its evil quality, so repeated avoidance of evil acts may weaken one's natural disposition toward them. Thus, Hamlet advises his mother to weaken her passion for Claudius by avoiding his embraces:

> Good-night; but go not to mine uncle's bed.
> Assume a virtue, if you have it not.
> That monster, *custom,* who all sense doth eat,

Of habits evil, is angel yet in this,
That to the use of actions fair and good
He likewise gives a frock or livery,
That aptly is put on. Refrain tonight,
And that shall lend a kind of easiness
To the next abstinence; the next more easy;
For *use* almost can change the *stamp of nature,*
And either [master] the devil or throw him out,
With wondrous potency. (III. iv. 159-170)

This passage reflects the language of the *Zodiake:*

116 Of *custome* long is *nature* bred, and yeldes hir sore alway, (p. 77)
To *vse* that long time hath bene kept: yet ought we for to pray
To God, within the mothers wombe that he may giue good seede:
For so we shewe our selues in lyfe, as wee therein doe breede.
Whosoeuer doth come nought from thence wil seldom vertuous proue, (p. 78)
Though manners good, the schole hym teach & thousand masters moue,
Well maist thou nature rule sometime, but neuer her expell:
For shee is still of greater force than all thy guiding well.
Yet something will shee altred be with vse and daily toyle.

117 To winne and vanquishe *nature,* doth require no litle paine. . . (p. 94)
For *custome* wonted is to breake the force of nature sure,
If that by many yeares it hath beene vsed to indure.

118 Who all Affections ouercomes, and wholy doth restraine, (p. 144)
He that from youth doth Vertue vse, may well to this attaine:
Such force hath *vse,* nothing more strong.

In these lines we find Hamlet's "custom" and "use" that "almost can change the stamp of nature." They cannot completely change it, but they can subdue and rule it. I have discussed elsewhere the development of this idea from Aristotle through La Primaudaye, Montaigne, and Richard Hooker, all of whom may have furnished contributory sources for this passage.[7] The appearance of "custom," "use," and "nature" furnishes the verbal links which would associate them with the lines from the *Zodiake,* the primary source.

In Q. 116 Palingenius also sets forth a theory of heredity. Our innate qualities and future course of life are likely to be determined within the mother's womb accordingly as the "seed" is good or bad.

[7] *The Character of Hamlet,* pp. 210-213.

This determines man's "nature"; while good habits may aid in controlling this "nature," they can never expel or completely change it. One should pray for "good seede" in the first conception of the child within the womb as the surest means of enabling him to lead a virtuous life. This concept has influenced the character of Edmund in *King Lear*. He twice refers to his "nature" as an innate disposition to evil (I. ii. 1, V. iii. 244), perhaps in consequence of his bastardy. Edgar recognizes that Edmund's evil "nature" proceeded from his birth, saying of their father:

> The dark and *vicious* place where thee he got
> Cost him his eyes. (V. iii. 172-173)

The "vicious place" is apparently the womb of Edmund's mother, where his evil character was determined before he was born.

In Hamlet's "vicious mole of nature" speech, he refers to the "stamp of one defect" as being either "nature's livery or fortune's star." This phrase reflects another passage from the *Zodiake,* in which "naughty seede" and "naughty starres" are combined as possible alternate causes of ill health, including mental illness. The passage further analyzes the relations of mind and body, with the influence of the mind upon the health of the body. Googe provides a marginal note:

119 Affections of the mind cause of sickness.

Palingenius advises against worry, against overeating, and in favor of cheerfulness as an aid to health. As we shall see, his lines find numerous apparent echoes in Shakespeare:

120 *a* For health is far more worth than gold. The healthy deluing
lout, (p. 79)
In better state accounted is than crased kyng, no doute. . . .
b The causer first of each disease is chiefest Nature sure,
As oft as vnder *naughty starres* the *byrth* she doth procure:
While as the childe doth inwarde take the motions of the skie,
Or else *begot of naughty seede;* the cause doth often lye
Amyd the parentes of the childe, when they perfourme the acte
Disposed ill, with naughty bloud, or sore diseases racte.
c More causes are there yet beside, as labour, toyle, and rest,
Both colde, and heate, with sleepe, and meat, and ioyes of Venus nest.

Eche one of these, doth strength abate and hurt the liuely sprite,
As oft as we to much them vse, or vse them else to lyght.
d *Excesse* of both doth sicknesse bring. Of *measure* health proceedes.
e The *perturbations* of the minde diseases often breedes.
And to much sadnesse, feare, and griefe, and to much myrth, as well
Doth kyll, if we will credit such, as histories doe tell. . . .
f If thou be sick (as nedes thou must sometime) what wilt thou
doe? (p. 80)
Deferr not then the medcine long, but loke thou soone thereto:
While as thy sore is yet but greene, nor yet thy mortall foe
Possessed hath his pitched place, amyd thy corps. For, loe,
g A litle water doth suffice, to *quench the breeding Fire:*
But when that it is fully growne, and flames begin to spire
Wyth vaunting course agayne the starres: scarce *Riuer,* Spring, or Lake
Will then suffice to *quench* it out. . . .
h See that thy diet holsome be, and eate not thou to much: (p. 81)
For mischiefe great hath come to men, by ouer feeding such.
Hereof doe most diseases breede, beware especially
As of a poyson strong, that doth enforce the corps to dye,
That thou no meate agayne do take, till that receiued last
Be well consumd, and perfectly his full digestion past.
And euery day vse exercise, by pace, or other feate:
Wherby the ioyntes thus moued, may procure a warming heate.
For mouing is the cause of warmth, and aydes the stomack well:
Encreaseth strength, and humors nought from out the fleshe expell.
i Breake not beside thy quiet *rest,* for *sleepe the body feedes,*
And *helps the mind:* wher harm to both, excessiue *watching* breedes.
Expell thou *sorrow* farre from thee, and *heauinesse* exile:
j For it *dries vp the synowes* all, and makes the body vile,
k And grisled haires vntimely plants. The *ioyfull heart* agayne
Doth make the limmes & members strong, and ioyful yeares retayne.

The influence of the stars is discussed at greater length in a subsequent chapter, but from 120*b,* above, we can see how the "vicious mole of nature" resulting from man's birth could be either "nature's livery or fortune's star."

With 120*d* compare Portia's exclamation when Bassanio chooses the leaden casket containing her portrait:

O love, be moderate; allay thy ecstacy;
In *measure* rein thy joy; scant this *excess!*
I feel too much thy blessing; make it less,
For fear I surfeit. (*Merchant of Venice,* III. ii. 111-115)

This apparently reflects Palingenius' statement that "measure" produces health and that "excesse" of any kind, particularly of the affections, can bring sickness or even death.

The power of the "ioyful heart" to make the limbs strong (120*k*) seems to be reflected in Autolycus' song:

> Jog on, jog on, the foot-path way,
> And merrily hent the stile-a;
> A merry heart goes all the day,
> Your sad tires in a mile-a. (*Winter's Tale,* IV. iii. 132-135)

We cannot be sure whether this stanza is original with Shakespeare or is part of an old folksong,[8] but the same sentiment occurs again in *The Taming of the Shrew:*

> For so your doctors hold it very meet,
> Seeing too much sadness hath congeal'd your blood,
> And melancholy is the nurse of frenzy.
> Therefore they thought it good you hear a play
> And frame your mind to *mirth and merriment,*
> *Which bars a thousand harms and lengthens life.*
> (Induction, ii. 133-138)

Several biblical verses are probable contributory sources of these passages. It is worth while to quote Prov. 17:22 in two versions:

121 A joyful heart causeth good health: but a sorrowful mind dryeth the bones. (G)

122 A merry heart maketh a lusty age: but a sorrowful mind dryeth up the bones. (C, B)

Mr. Noble cites the following verses:

123 The joy and cheerfulness of the heart is the life of man, and a man's gladness is the prolonging of his days. . . . Zeal and anger shorten the days of life; carefulness and sorrow bring age before the time. (Ecclesiasticus, 30:22, 24) (B)

The second sentence is compared with Sir Toby's remark that "care's an enemy to life" (*Twelfth Night,* I. iii. 3).

Palingenius' simile of the fire (120*g*) recalls an earlier use in 79*f*. The present passage seems to be echoed in *3 Henry VI:*

> A little fire is quickly trodden out,
> Which, being suffer'd, *rivers cannot quench.* (IV. viii. 7-8)

The images of 120*i, j,* appear briefly in Kent's words concerning Lear:

[8] Cf. Chappell's *Popular Music of the Olden Time,* I. 211-212.

Oppressed nature sleeps.
This *rest* might yet have balm'd thy broken *sinews*. (III. vi. 104-105)

One should remember that "sinews" meant "nerves" to the Elizabethans. The "crased kyng" of 120*a* is especially applicable to Lear, who is breaking physically and mentally. There is also a possible reminiscence of 132*h,* below, on the healing power of sleep for troubled minds, later echoed in the Doctor's words to Cordelia:

Our foster-nurse of nature is repose,
The which he lacks; that to provoke in him,
Are many simples operative, whose power
Will close the eye of anguish. (IV. iv. 12-15)

The power of sorrow to dry up the body (120*j*) appears in *Romeo and Juliet:* "Dry sorrow drinks our blood" (III. v. 59).

In several passages Shakespeare combines the heaviness of sorrow with melancholy, going beyond the *Zodiake* in that regard:

For she is lumpish, heavy, melancholy.
(*Two Gentlemen of Verona,* III. ii. 62)

He made her melancholy, sad, and heavy.
(*Love's Labour's Lost,* V. ii. 14)

These were commonplace notions concerning melancholy. While there were many treatises upon the subject, it seems to me that the verbal echoes in Shakespeare from the following passage in *The French Academie* point to it as a specific source. La Primaudaye is discussing the functions of reason and fancy in guiding the affections of men and the influence of these affections upon the physical health of the body. He urges joy and a merry heart as a preserver of health and life. In the midst of this discussion, he writes:

124 We see also by experience, that there is great agreement betweene the qualities and temperature of the body, and the affections of the soule: insomuch that as the bodies of men are compounded of the qualities of heate, colde, moisture, and drinesse, so among the affections some are hot, others colde; some moist, others dry, and some mingled of these diuers qualities. So that euery one is most subject to those affections that come neerest to the nature, temperature, and *complexion* of his body. As for example, the affection of ioy is hote and moist, and therefore they that are hot and moist, as children, young men, sound

> and healthy folkes, and idle persons, are more easily inclined to that affection. Contrariwise, sorrow is a cold and dry affection, and therefore they that are colde and drie are most giuen to that affection; and such are old folkes and they that are of a melancholy humor, which is earthy, cold and dry. For the like reason, they that haue a *soft* and tender heart, receiue more easily the *impression* of ioy & griefe, *as waxe taketh the print of a seale.* (Pt. II, ch. 39)

The final sentence is particularly suggestive. In *Measure for Measure,* when Angelo taxes women with frailty, Isabella says:

> Women! Help, Heaven! men their creation mar
> In profiting by them. Nay, call us ten times *frail;*
> For we are *soft* as our *complexions* are,
> And credulous to *false prints.* (II. iv. 127-130)

The nature of these "prints" is made clear by Viola's comment upon Olivia's falling in love with her as Cesario:

> How easy is it for the proper-*false*
> In women's *waxen* hearts to set their forms!
> Alas, our *frailty* is the cause, not we! (*Twelfth Night,* II. ii. 30-32)

In these passages Shakespeare makes the speakers say that women have soft and tender hearts and hence are more easily deceived by men, who can impress their hearts just as a seal-ring sets its imprint in soft wax. This "complexion" causes their frailty and errors of the heart, which do not usually proceed from a love of sin or vice. In *Lucrece,* the poet pleads for greater sympathy for women on these same grounds:

> For men have marble, women *waxen,* minds,
> And therefore are they form'd as marble will;
> The weak oppress'd, the *impression* of strange kinds
> Is form'd in them by force, by fraud, or skill.
> Then call them not the authors of their ill,
> No more than *wax* shall be accounted evil
> Wherein is stamp'd the semblance of a devil. (1240-1246)

The passage from La Primaudaye also seems to be reflected in the exchange of remarks between Othello and Desdemona:

> *Oth.* Give me your hand. This hand is moist, my lady.
> *Des.* It yet hath felt no age nor known no sorrow.
> *Oth.* This argues fruitfulness and liberal heart
> Hot, hot, and moist. This hand of yours requires

> A sequester from liberty, fasting and prayer,
> Much castigation, exercise devout;
> For here's a young and sweating devil here
> That commonly rebels. (III. iv. 36-43)

Desdemona's reply reflects La Primaudaye's statement that heat and moisture were dominant qualities in the young and joyful, as opposed to the cold and dryness of the aged and sorrowful. Yet Othello seems to give these good qualities a different significance, to find in them evidence of a lustful disposition, to believe that his wife's "liberal heart" would be indiscriminately liberal with her sexual favors. There is no precedent for this in La Primaudaye, but I have observed in the writings of Marsilio Ficino, the translator of Plato into Latin, a statement that a hot and moist complexion was one particularly inclined to lust.[9] Shakespeare is clearly familiar with both theories concerning the hot and moist complexion of the body.

Shakespeare also seems to have recalled La Primaudaye's statement that a temperate youth insures a healthful old age:

> 125 And as in calme weather when a man is vpon the sea, hee must prouide such things as are necessary against a storme: so in time of adolesency, men must furnish themselues with temperance, sobriety, and continency, laying vp store of prouision in due time, whereby to sustaine olde age the better. This is that which Plato saith, that a moderate youth maketh an easie old age: but that which is immoderate maketh it grieuous and irkesome. (Pt. I, ch. 52)

In *As You Like It,* Adam says to Orlando:

> Though I look old, yet I am strong and lusty;
> For in my youth I never did apply
> Hot and rebellious liquors in my blood,
> Nor did not with unbashful forehead woo
> The means of weakness and debility;
> Therefore my age is as a lusty winter,
> Frosty, but kindly. (II. iii. 47-53)

In the various instances quoted in this chapter, we can see that Shakespeare had a consistent theory concerning mental sickness of several kinds and its relation to physical health. We have also observed some of his probable sources in *The French Academie* and

---

[9] *Commentarium in Convivium (Symposium),* VII. iv.

The Zodiake of Life. It would be a mistake to insist on these as the only sources, for health and sickness are now and doubtless were then matters of everyday discussion. Yet the verbal resemblances suggest these as the primary sources, as the original suggestions around which other associations may have clustered. They enable us to perceive in his plays a sustained and consistent attitude on this subject, when otherwise we might see only isolated references to it.

Chapter 8
Sleep

We have already observed several instances in which sleep appears as a cure for mental troubles. Conversely, such troubles may cause a lack of sleep or broken slumbers. Shakespeare secures strong poetic effects through his imagery of sleep. We find echoes of Q. 120 in some of these.

In commenting upon Lady Macbeth's sleepwalking, the Doctor says:

> A great perturbation in nature, to receive at once the benefits of sleep and do the effects of watching. (V. i. 10-12)

Here "watching" means "waking," as in 120*i*. We have already observed La Primaudaye's use of "perturbation" to describe the war of the affections (*supra,* p. 79). This recollection may have combined in Shakespeare's mind with 120*e:* "The *perturbations* of the minde diseases often breedes" to furnish the Doctor with his comment on Lady Macbeth. The perturbations occurring during sleep appear in Richard III's dream when the ghost of Lady Anne "now fills thy sleep with perturbations" (V. iii. 161). The cause of Richard's perturbations is the same as the cause of Lady Macbeth's, a guilty conscience, but it does not so affect him as to make him walk in his sleep.

The perturbations of the mind as a cause of physical illness appear in *2 Henry IV,* in Falstaff's description of the King's illness:

> This apoplexy, as I take it, is a kind of lethargy. . . a kind of sleeping in the blood. . . . It hath it original from much grief, from study, and *perturbation of the brain*. . . . It is a kind of deafness.
> (I. ii. 127-134)

Coriolanus gives a similar list of symptoms of apoplexy as a contemptuous analogy for peace: "Peace is a very apoplexy, lethargy, mulled, deaf, sleepy" (IV. v. 239). Using the same image as Falstaff does, Prince Hal assumes that his father's "perturbations" proceed from the cares of the kingship and applies the term to the symbol of kingship, the crown. Here he also recalls the first two lines of Q. 120, lines which we find echoed in several later speeches as well:

> 126 For health is far more worth than gold. The healthy deluing lout,
> In better state accounted is than crased kyng, no doute.

"Crased" could refer to physical feebleness as well as mental
infirmity in the sixteenth century, as evidenced in *1 Henry*
[127] *VI,* III. ii. 89: "fitter for sickness and for crazy age." Besides,
Palingenius' Latin reading, "rege aegro," leaves no doubt that physical illness is meant (V. 755). The contrast between the healthy laborer and the ailing king combined in Shakespeare's mind with the healing effects of sleep, which are briefly set forth in 120*i*. Prince Hal says:

> Why doth the crown lie there upon his pillow,
> Being so troublesome a bedfellow?
> O polish'd *perturbation!* golden care!
> That keep'st the ports of slumber open wide
> To many a watchful night! Sleep with it now!
> Yet not so sound and half so deeply sweet
> As he whose brow with homely biggen bound
> Snores out the watch of night. (*2 Henry IV,* IV. v. 21-28)

The "watchful night" refers to the wakefulness of the king. Earlier in the same play, Henry IV makes the same contrast when he is troubled with insomnia. His poorest subjects, the common laborer, the sailor tossed upon the high mast, can sleep, but the sick king cannot sleep:

> How many thousand of my poorest subjects
> Are at this hour asleep! O Sleep, O gentle Sleep,
> Nature's soft nurse, how have I frighted thee
> That thou no more wilt weigh mine eyelids down
> And steep my senses in forgetfulness?
> Why rather, Sleep, liest thou in smoky cribs,
> Upon uneasy pallets stretching thee. . . .
> Deny it to a king? Then happy low, lie down!
> Uneasy lies the head that wears a crown. (III. i. 4-31)

The same contrast is evident in Henry V's long soliloquy on the eve of the Battle of Agincourt:

O hard condition,
Twin-born with greatness, subject to the breath
Of every fool whose sense no more can feel
But his own wringing! What infinite heart's-ease
Must kings neglect, that private men enjoy!
And what have kings, that privates have not too,
Save ceremony, save general ceremony? . . .
O, be sick, great greatness,
And bid thy Ceremony give thee cure!
Think'st thou the fiery fever will go out
With titles blown from adulation?
Will it give place to flexure and low bending?
Canst thou, when thou command'st the beggar's knee,
Command the health of it? No, thou proud dream,
That play'st so subtly with a king's repose;
I am a king that find thee, and I know
'Tis not the balm, the sceptre, and the ball,
The sword, the mace, the crown imperial,
The intertissued robe of gold and pearl,
The farced title running 'fore the King,
The throne he sits on, nor the tide of pomp
That beats upon the high shore of this world,—
No, not all these, thrice-gorgeous Ceremony,
Not all these, laid in bed majestical,
Can sleep so soundly as the wretched slave,
Who with a body fill'd and vacant mind
Gets him to rest, cramm'd with *distressful bread,*
Never sees horrid night, the child of hell,
But like a lackey from the rise to set
Sweats in the eye of Phoebus, and all night
Sleeps in Elysium; next day after dawn,
Doth rise and help Hyperion to his horse,
And follows so the ever-running year
With profitable labour to his grave:
And, but for ceremony, such a wretch,
Winding up days with toil and nights with sleep,
Had the fore-hand and vantage of a king.
The slave, a member of the country's peace,
Enjoys it, but in gross brain little wots
What watch the King keeps to maintain the peace,
Whose hours the peasant best advantages. (IV. i. 250-301)

Here are stressed the superior conditions of the poor laborer: health, freedom from care, ability to sleep soundly. Furthermore, private men feel free to criticize the king, not realizing how much care and worry he expends for their benefit; they are deceived by the outward show of pomp and grandeur. The "heart's-ease" which they can enjoy is not available to him.

This last element of Henry's speech is indebted to another passage in the *Zodiake:*

128 *a* So Kings that haue the supreme power and rule of relmes in
hand, (p. 70)
With greater cares tormented are, and greater griefes of minde,
b Although the common people yet, these wounds doe neuer finde.
For secretly within their heartes their torments they do hide. . . .
c Full oft a king therefore (p. 71)
May liue in wretched case no doubt, nor makes him happy more
(Beleue me now) his regal crowne. But on the outward show
The fooles do gase, and what within remaynes they little know.

These lines express the spirit of Henry's speech. The "regal crowne" has been associated by Henry with all the other badges of office, and he likewise concludes that they cannot make the king happy. The hidden care and grief which the outer world little suspects are also reminiscent of the above passage.

The Scriptures provide two contributory sources of Henry's speech. One occurs in Ecclesiastes 5:12:

129 A labouring man sleepeth sweetly whether it be little or much that he eateth: but the abundance of the rich will not suffer him to sleep. (B)

Henry's phrase "cramm'd with *distressful bread*" seems indebted to Psalms 127:3:

130 It is but lost labour that ye haste to rise up early, and so late take rest, and eat the *bread of carefulness;* for so he giveth his beloved sleep.

Mr. Noble cites this phrase but doubts that it is really Shakespeare's source. We should note, however, that the Psalmist is echoing God's condemnation of Adam after the Fall:

131 Cursed is the earth for thy sake: in sorrow shalt thou eat of it all the days of thy life. Thorns also and thistles shall it bring forth to thee, and thou shalt eat the herb of the field. In the *sweat* of thy face shalt thou eat *bread*. (Gen. 3:17-19) (G)

It seems likely that Shakespeare made this rather obvious association, for his phrase "distressful bread" does not imply grief in the people eating the bread; it is rather the biblical characterization of bread which must be earned by sweat and hard labor. In this sense, the laborer's bread is "distressful" because he worked for it, but he may enjoy it very much; the king's bread is not "distressful," since he does not work to produce it, yet he may not enjoy it at all.

The relation of sleeplessness to health, sickness, and mental perturbations appears again in Friar Laurence's speech to Romeo:

> Young son, it argues a distemper'd head
> So soon to bid good morrow to thy bed.
> Care keeps his watch in every old man's eye,
> And where care lodges, sleep will never lie;
> But where unbruised youth, with unstuff'd brain
> Doth couch his limbs, there golden sleep doth reign;
> Therefore thy earliness doth me assure
> Thou art up-rous'd with some distemp'rature. (II. iii. 33-40)

Besides the quotations already given, Palingenius discusses sleep in several other passages. He presents sleep as a curative and solacing force, a relief from worry and torment of mind. But excess of sleep can have its undesirable qualities. It dulls the mind, making it unfit for study or worthy enterprises. Particularly bad is the sleep which accompanies gluttony and results from an overfilled stomach. It is necessary to quote at considerable length to show the probable influences upon Shakespeare. In the following lines, these several elements appear. In a few lines not here quoted, Gluttony has been personified as a woman; in the quoted lines she leads her son Sleep, begotten by Labour, suggesting the fatigue of manual labor as causing a desire for sleep:

> 132 *a* For nothing is more vile than this, nor harmeth more the state (p. 37)
> Of Man: The beastes for onely lyfe did Ioue aboue create.
> But man for life and reason to, and that he should excell:
> And so be like vnto the Saints, which in the heauens dwell,
> He hath ordainde to rule the earth. But they that loue the yoke
> *b* Of Greedines and Belly ioyes, are dull, and with the smoke
> Of *fuming meates* their wit is darckt, (like as with cloudes the Sunne)
> Ne may they yet the truth discerne, but chiefly when begunne
> Hath *boyling wines* within the brest, to blinde and dull the witte:
> And when the *paunch* is stuffed ful, for bookes they be vnfitte.
> Whereby it often comes to passe, their *witte* but small to bee:
> The end that nature plaste them for, they cleane forsake we see.
> *c* Nor more they knowe, than doth the herd of Shepe or Oxen dull,
> Yea lesse sometyme, when as with wine, their beastly braynes be full. . . .

d I haue thee here declared now, the woman what she hight:[1] (p. 39)
And now the Boy with drousy noule,[2] I will thee here recite.
The Boy is hers, and of her borne, and Labour him begat,
e His name is Sleepe, his nourse is *Leth,* his foode is *poppy fat.*
He brother germane is to Death, but not as she, doth last.
f He doth refresh the weried limmes, with dayly labour past.
He doth expell the cares of men, and calleth strength agayne;
Without the ayde of him, no man hys lyfe may well sustayne.
g Yet hurts he much, and doth the minde, in certaine wise oppresse:
Diseases breedes, and duls the corps, oft vsed with excesse.
If foode be small, he small wil be, for when the meate is spent,
The corps doth wake or else doth rest, with litle slepe content.
More lightly then his rest he takes, and better sleepes doth breede,
h But vnto troubled mindes it is, a *comfort* greate in deede.
And much it is to be desired, when loue the hart doth payne,
When sicknesse greues, or when the man doth heauy chaunce sustayne:
Then is it more to be estemde than golde or precious stone.
i As death, so sleepe doth make the wretch and happy man as one.
j But he whome nature hath endewed, with long and happy dayes,
That doth desire expert to be in euery kinde of wayes,
By vertue eke a famous name in earth for to obtayne,
Must watche: for famous things, by sleepe none are perfourmed plaine
k And for to sleepe in feathers soft, renowne doth eft refuse:
Shun thou this same, with all thy might thy selfe to watching vse.
l For, O what times of quiet length shall fates permit to thee:
When last of all *the night shall come and day shall banisht bee,*
And breath hath left the quiuering ioynts lyke ayre that fleeting flyes,
With long and euerlasting sleepe, then shalt thou shut thine *eyes.*

In this and in 120*i,* we find the possible sources of several images occurring in Macbeth's description of sleep:

Sleep that knits up the ravell'd sleeve of care,
The death of each day's life, sore labour's bath,
Balm of hurt minds, great nature's second course,
Chief nourisher in life's feast. (II. ii. 37-40)

The final image apparently stems from 120*i,* "sleepe the body feedes." The same phrase suggests "great nature's second course." It is the second course because in both quotations eating and sleeping are discussed in that order; eating would be the first course. The phrase "life's feast" probably stems from yet another passage in the *Zodiake* in which life is compared to an inn where travelers sit for a time at a feast provided by Nature (*infra,* p. 216). "Balm for hurt

[1] *hight.* Was named.
[2] *noule.* Head.

minds" may be a transformation of 132*h,* "comfort to troubled minds."[3] The phrase is echoed again in *The Tempest* in Sebastian's words concerning sleep:

> It seldom visits *sorrow;* when it doth,
> It is a *comforter.* (II. i. 195-196)

The power of sleep to relieve the heaviness of sorrow appears in *A Midsummer Night's Dream:*

> So sorrow's heaviness doth heavier grow
> For debt that bankrupt sleep doth sorrow owe. . . .
> And sleep, that sometimes shuts up sorrow's eye. (III. ii. 84-85, 435)

Macbeth's phrase "the death of each day's life" may reflect 132*l,* in which the "long and euerlasting sleepe" of death is described in terms of the banishing of day and the onset of night. The same lines appear again in *Romeo and Juliet,* IV. i. 100-101:

> Thy *eyes'* windows fall,
> Like *death* when he *shuts* up the *day of life.*

A most interesting association occurs in Palingenius' personification of sleep:

134 His name is Sleepe, his nourse is Leth, his foode is poppy fat.

Again, on p. 84, the *Zodiake* shows the River Lethe as a dark stream winding among poisonous fields of poppies. These passages were probably recalled in connection with Ovid's description of the dwelling of Sleep beside the River Lethe among fields of poppies (*Metamorphoses,* XI. 602-607). Iago uses the poppy as a sleep-producing opiate in his words concerning Othello:

> Not *poppy,* nor mandragora,
> Nor all the drowsy syrups of the world,
> Shall ever medicine thee to that *sweet sleep*
> Which thou ow'dst yesterday. (III. iii. 330-333)

"Sweet sleep" is biblical (Prov. 3:24, Eccl. 5:12, Jer. 31:26).

---

[3] These images, however, may also be reminiscent of lines in Ovid's *Metamorphoses,* cited by Kittredge from Rushton:

133 Somne, quies rerum, placidissime, Somne, deorum,
Pax animi, quem cura fugit, qui corpora duris
Fessa ministeriis mulces reparasque labori! (XI. 623-625)

In "poppy fat" Googe has reversed the normal word order to secure his rhyme, for he refers to the "fat poppy." This description accounts for a puzzling phrase in Shakespeare, when the Ghost is charging Hamlet with his mission of revenge:

> And duller shouldst thou be than the *fat weed*
> That rots itself in ease on *Lethe wharf,*
> Wouldst thou not stir in this. (I. v. 32-34)

Palingenius' association of Lethe with the poppy, described by Googe as the "fat" poppy, has resulted in Shakespeare's phrase "fat weed." The reference to Lethe naturally recalled to Shakespeare's mind Aeneas' visit to the underworld. There Lethe is the river of oblivion (*Aeneid,* VI. 749), located in the Elysian Fields. Shakespeare, identifying the "poppy fat" as a "weed" producing Lethean dullness, promptly attached it to the only weeds in Virgil's underworld. These are not beside the River Lethe but beside the River Acheron, on the very spot where Charon disembarks his passengers:

135 Tandem trans fluvium incolumes, vatemque virumque,
> *Informi limo, glaucaque* exponit in *ulva.* (VI. 415-416)

The "formless slime" and "bluish-gray weed" suggest the rotting weed; their landing on it from a boat suggests that it grows on a wharf. Without the two works in view, we cannot see clearly how the associative process has produced Shakespeare's images. Thus, Professor Baldwin (*op. cit.,* II. 468-472) showed considerable ingenuity in tracing Shakespeare's image of Lethe to Virgil, and his conclusions are basically correct; but he failed to observe the connecting links between Lethe, poppies, and the "fat" weed which are furnished by Googe's translation of Palingenius. The "fat" is
[136] Googe's addition, for the Latin line reads: "Nutriit hunc
Lethe, multoque papavere pavit" (III. 638). Possibly Googe was trying to convey the implications of "pavit," a verb which suggests cramming or forced feeding. His mistranslation helps us to determine more precisely the manner in which the image was adapted and has resulted in a striking Shakespearean phrase.

The association of Lethe with sleep, gluttony, and dullness appears again in Pompey's words concerning Antony:

> Tie up the libertine in a field of feasts,
> Keep his brain fuming; Epicurean cooks
> Sharpen with cloyless sauce his appetite,
> That *sleep and feeding* may prorogue his honour
> Even till a *Lethe'd dulness.* (II. i. 23-27)

At the drinking party given aboard Pompey's vessel, Antony expresses the voluptuary's ideal in these words:

> Come, let's all take hands.
> Till that the conquering wine hath steep'd our sense
> In soft and delicate *Lethe.* (II. vii. 113-115)

It is very likely that in the uses of Lethe[4] quoted from Shakespeare he is recalling from Ascham's *Scholemaster* the word *lethen,* given there in the Greek script (Arber's Reprint, p. 155). As Homer feigned that Circe changed men into beasts, so Plato declares that yielding oneself up to pleasure will change one's character by developing four notorious properties. Of these the first is
[137] *lethen,* the "forgetfulness of all good thinges learned before. . . . For, if a man inglutte himself with vanitie, or walter in filthines like a Swyne, all learnyng, all goodnes, is sone forgotten." Ascham's comparison to those who drink of Circe's cup may have contributed to the notion of "bestial" oblivion for this kind of dullness. In Hamlet's fifth soliloquy, where the phrase is used, he omits any reference to Lethe, but he does repeat Pompey's image of sleep and feeding causing the decline of honor. This association shows that he has in mind the same kind of dullness which the Ghost had identified with the weed on Lethe wharf. Hamlet says:

> *What is a man,*
> If his chief good and market of his time
> Be but to *sleep and feed?* A *beast,* no more.
> Sure, he that made us with such large discourse,
> Looking before and after, gave us not
> That capability and *god-like reason*
> To fust in us unus'd. Now whether it be
> *Bestial oblivion,* or some craven scruple

[4] For other uses of Lethe, see p. 206, *infra.*

Of thinking too precisely on th' event. . . .
Rightly to be great
Is not to stir without great argument,
But greatly to find quarrel in a straw
When honour's at the stake. How stand I then,
That have a father kill'd, a mother stain'd,
Excitements of my reason and my blood,
And let all sleep? (IV. iv. 33-41, 53-59)

I have elsewhere interpreted Hamlet's character in terms of the "honour" found in the fifth soliloquy,[5] and I shall not repeat the discussion here except to point out that "bestial oblivion" is Hamlet's disgusted self-accusation and does not represent Shakespeare's interpretation of his character.

The reader will immediately notice the resemblance of Hamlet's lines to 132*a*. Man is elevated above the beasts by the use of reason; by it he rules the earth and is like the dwellers of heaven. But, the subsequent lines declare, he obscures this faculty by excessive sleeping and feeding. The idea occurs elsewhere in the *Zodiake,* with phrasing much nearer to that used by Shakespeare:

138 *a* For vnderneth the kinde (p. 114)
Of Man, the wilde and sauage *Beastes* consist of brutish minde,
To sleepe and foode, addicted all. And if he had not framed
No better things than here we see, the worlde might well be named,
b A folde of filthy feeding flocks, with thornes and donge set out. . . .
c For *what is Man?* a foolishe *beast,* a creature full of spight,
And wretched farre aboue the rest if we shall iudge vpright.

139 *a* O learne you mortall men at length, put darkeness from your minde, (p. 20)
Lyft vp a loft your dimmye eyes: wherto doth will so blinde
You leade? take heede in any wyse you thither doe not goe.
b *By reason, lyke the gods* aboue, you are created, Loe,
By reason are the seas and land, vnto your power subiect:
Let errors not therefore as now, but reason you direct. . . .
c But happy he that is content, with litle to remaine:
Nor puts his trust in things so frayle, that death will him constrayne
To leaue behinde as none of his: and wayeth well in minde. (p. 21)
How short the space is of our life, how all things vayne we finde
d That here on earth created be: *who alwayes one remaynes*
In prosperouse eke and aduerse chaunce, the iudge, nor Stygian paynes
Regardeth not, and nought esteemes what euer *fortune* flyng.

[5] *The Character of Hamlet,* pp. 57-83.

In the first passage we find the sentiment that man is no more than a beast if his sole concern is "but to sleep and feed," and the rhetorical question with its answer: "What is man? A . . . beast." In the second is the statement that his reason makes him like the gods. The statements are close parallels to Hamlet's phrasing and are probably contributory sources of his speech. We may note that the latter part of Q. 139 resembles Hamlet's words to Horatio:

> Nay, do not think I flatter,
> For what advancement may I hope from thee,
> That no revenue hast but thy good spirits
> To feed and clothe thee? . . . for thou hast been
> As one, in suffering all, that suffers nothing,
> A man that Fortune's buffets and rewards
> Hath ta'en with equal thanks. (III. ii. 61-73)

In 139*c* is the reference to cheerful poverty, in 139*d* the reference to equanimity in favorable or adverse fortune.

In 132*b, j,* and in other passages from the *Zodiake,* excess in food or sleep is pronounced an enemy of learning. One cannot study if overstuffed with food or drowsy with sleep. This emerges in Rosalind's remark that "a priest that lacks Latin . . . sleeps easily because he cannot study . . . lacking the burden of lean and wasteful learning" (*As You Like It,* III. ii. 337-341). The most elaborate use of the idea occurs in *Love's Labour's Lost,* where it is an important element of the plot. The King and his followers agree to devote themselves to study for three years. The conditions are: to fast one day a week and eat only one meal per day; to sleep only three hours each night and not at all in the day; to see no women; to study constantly. The purpose to sleep sparingly in order to obtain glory through study may possibly have been suggested by 132*j, k*. With 132*b,* compare Longaville's lines:

> The mind shall banquet, though the body pine.
> *Fat paunches* have lean pates, and dainty bits
> Make rich the ribs, but bankrupt quite the *wits*. (I. i. 25-27)

Professor Baldwin (*op. cit.,* I. 712) cites an analogue to this from Withal's *Dictionarie:*

140 Repletus venter, non vult studere libenter: A Belly full with gluttony, will never study willinglie.

It is quite possible that this is a contributory source of Longaville's lines, which show, however, another reminiscence of the *Zodiake* (*infra,* p. 211).

The reference to the heavy eater who will not study and is like a sheep or ox (132*b, c*) may have suggested Nathaniel's description of Dull:

> Sir, he hath never fed of the dainties that are bred in a book; he hath not eaten paper, as it were; he hath not drunk ink; his intellect is not replenished; he is only an animal, only sensible in the duller parts.
> (*Love's Labour's Lost,* IV. ii. 25-28)

In these various passages, we have seen that Shakespeare used sleep in a variety of ways and that most of these find parallels in the *Zodiake.* Many of the images are rather commonplace and lack the uniqueness which would enable us to pick their sources with certainty. Since we have seen in other chapters how extensive was Shakespeare's knowledge of the *Zodiake,* we may assume that the parallels here given are at least contributory sources, and probably his primary ones.

Chapter 9

The Sleep of Death

IN VARIOUS QUOTATIONS from Shakespeare, notably in Hamlet's third soliloquy, we find references to the sleep of death. This is so prevalent a figure in literature (cf. Psalms 13:3) that it is difficult to assign it to particular sources. Still, the test of internal probability, of several derived images reappearing in conjunction, indicates an indebtedness to the *Zodiake*. In planning the murder of Duncan, Lady Macbeth says:

> His two chamberlains
> Will I with wine and wassail so convince,
> That memory, the warder of the brain,
> Shall be a fume, and the receipt of reason
> A limbeck only. When in swinish sleep
> Their drenched natures lie as in a death. . . . (I. vii. 63-68)

"Swinish" bears a general resemblance to the beastliness of excessive food and sleep as described in 132*c* and 138*a*, with a possible reminiscence from Ascham (Q. 137). The resemblance of sleep to death appears in 132*i, l,* as well as in other places in the *Zodiake*. These examples are commonplace enough, but they occur in conjunction with the "fume" of wine and wassail which will obscure the memory and thus disarm the brain. The reference to the limbeck or retort indicates that the receptacle of reason, the brain, is "boiled" by these fumes. This reference seems to proceed from the "fuming meates" and "boyling wines" which "blinde and dull the witte" (132*b*). We should observe that "fuming" and "boyling" refer to the action of the food and wine within the body, not to their qualities before they were consumed. The physical effect of excessive wine-drinking is again described in Timon's words to the thieves:

> Go, suck the subtle blood o' the grape
> Till the high fever *seethe your blood to froth,*
> And so 'scape hanging. (IV. iii. 432-434)

Here the "boiling" is pictured as fatal if enough wine is consumed to cause the blood itself to vaporize, as it will do in a fever of sufficient violence.

The "fumes" from excessive eating and drinking appear again in the *Zodiake:*

141 All drunkennes must eschewed be, and surfets must be fled (p. 185)
For these the stomacke ouercharge, and muche annoy the head,
And round with *fumes* beset the brain: by this doth alwayes come
The dul appalled sense and sprite, and *sleepes of afternoone.*

These lines receive a most interesting treatment in *Hamlet.* The Ghost describes the time of his murder thus:

Sleeping within mine orchard,
My custom always *in the afternoon,*
Upon my secure hour thy uncle stole. . . . (I. v. 59-61)

These lines would have no special significance except for Hamlet's later comment upon his father's death:

He took my father *grossly, full of bread,*
With all his crimes broad blown, as flush as May;
And how his audit stands who knows save Heaven?
But in our circumstance and course of thought
'Tis heavy with him. (III. iii. 80-84)

Here the fact that the elder Hamlet died while sleeping off the effects of a big meal seems to imperil his soul in the future life. Likewise, if Hamlet can catch Claudius "drunk asleep" or in other activities having "no relish of salvation," he can send Claudius' soul to hell. This danger of dying with an over-full stomach seems to be something apart from the danger of dying with crimes unrepented, to which the Ghost had also referred in his line, "Unhousel'd, disappointed, unanel'd" (I. v. 77). Though the phrase "full of bread" is a biblical reminiscence (Ezek. 16:49), the meaning of Hamlet's line must be sought elsewhere. The clue is found in Palingenius' phrase, "the dul appalled sense and sprite." The soul is brought to this condition by the "fumes" from excessive eating and drinking. If it is in this condition at the moment of death, it is not fitted to take its flight to the heavens and must spend a correspondingly longer time in the cleansing pains of purgatory. This idea seems to derive ultimately from Macrobius, from whom Shakespeare may have taken it. I have already discussed at some length elsewhere the biblical and theological implications of this doctrine.[1]

[1] *The Character of Hamlet,* pp. 24, 185, 233.

The comparison of sleep and death is more extensively developed in another passage from the *Zodiake:*

142 *a* Sleepe onely peace to man doth bring amid his fleeting life, (p. 103)
Nothing than this *(if dreames fray not)* more sweete or voide of strife:
For cares and labour it exiles, and with his pleasaunt wings
The wretched body resting brodes, and sweete estate him brings,
b Yet nature seemes this rest to hate and ordaind hath hereby,
The stinging Gnat and byting Flea, to vexe continually
With twinging prick this pleasant ioy, wherby both night and day
c Might mischiefes euer present bee. More better farre away
Therfore is *death, than Picture his.* No wise man will gainesay.
d For who so once the *seas of lyfe* in ioyfull bote hath past,
And in the quiet hauen faire his Anchor safe hath cast,
With mery heart doth laugh to scorne the blastes of ragyng wyndes
With tempestes black, & Leucoths hed which floury Garlands bynds,
Doth honor much, and Melicert with giftes he doth salute,
And safe amid the shores he ioyes with playes of sundry sute.
e *Death endes all pain, all bonds doth lose, death causes feare to flie,*
And *daungers* all *by death* are forste to *rest eternally.*
f And as no griefe nor paine thee vext before thy Syre thee got,
So shalt thou feele no griefe nor paine, when death her dart hath shot.
Who can conceiue the times as yll, he felt his byrth before?
Or iudge of dayes he neuer saw or neuer shall see more?
g Or who will once dispraise the night as wretched, nought or yll,
Wherein possest of deadly sleepe he sen[s]lesse lay full still?
For *what is death? continuall sleepe.* What sleepe? for small time death.
h But many thinke soules neuer die, but after losse of breath
The dead they say doe liue againe, and flesh forsaking quite
As cockels from the shell outdrawne to Pluto take their flight:
i And downwarde hedlong fast they run in kingdome blacke to sayle.
There faine they woods of Mirtle trees, where wofull louers wayle. (p. 104)
There riuers run with *flaming flouds,* and dreadful Monsters bee
That poyson fome with gaping throtes, there places may you see
Of diuers forme, where Infants crye, and where the guilty Ghostes
The furies fierce of Hell doe burne, and whipp fast lynckt to postes,
j And where the pleasaunt fieldes doe lye with goodly greene arayde,
As due to blessed men that here their pagents well haue playde.

In 142*c* occurs the image of sleep as the "picture" of death. It promptly recalls another passage in the *Zodiake,* p. 141:

143 Or they whose eyes the heauy sleepes haue shut & closed sure:
For *Sleepe* is counted plaine *of death, the liuely portrature.*

Beside these lines Googe has printed a marginal note:

144 Sleepe, the *Image* of Death: and (as Socrates called it) the cousine Germane.

It should also be noted that for "picture" and "portrature" in Googe the original Latin reads "*imago* mortis" (VI. 814, VIII. 390). These readings are perhaps reflected in the Induction to *The Taming of the Shrew,* when the noble lord says of Christopher Sly's drunken sleep:

> O monstrous beast! how like a swine he lies;
> Grim *death,* how foul and loathsome is thine *image!* (i. 34-35)

The foulness of swinish drunkenness repeats the image of Lady Macbeth's phrase "swinish sleep" and may be traced to the same sources. We may observe that sleep as the image of death also occurs in Cicero's *Tusculan Disputations,* I. xxxviii. 92.

The image of sleep as a "picture" of death influences several other passages. In *A Midsummer Night's Dream,* the lovers fall into "death-counterfeiting sleep" (III. ii. 364). In *The Winter's Tale,* Hermione's statue, called by the Clown "the Queen's *picture*" (V. ii. 188), is described by Paulina:

> Prepare
> To see the life as *lively* mock'd as ever
> Still *sleep mock'd death.* (V. iii. 18-20)

This seems to reflect Palingenius' phrase "liuely portrature." A similar comparison occurs in Imogen's chamber, when Iachimo hopes that she will not awake: "O *sleep,* thou *ape of death,* lie dull upon her!" (*Cymbeline,* II. ii. 31).

Sleep as the picture of death has probably suggested Lady Macbeth's reproach to her husband for his cowardice in refusing to revisit the chamber of the murdered Duncan:

> The sleeping and the dead
> Are but as pictures; 'tis the eye of childhood
> That fears a painted devil. (II. ii. 53-55)

Here sleep and death are both thought of as "pictures" of the waking consciousness of a person. They are only pictures because they lack motion and perception; therefore, they can do no harm. The dead Duncan and the sleeping grooms are no more dangerous than is a painting of the devil as contrasted with his real presence. The poet has extended Palingenius' use of sleep as a picture of death to make both unconscious states of mind "pictures" of the conscious state of mind. The second part of Lady Macbeth's sentence, in reference to "a painted devil," has no precedent in the *Zodiake* and was probably recalled from elsewhere. Professor Kittredge cites from *Selimus* (1594) these lines:

145 A tale to terrifie yoong babes:
Like *diuels* faces scor'd on *painted* poasts.

He also notes a later parallel in John Webster's *The White Devil,* III. ii. 151:

146 Terrify babes, my lord, with painted devils.

A further extension of the "picture" usage occurs in Macduff's horror-stricken cry when he discovers Duncan's murder:

Banquo and Donalbain! Malcolm! awake!
Shake off this downy *sleep, death's counterfeit,*
And look on *death* itself! Up, up, and see
The *great doom's image!* Malcolm! Banquo!
As from your graves rise up, and walk like sprites,
To countenance this horror! (II. iii. 80-85)

As sleep is the image of death, so the death of a king, Duncan, is an image of the world's death at Judgment Day. Here there is involved the idea of the microcosm and the macrocosm. Man is a "little world," the model or pattern of the great world, and his death is therefore an image of the world's destruction. This is another instance of what I have called Cosmic Despair upon the death of a loved one, the speaker attributing to nature a corresponding disorder to that in his own mind. In these phrases Shakespeare is recalling images already used in *King Lear.* At Cordelia's death Kent, Edgar, and Albany successively exclaim:

Is this the promis'd end? —
Or *image* of that horror? —
Fall, and cease! (V. iii. 263-264)

The "promis'd end" is the final Judgment; Cordelia's death is its image, so horrifying that it seems impossible except as part of universal destruction. This is another vivid instance of Cosmic Despair.

Macduff's cry, "As from your graves rise up, and walk like sprites," involves a double biblical reminiscence. "Sprites" is an alternative spelling of "spirits." The first reminiscence is from Rev. 20:13, describing the spirits of the dead which shall arise to be called before the Judgment. This in turn recalled the phenomena attending Christ's death:

> 147 And, behold, the vail of the temple was rent in twain, from the top to the bottom; and the earth did quake, and the stones did rent; And graves did open; and many bodies of the saints which slept, arose, And came out of the graves after his resurrection, and came into the holy city, and appeared unto many. (Matt. 27:51-53) (G)

The horror of Duncan's death seems to Macduff comparable to that of the last Judgment or of Christ's crucifixion. The attendant convulsions of nature, such as the earthquake, probably suggested his words a moment earlier:

> Confusion now hath made his masterpiece!
> Most sacrilegious murder hath broke ope
> The Lord's anointed temple, and stole thence
> The life o' th' building. (II. iii. 71-74)

"Confusion" is the reverse of the principle of order in the universe, the disruptive force that seeks a return to primeval chaos for the physical world. It has made a master stroke at the principle of order by the murder of Duncan, a king. Matthew's account of the rending of the stones of the temple may have suggested the breaking open of the "Lord's anointed temple" as a suitable description of the murder. This involves yet another biblical association, St. Paul's definition of the body of man as the temple of God (1 Cor. 3:16, 6:19). The description of the king as "the Lord's anointed" is used by David in sparing Saul (1 Sam. 24:6,10; 26:11) (G, B). This tissue of biblical images is a remarkable instance of Shakespeare's assimilative powers.

The germinal idea of Hamlet's third soliloquy appears to be indebted to Q. 142. Hamlet says:

> To be or not to be: that is the question.
> Whether 'tis nobler in the mind to suffer
> The slings and arrows of outrageous fortune,
> Or to take up arms against a sea of troubles,
> And by opposing end them. *To die; to sleep;*
> *No more;* and by a sleep to say we end
> The heart-ache and the thousand natural shocks
> That flesh is heir to. 'Tis a consummation
> Devoutly to be wish'd. *To die; to sleep;—*
> *To sleep? Perchance to dream!* Ay, there's the rub;
> For in that *sleep of death* what *dreams* may come,
> When we have shuffl'd off this mortal coil,
> Must give us pause. (III. i. 56-68)

The soliloquy is built upon the figurative use of death as a sleep. The turning point comes when Hamlet realizes that it may not be an untroubled sleep. The possible pains or torments of a future life are then figured as dreams which may trouble the sleep of death and which may be worse than any mental anguish endured in this life. Sleep as an absence of consciousness would bring a welcome surcease of pain, but a future conscious existence might be worse than this one. The central question is one of immortality. Can the consciousness of the soul be extinguished by death, even if one should desire this? A belief that it cannot be extinguished makes us hesitant to seek the relief of death.

The reader will find the same progression of thought in 142*a, e, g, h, i.* Sleep brings peace "if dreames fray not"; i.e., if dreams do not frighten us. Death ends all fear, pain, and danger. Death is a continual sleep. *But*—and the transition is emphasized by the indention for a new paragraph—the soul of the dead may live again among the pains of hell or in the place of the blest, in which case it cannot have the dreamless sleep it had desired.

The use of "dreams" as a term for the expected punishments or rewards of a future life may have drawn a hint from a sentence in *The French Academie:*

148 First, he [Pliny] derideth all that men haue spoken or written of the being of soules after the death of the bodies, accompting all this to be but toyes & *dreames*. . . . (Pt. II, ch. 98)

A similar usage of "dreams" occurs in the *Zodiake* in a passage which describes the supposed pains of hell in terms of Greek mythology and would promptly have been associated with 142*i*. Epicurus, expounding his philosophy, is made to declare that there is no future conscious existence and that supposed penalties or rewards after death are nothing but dreams:

149 *a* For when that once our vitall breath is faded cleane away, (p. 27)
No more we be, than first we were before our natall daye.
b O to much weake, to fraile, and proude, O nature bolde of man,
Whereby doest thou perswade thy selfe to liue for euer than?
c Leaue of therefore thou *lumpe of claye,* the yeares of Gods to wyll:
d All things begonne shall haue an ende, nothing remaineth styll.
Both cities great, and mighty men, and vasty realmes withall:
The hautiest hylles, and greatest flouds, doth Time at length let fall.
e And thinkest thou (O fading *dust*) for euer to remaine?
Is hope of minde with thee so great? we trauaile but in vaine
f In trusting *dreames* for vertues sake, and fayning fansies straunge.
They be but fooles that things assurde, for vnassurde will chaunge.

We have already observed that this passage combines the dust-image with the "lumpe of claye,"[2] both of which are used by Shakespeare (*supra,* p. 45), who also has other echoes of the passage (*infra,* p. 224). The use of "dreames" in reference to the supposed sensations of a future existence may have suggested Shakespeare's allusion to such sensations as "dreams" in the "sleep of death." It will be noticed that 149*a* repeats the argument of 142*f,* on the complete absence of consciousness after death, and may have caused Shakespeare to associate the two passages.

Professor Kittredge cites a significant contributory source for Hamlet's lines from Montaigne's *Essais,* III. xii:

150 If it bee a *consummation* of ones being, it is also an amendment and entrance into a long and quiet night. Wee finde nothing so sweete in life, as a quiet rest and gentle sleepe, and without dreames. (p. 952)

Since the key-word "consummation" does not appear until the Second Quarto of *Hamlet* (1604), it could easily have been borrowed from Florio's translation, which appeared in 1603 (*supra,* p. 6).

[2] This phrase also occurs in Marlowe's *Jew of Malta,* I. ii. 217.

For Hamlet's "sea of troubles" we find the clue in 142*d,* "the seas of lyfe." This phrase immediately associates itself with another passage in the *Zodiake:*

151 *a* Of all good things that vnto man, may any waies arise, (p. 240)
While as of this his present *life,* the *troublous seas* he tries.
b And when *escapte from mortall chaine,* the Soule hath passage straight,
Conueying with hir selfe these three, that alwaies on hir waite,
c The Minde the Sense and Mooueing force vnto the heauens hie,
Shall ioyfull go, and there remaine, in blisse perpetually.

In this second quotation, life is not merely a "sea" but a "troublous sea." This satisfactorily accounts for Hamlet's "sea of troubles."

Considerable speculation has attended Shakespeare's line, "When we have shuffl'd off this mortal coil." The word "coil" is generally taken to mean "tumult" or "turmoil," its usual signification in his plays. But it could also mean a coil of rope or cable, in which case the image would be that of a prisoner putting aside his bonds. The *Variorum* gives considerable debate on this point. The sense of the passage really depends upon the word "shuffl'd," which can refer to a manner of walking, as in "the forc'd gait of a shuffling nag (*1 Henry IV,* III. i. 135); which can mean "to evade or escape from," as in Claudius' "There is no shuffling" (*Hamlet,* III. iii. 61); and which can likewise mean "to put aside," as in *Twelfth Night,* III. iii. 16.

Shakespeare could have visualized the image in two ways. If "shuffl'd" refers to a manner of walking, he is perhaps thinking of the same figure as Macbeth's "poor player" who must leave the stage of the world (*supra,* p. 38). The "mortal coil" would correspond to the "sound and fury" which characterize human life. The player would walk out of this tumult slowly, ungracefully, dragging his feet as though reluctant to go.

The second visualization would show a prisoner in bonds. These bonds are figuratively the worries and distractions of life, the confused excitement from which he seeks escape. Shakespeare quite often uses double meanings of words for a punning effect, and he may imply both uses in this image: the coil of rope symbolic of the "coil" or tumult of mortal existence. The prisoner strains at his bonds and finally slips out of them and puts them aside. In the first visualization, the player would leave life unwillingly; in the second, the prisoner would leave life willingly. The second seems more in harmony with the general purport of Hamlet's soliloquy.

If this second visualization of the image is accepted, it may very well have proceeded from Palingenius' phrase "escapte from *mortal* chaine," which occurs in the next line after "troublous seas" (151*b*). The proximity of these two images suggests that Shakespeare remembered them both while writing Hamlet's lines. The use of the word "mortal" is the same as in his speech, and the figurative signification of an escape from life into death is likewise the same. It therefore seems probable that Shakespeare has borrowed the image from Palingenius, transforming his phrase into the line as we now have it.

A remarkable instance of adaptation is represented in Hamlet's description of the next world:

> The undiscover'd country, from whose bourn
> No traveller returns. (III. i. 79-80)

Shakespeare has here given the most nearly perfect expression to a sentiment which he must have found in several places. The image of man as a traveller or pilgrim toward a future world was such a commonplace in religious and sermon literature that no particular source is needed for it, though it does occur in the *Zodiake* (*infra,* p. 216). The idea of no return from the other world occurs in the same volume:

> 152 But yet is no man sure of this, for who doth know so well, (p. 119)
> God's misteries? *who hath bene there, and turnde againe to tell?*

Job writes in a similar vein:

> 153 Before I go and *shall not return,* even to the *land* of darkness and shadow *of death.* (10:21) (G)

This verse is near other images used by Shakespeare (*supra,* p. 45). Mr. Noble has observed it and has added another parallel from Wisdom 2:1:

154 Our life is short and tedious, and in the death of a man there is no remedy, neither is there any man known to have returned from the grave. (B)

We have already noted Shakespeare's probable use of the first part of this verse (*supra,* p. 38).

The unknown "country" appears in *The French Academie:*

155 . . . they who stay onely in their corporall senses, as bruit beasts doe, propound commonly against the immortality of Soules, that which is vsually spoken of the common people, namely, that it is not knowne what becomes of mens soules after the death of the body, or *to what countrey they goe, because none euer returned* from thence to bringe any newes. Wherefore (say they) no body can tell what is done there, neither can any thing be knowne. (Pt. II, ch. 89)

Finally, there is almost certainly an echo of Young Mortimer's last words in Marlowe's *Edward II,* as pointed out by A. W. Ward:

156 Weep not for Mortimer,
That scorns the world, and, as a *traveller,*
Goes to *discover countries* yet unknown. (V. vi. 64-66)

Hamlet's short phrase is a notable instance of composite imagery. Mortimer's speech does not include the idea of "no return," but it has close affinities with other passages which do stress this idea. His "countries yet unknown" would recall La Primaudaye's "it is not knowne . . . to what countrey they goe," with the subsequent reference to "no return." Mortimer's speech probably suggested the words "traveller" and "undiscover'd." Since it is very likely that Shakespeare had read every one of the passages I have quoted, he may well have been indebted to them all. He has said nothing new but has adapted a familiar image, phrasing it better than it had ever been uttered before. This technique, perhaps largely unconscious on his part, is most evident when his poetic imagination is working at high pitch, for then the recollected images flow from many sources and are fused into a single memorable phrase.

The images of Q. 142 and Q. 149 seem to be reflected in *Measure for Measure,* when Claudio contemplates the terrors of death:

To bathe in fiery floods, or to reside
In thrilling region of thick-ribbed ice;
To be imprison'd in the viewless winds,

And blown with restless violence round about
The pendent world; or to be — worse than worst —
Of those that lawless and incertain thought
Imagine howling — 'tis too horrible!
The weariest and most loathed worldly life
That age, ache, penury, and imprisonment
Can lay on nature is a paradise
To what we fear of death. (III. i. 122-132)

The last four lines repeat the essential argument of Hamlet's third soliloquy. The imagination of future ills makes us prefer to risk the present life. A more complete discussion of the pains of hell must await presentation elsewhere, but here we may notice that both the "fiery floods" and the region of ice appear in the *Zodiake*. We find "flaming flouds" in 142*i*. In enumerating the pains of Tartarus just before Q. 149, Palingenius writes:

157 Where *flames* the *flouds* of Phlegeton that burnes with roaring yell . . . (p. 27)
Wyth dreadfull darkenes voide of light, and fyres whose flaming heat,
Consumes no wood, where *frieseth cold,* without the wynters space.

In describing Hercules' visit to hell, he writes:

158 Nor quiuering Tartares *frosty colde,* nor *flames* of Phlegethon. (p. 34)

It seems likely that the word "floods" in Claudio's speech is recalled from the *Zodiake,* and possibly the double punishments of heat and cold, though other sources have doubtless contributed to the passage.

The Duke-Friar's advice to Claudio at the beginning of the same scene involves the comparison of sleep and death. With 142*g,* compare these lines:

Thy best of rest is sleep,
And that thou oft provok'st; yet grossly fear'st
Thy death, which is no more. (III. i. 17-19)

The folly of fearing death appears twice more in the same speech:

Reason thus with life:
If I do lose thee, I do lose a thing
That none but fools would keep. (III. i. 6-8)

These lines reflect a passage in the *Zodiake,* accompanying Googe's marginal note, "To feare Death a great folly":

159 Therefore *who feares to dye* (p. 107)
Is but a foole, since he desires such hurt and harme to byde
Both of the body and the minde, with labours long besyde.

The Duke-Friar again says:

Yet in this life
Lie hid moe thousand deaths; yet death we fear
That makes these odds all even. (III. i. 39-41)

Shakespeare's implied reference to odd and even numbers is probably derived directly or indirectly from the moral writings of Seneca:

160 Inpares nascimur, pares morimur. (*Epistulae Morales,* xci. 16)

161 Venit ecce mors quae vos pares faciat. (*De Ira,* III. xliii. 1)

In Latin the words *pares* and *inpares* signify even and odd numbers, as well as other forms of equality and inequality. Shakespeare has transferred this double usage to English. In life we may be "odds," i.e., of unequal fortunes; but at death we become "evens," i.e., equal in fortune.

The "thousand deaths" of the Duke's speech are explained by a speech of Julius Caesar on the fear of death:

Cowards die many times before their deaths;
The *valiant* never taste of death but once.
Of all the wonders that I yet have heard,
It seems to me most strange that men should fear,
Seeing that death, a *necessary end,*
Will come when it will come. (II. ii. 32-37)

These "deaths" are the imagined deaths which the fearful man suffers in his own mind. Caesar's speech is indebted to Plutarch, but his phraseology has echoes of the *Zodiake:*

162 *a* We all are borne to this intent, to render lyfe agayne. (p. 77)
b For of our fyrst beginning doth the *fatall ende* depende,
And *certaine is the time decreed* for all away to wende.
And either soone or latter doth eche man his graue descende,
c To death which is of euils all the last and finall ende,
Not of the valiaunt to be feared.

The observation that death is "not of the valiaunt to be feared" and that it will come to all at predetermined times may be reflected in

Caesar's lines. Mr. Noble traces "taste of death" to biblical sources (Matt. 16:28, Mark 9:1, Luke 9:27, John 8:52).

We have seen in this chapter the various uses of the "sleep of death" in Shakespeare's plays. As an image, it powerfully affected his mind and resulted in several notable passages, of which the best is Hamlet's third soliloquy. There it gave rise to what is probably Shakespeare's most profound piece of philosophic speculation, certainly the one that is best known. To trace its probable sources, as we have done, is better to understand the imaginative processes of its author.

Chapter 10

Vile Bodies

PALINGENIUS VARIES HIS treatment of death by personifying Death, allowing him to speak, then reflecting upon what he says. The following passage seems to have a number of echoes in Shakespeare:

163 *a* How many men hath this my hand downe cast from state on
hie? (p. 85)
And hedlong shoued with mortall might, in darksome graue to lie?
I well remember Priam once, when slaine at Altar stone
b He sacrificed was to me, *the guide of Macedone*
The proud, with fighting hand that put so many realmes to flight,
To whom no like could then be found, by force and deadly might,
Of this my dart, in Babilon, sore wounded downe did fall.
c What should I here the Latine Lordes, and Mars his nephues call
To minde, the Lordes of all the earth, whose valeant vertue plaine:
Did ioyne their rule to Ocean seas, and fame with starres to raigne.
d Could I not when me list, all these destroyd to hell throw downe?
Depriude theyr hands of scepter stout, theyr heades of regall crowne?
Of wordes their mouthes, of sight their eyes, of mouing members all?
And eke their bodies thus destroyde, in filthy graue let fall?

[After describing his terror, the author reflects as follows:]

e What are wee wretches here but *dust,* with winde and rayne
vpcast? (p. 86)
And like the *brittle breaking glasse* and *shadowes* fading fast?
f Much like to *Roses* that doe shewe a gorgeous gaudy face
When sunne doth rise, and when the night appeares do lose their grace.
g To day with myrth aliue, and foode to wormes within a while,
This day in fayre and lusty plight, and straight a Carrian vile.
h Alas, what doth it vs auaile to hourd vp heapes of Gold?
And place to haue, and clothing riche, and Gems of price to holde?
Great realmes and cities strong to guide, in houses fayre to lye?
Aloft to loke, and thinck our selues full like to Gods on hye?
i If death do al things take from hence, if wee *like smoke, or dust,*
As wretches fade, if that so sone our pride, our pompe and lust
Do passe, and end for euermore. . . .
j Shee takes from vs both life and goods, delightes and all at ones, (p. 87)
The corps to nought resolues, for what remaines but dust and bones,
Which bones in tyme returne to dust. In fine all goodly things
Shee here from vs doth take away, and chiefest mischiefe brings.
k Whom would not therefore such a beast and *vgly Monster* feare:
Except his heart were made of steele.

The poet represents himself as saying these words to Nature, who replies with a demonstration that death should not be feared. The passage quoted is Palingenius' longest meditation upon the temporal nature of human bodies, which fall to decay and cannot survive inevitable death. The theme occurs often, both in the *Zodiake* and in Shakespeare. It has numerous biblical parallels, especially in the Psalms and the Book of Job. Here, however, certain specific parallels suggest Shakespeare's indebtedness to Palingenius' lines. We have already mentioned the "dust" (163*i*) and the "shadow" (163*e*) as descriptive images of man. The comparison of life to a rose (163*f*) was possibly Othello's source for the image (*supra*, p. 50). The personification of Death as an "vgly Monster" (163*k*) may have suggested Romeo's personification of it as "the lean abhorred monster" (V. iii. 104).

The passage seems to have influenced Hamlet's meditation on death in the Gravediggers' scene, for several of the same images appear there in conjunction. Hamlet inspects the skull, is nauseated by it, and reflects that all men must come to "my Lady Worm" in the same manner. When he learns that it is the skull of Yorick, he says:

> Alas, poor Yorick! I knew him, Horatio; a fellow of infinite jest, of most excellent fancy. . . . Where be your gibes now, your gambols, your songs, your flashes of merriment, that were wont to set the table on a roar?. . . Dost thou think Alexander look'd o' this fashion i' th' earth? . . . Alexander died, Alexander was buried, Alexander returneth into dust. . . . Imperial Caesar, dead and turn'd to clay. . . .
> (V. i. 202-236)

As a marginal note to 163*b,* Googe prints "Great Alexander," explaining the reference to "the guide of Macedone" in the text. The mirth of Yorick, who is now reduced to a foul-smelling skeleton, may have been suggested by 163*g:*

164 To day with myrth aliue, and foode to wormes within a while
This day in fayre and lusty plight, and straight a Carrian vile.

The downfall of the wealthy and powerful (163*h, i*) has some resemblance to Hamlet's speculations on the politician, the courtier, the lawyer, and the painted lady, all of whom come to the same end.

There is also the parallel of "foode to wormes" and Hamlet's phrase "my Lady Worm." None of the images mentioned is unusual, but it is unusual to find these particular ones in conjunction. The presence in both passages of mirth, dust, worms, and Alexander, together with the general resemblance of subject matter, suggests that the *Zodiake* was the primary source.

Before following the image of "vile bodies" through other lines of the two authors, it is necessary to pursue a chain of images suggested by 163*e,* the comparison of human bodies to "brittle breaking glasse." Richard III uses the phrase in a different sense:

> I must be married to my brother's daughter,
> Or else my kingdom stands on *brittle glass.* (IV. ii. 61-62)

Richard II, beholding his own face in the glass, exclaims before breaking the glass:

> A *brittle* glory shineth in this face;
> As *brittle* as the glory is the face. (IV. i. 287-288)

He dashes the glass to the ground, destroying it. He obviously intends a symbolic meaning. As the glass is so brittle and easily destroyed, so is the pomp of kingship easily destroyed. Equally brittle is the fleshly face shadowed in the mirror, for it is destroyed easily, too; i.e., life itself is brittle. As though to confirm this interpretation, we find Hotspur's dying speech to Prince Hal:

> O, Harry, thou hast robb'd me of my youth!
> I better brook the loss of *brittle life*
> Than those proud titles thou hast won of me.
> (*1 Henry IV,* V. iv. 77-79)

The exact form of Hotspur's phrase is recalled from another passage in the *Zodiake,* immediately following Q. 149. Epicurus is expounding his philosophy of seizing pleasure while one can, since nothing remains after death. Some may say that the fame of having done great deeds or having made the world better is a reward for hardship and toil; but, he asks, of what use is fame when the body is in the grave and man is as nothing? He cannot feel it or enjoy praise any more than a stick or stone could:

165 *a* But yet of olde and auncient *fame,* rewardes remaineth sweete. (p. 28)
b Of little force this nothing is, when death hath had his right
Thou nothing art, for what is fame, if it doe nought delight
c The corps in graue? what doth the stone or stocke reioyce in prayse?
If here thou hast not them, thou shalt haue neuer happy dayes.
d Therefore whyle this our *brittle lyfe,* vncertaine eke, doth last:
e The wyse man, to his power, will ioy: nor straite wyll downe be cast.
As oft as fortune on him frownes, wyll seeke the pleasaunt life:
If any thyng to him shall hap, of bitter eagre strife.

The occurrence of "brittle life" in Hotspur's speech suggests that Shakespeare had the above passage in mind when writing *1 Henry IV*. He has used Epicurus' argument for humorous effect in the characters of Falstaff and his associates. Professor Baldwin (*op. cit.,* I. 678-679) expresses the opinion that Falstaff's speech on honor is indebted to the above passage. Falstaff says of honor:

> Who hath it? He that died o' Wednesday. Doth he feel it? No! Doth he hear it? No! 'Tis insensible, then? Yea, to the dead. . . . Therefore I'll none of it. (V. i. 137-142)

Later, seeing Sir Walter Blunt dead, he says:

> I like not such grinning honour as Sir Walter hath. Give me life. (V. iii. 62-63)

It is easy to see the resemblance of this attitude to Epicurus' point of view as described above, though the latter uses "fame" as the object of bootless endeavor. In *Henry V,* we have Falstaff's sentiments repeated, this time using the word "fame." Pistol boastfully sings at the Battle of Harfleur:

> And sword and shield in bloody field
> Doth win *immortal fame.*

His attendant boy replies:

> Would I were in an alehouse in London! I would give all my *fame* for a pot of ale and safety. (III. ii. 9-14)

The "brittle breaking glasse" as a symbol of life serves to explain two passages in *Measure for Measure.* When Angelo declares that women are frail, Isabella says:

> Ay, as the *glasses* where they view themselves,
> Which are as *easy broke* as they make forms. (II. iv. 125-126)

The image is essentially the same as that used by Richard II. The mirror easily makes the reflected form of a face, but the form and the mirror are both easily broken; likewise, the person herself is "frail" and easily broken too. Shakespeare puns on the word "frail," using it in the double sense of physically fragile and morally weak.

These lines serve to explain an earlier passage spoken by Isabella:

> O, it is excellent
> To have a giant's strength; but it is tyrannous
> To use it like a giant. . . . But man, proud man,
> Dress'd in a little brief authority,
> Most ignorant of what he's most assur'd,
> His glassy essence, like an angry ape,
> Plays such fantastic tricks before high heaven
> As make the angels weep; who, with our spleens,
> Would all themselves laugh mortal. (II. ii. 107-123)

The "glassy essence" of which man is so ignorant is his physical nature, as in 163*e*. The "shadowes fading" in the same line suggest the sense in which man's essence is "glassy." His earthly being is as an image in a mirror; he is only one of the shadows in Plato's cave (*infra,* p. 219). He is "ignorant" of this shadowy nature of human life (cf. Q. 36) and cannot realize his ignorance. As the glass is easily destroyed, so is man.

Both the ape and the giant of Isabella's speech are apparently drawn from the *Zodiake*. A few lines following Q. 163, we read:

166 *a* An Ape (quoth shee) and iesting stock is man to God in skye, (p. 87)
b As oft as he doth trust his wit to much, presuming hye,
Dare searche the things of nature hid his secrets for to speake,
When as in very deede his minde is dull and all to weake,
c If he be *ignorant* of things that lye before his feete,
How thinkst thou those things shall he see, which God & nature sweete
Within their bosoms close haue hyd? yet al at fingers ends
This hasty, blinde, vnhappy foole, perswades himselfe he kends.[1]

These lines immediately recall another use of the ape (cf. Q. 30):

167 *a* And as the *Ape* that counterfets, to vs doth laughter moue: (p. 62)
b So we likewise doe cause and moue *the Saintes to laugh* aboue,
c As oft as stately steps we treade with looke of proude disdaine.

The Arden Shakespeare cites another verbal parallel from Thomas Dekker's *Old Fortunatus* (1600):

[1] *kends*. Knows.

168 When the old traveller my Father comes home, like a young *Ape,* full of *fantasticke trickes,* or a painted Parrot.

In these three passages we can see the probable sources of Isabella's figure of the ape. The "fantastic tricks" are a verbal reminiscence from Dekker. The overweening presumption of man, who thinks his judgment infallible when he is actually "ignorant" of the things closest to him, comes from 166*c*. The fact that he "plays . . . before high heaven" comes from the comparison of the ape that "counterfets" for our amusement to human beings whose actions amuse the "Saintes" of the heavenly audience. The laughter of the saints, who have been human beings on earth, as distinct from the angels, who were always dwellers of heaven, has suggested Shakespeare's image of the angels who weep but would laugh if they had human spleens. Our "stately steps" and "proud disdaine" have suggested the man proud of his brief authority. The "Ape" is the verbal link that associates these three passages, from all of which Shakespeare seems to have drawn his image.

The probable source of the "giant" in Isabella's speech occurs in a passage explaining God's attitude toward men:

169 Is not this God of passions void, and free from griefe or paine: (p. 150)
And thereby liues in blessed state, and alwaies doth remaine?
Doth it become a Prince to fume when foles do fondly prate:
Or rather them for to contemne? seemes it a *Giants* state,
With litle children for to fight?

Isabella's statement is that the strength of a giant is good in itself but that the oppressive use of it is not good—and such oppressive use is typical of the giants of British folklore. This parallels Palingenius' suggestion that it is not suitable for a giant to fight little children; i.e., that God's great power will not be used oppressively against man. In Isabella's mind, the image of the giant seems to have coalesced with another passage in which Palingenius discusses the proper use of "strength," which is good in itself but the use of which may be either good or evil:

170 These are the bodies outward giftes, vse makes them good or nought: (p. 63)

> As if a man his countrey saue by *strength,* this *strength* is thought
> Then good to be, but if he harme the giltlesse innocent:
> And with this *strength* his countrie wast, then now incontinent,
> This *strength* shall counted be for yll.

We return again to the images of "vile bodies" as treated by Palingenius and by Shakespeare. Both authors are fond of dwelling upon the image of the grave-worms that devour the corpses of the dead. The general resemblances are apparent, and in some cases we can note parallels between particular passages, most notably in Hamlet's ironic comments upon Polonius' corpse. Palingenius writes:

171 O *dust,* what makes thee proud to be? whose *stinking guttes* in graue
The filthy *wormes* anone shall teare. . . . (p. 52)

Hamlet remarks of Polonius' body that he has "compounded it with *dust,* whereto 'tis kin" (IV. ii. 6). He likewise uses "guts" as a term for the corpse: "I'll lug the *guts* into the neighbour room" (III. iv. 212). The "stink" of the corpse occurs in his remarks: "If you find him not within this month, you shall *nose* him as you go upstairs into the lobby" (IV. iii. 38). These are only general parallels, but we find a more definite one in Hamlet's speculation on the worm that may feed on a king:

> Your worm is your only emperor for diet. We fat all creatures else to fat us, and *we fat ourselves for maggots.* (IV. iii. 22-24)

This unmistakably echoes Palingenius' account of the voluptuary who

172 Runnes headlong into whoredome vile, and *fattes himself* with meate,
A foolish man, *that so the wormes, may haue more foode to eate.* (p. 199)

There is also a possible reminiscence of Florio's Montaigne, cited from Brandes by Kittredge:

173 The heart and life of a mighty and triumphant Emperor, is but
the *break-fast* of a seely little Worme. (*Essais,* II. xii; p. 409)

Here "break-fast" may have suggested Hamlet's statement that Polonius is "at supper" where he is eaten by worms.

As Romeo breaks open the tomb of the Capulets to die by Juliet's side, he speaks as follows:

> Thou detestable maw, thou womb of death,
> Gorg'd with the dearest morsel of the earth,
> Thus I enforce thy rotten jaws to open,
> And, in despite, I'll cram thee with more food.
> . . . Ah, dear Juliet,
> Why art thou yet so fair? Shall I believe
> That unsubstantial Death is amorous,
> And that the lean abhorred monster keeps
> Thee here in dark to be his paramour?
> . . . Here, here will I remain
> With worms that are thy chambermaids. (V. iii. 45-48, 101-109)

The image of the grave as a "maw" whose "rotten jaws" devour human beings may be compounded of several sources:

174 Let us swallow them up like the grave quick and whole, as those that go down into the pit. (Prov. 1:12) (B)

175 Death shall feed on them . . . and their beauty shall consume in the grave. (Psalms 49:14)

176 . . . as when Esay sayeth, 'Therefore Hell (that is to say, the graue) hath enlarged his soule, and hath opened his mouth without measure: and their glory, and their multitude, and their pompe, and hee that reioyceth among them, shall descend into it.' The Prophet propoundeth heere *the graue as a great and horrible monster,* that hath a throate, *with a stomach and belly,* as it were a deepe gulfe and bottomlesse pitte to swallowe vp and to consume all.
(*The French Academie,* Pt. II, ch. 79)

The biblical reference is to Isaiah 5:14. Palingenius writes:

177 Reioyce I say that here you lead your life (p. 197)
With thousand painfull labours great, in trauaile, toyl and strife:
And after in a litle space in paine you drop awaie,
And lumpishe lye in *lothesome vault* to *wormes* a gratefull *pray.* (p. 198)

Of these several sources, perhaps the most significant is La Primaudaye's personification of the grave as a monster with a stomach, the "maw" of Romeo's speech, though the same image is implied in the two biblical sources. The "lothesome vault" and "worms" of Palingenius' line have perhaps been echoed in the speech. We have already noted Death as a monster in 163*k*.

The body as the "pray" of worms in the last line of Q. 177 finds two probable echoes in Shakespeare. In *Richard III,* Queen Elisabeth speaks of the two dead princes as "bedfellows for dust" and "the prey for worms" (IV. iv. 385-386). In Sonnet 74 we read:

> So then thou hast but lost the *dregs of life,*
> The *prey of worms,* my body being dead.

The use of the "dregs of life" as a description of the human body may be indebted to another passage from the *Zodiake* in which the vileness of the body receives perhaps its fullest expression:

> 178 How filthy and how miserable, mans body doth appere, (p. 200)
> Of fading flesh, and brittle bones, with skinne incompast here:
> Al flowing ful with *dregges* vncleane, and bloud corrupt and *vile,*
> Still durty, foule, and filthy lookes, except it euery while
> Be washt, and kept with daily care, and so made fayre and white.
> O dolefull hospitall of minde, and vessell of the sprite,
> By which such sycknesse great we feele, by which such neede we haue.
> O heauie garment, *pryson* strong, *O quick and liuely graue:*
> That chokest here both minde, and sense, and them in darknesse hide,
> Whereby so great an ignorance, in brest of man doth bide.
> O earth to earth returning soone, that in a smallest while (p. 201)
> In tumbe shalt freshly *feede the wormes,* with foode of *carcasse vile.*

Several images like these in this passage appear in *King John.* After Constance has heard of her son Arthur's death, King Philip says of her:

> Look, who comes here! *a grave unto a soul;*
> Holding th' eternal spirit, against her will,
> In the *vile prison* of afflicted breath. (III. iv. 17-19)

The comparison of Constance's living body to a grave may be an echo of Palingenius' "quick and liuely graue," a phrase in which both adjectives mean "alive." It is possible that his description of the body as the "vessell of the sprite" has determined the image of Constance's body holding the "spirit" against its will. Immediately following these lines, Constance utters an elaborate personification of Death:

> Death, death. O amiable lovely death!
> Thou odoriferous stench! sound rottenness!
> Arise forth from the couch of lasting night,
> Thou hate and terror to prosperity,

> And I will kiss thy detestable bones,
> And put my eyeballs in thy vaulty brows,
> And ring these fingers with thy household worms,
> And stop this gap of breath with fulsome dust,
> And be a carrion monster like thyself.
> Come, grin on me and I will think thou smil'st
> And buss thee as thy wife. (III. iv. 25-35)

Here are repeated most of the images already quoted from *Romeo and Juliet,* including the description of Death as a monster and the suggestion of amorous dallying with him. The "carrion" may be an echo of 163*g,* where the "Carrian vile" of the human corpse occurs in the lines which suggested the speech on Yorick.

The "vile prison" of Philip's lines finds its source in another passage from the *Zodiake:*

179 *a* Some thinke the soule doth not remaine when fleshe from it is gone,
Because the heuy, sluggish sleepe, the neerest thing that may: (p. 130)
Resemble death, doth seeme to take, both sense and minde away. . . .
b And if perforce she be compeld in *carcasse caue* to ly,
Who doth constraine? Doth God himself? then her he naught esteemes:
c Nay, which in *prison vile* he puts to hate he rather seemes.

The "pryson strong" of Q. 178 has associated itself with the "prison vile" of this passage, likewise a figurative description of the human body. The "carcasse caue," or cave of the body, emerges in Juliet's angry line upon learning that Romeo has killed Tybalt:

> Did ever dragon keep so fair a cave? (III. ii. 74)

The cave is Romeo's body, inhabited by a cruel, dragon-like soul. In almost the next breath, she retracts the charge.

While the *Zodiake* is Shakespeare's most likely source, we should point out that the image of the body as the grave or prison of the soul was very popular. Porter and Clarke cite Anders' mention of Plato (*Cratylus,* 400) and Farmer's mention of Sir Thomas More. The Arden Shakespeare cites parallels in Lyly's *Campaspe,* Marlowe's *Tamburlaine,* Peele's *Edward I* and *The Battle of Alcazar.*

[180] Nor should we forget Virgil's description of souls inhabiting bodies as "shut up in darkness and in a blind prison"—"clausae tenebris, et carcere caeco" (*Aeneid,* VI. 734). La Primau-

daye informs us that the "Platonicall Phylosophers" consid-
[181] ered the body a "darke & filthy prison" into which the soul
descended from above (Pt. II, ch. 83). Shakespeare was fond of the image, for he uses it in *Titus Andronicus,* "this hollow prison of my flesh" (III. ii. 10), and in *3 Henry VI,* "My soul's palace is become a prison" (II. i. 74).

The contemning of the body is a commonplace of both Christian theology and Platonic philosophy. With relation to the soul, the body is a grave, a prison, a rotting garment soon to be eaten by worms. For this gloomy, sepulchral, macabre element of his work, Shakespeare is in part indebted to *The Zodiake of Life.*

Chapter 11
Earth

IN PALINGENIUS, as in Shakespeare, the vileness of the human body is closely associated with the vileness of the earth. Since the body is of earth and shall return to earth (Gen. 3:19), the basis of the association is obvious. Also occurring in Shakespeare are references to the earth as the center of the universe, the drawing power of the earth's own center, and the figurative comparison to the soul as the center of the body. The language of these references shows a definite influence of passages in the *Zodiake.*

On p. 112 of the latter work, Googe has a marginal note:

182 The earth is the Ce[n]tre of the vniuersal world. The earth *grosest* and *basest* of all the elements.

Hamlet thus reproaches himself for delay:

> Examples *gross as earth* exhort me. (IV. iv. 46)

In Valentine's speech from *The Two Gentlemen of Verona* occur the lines:

> To bear my lady's train, lest the *base earth*
> Should from her vesture chance to steal a kiss. (II. iv. 159-160)

In *Richard II,* the King exclaims as Bolingbroke kneels:

> Fair cousin, you debase your princely knee
> To make the *base earth* proud with kissing it. (III. iii. 190-191)

Earlier in the same play Richard had said:

> Ah, Richard, with the eyes of heavy mind
> I see thy glory like a shooting star
> Fall to the *base earth* from the firmament. (II. iv. 18-20)

The text which accompanies Q. 182 reads as follows:

183 *a* For of all Elements the *Earth* the *vylest* hath beene thought. (p. 111)
And as the rubbish of the reste, cast by, when they were wrought.
b Therefore the wysest Workman first, did cause it lowe to lye, (p. 112)
That distant farre it should remaine, remoued from the Skye.
c And thick in *Ball* he cast it rounde, more lesse and small to bee,
That Saints might haue more plain prospect that list the world to see.

d For when that God had deckt the world, with Starres in trym aray,
What drosse remaynde he bad the winds, to clense and sweepe away.
Then in with hasty course they rushe their Lordes awarde to do,
The Northwinde blowes[,] the Southwind huffes, the West, & East set to:
e With striuing blastes they sweepe the fieldes & round in heape they cast
Whatsoeuer they finde, constrayning it, the earth is framd at last:
f Which, banisht from the heauens hye, *straight downe to Centre fell,*
g No place more farre nor *base* appears, wher nygher shee might dwell.

The first line of Q. 183 is echoed in *1 Henry IV,* in Prince Hal's speech over the corpse of Hotspur:

Ill-weav'd ambition, how much art thou shrunk!
When that this body did contain a spirit,
A kingdom for it was too small a bound;
But now two paces of the *vilest earth*
Is room enough. (V. iv. 88-92)

In the next play, *2 Henry IV,* Rumour says in the Induction: "The acts commenced on this *ball of earth*" (line 5). This image appears in 183*c* and in 189*b*.

Again Palingenius writes of the earth:

184 For earth is *stable* to all the worlde, wherein all filth doth hide, (p. 218)
Dust, dyrt, *dung,* bones and carion, and lothsome things beside.

This may account for the "dungy earth" in *The Winter's Tale,* II. i. 157, and *Antony and Cleopatra,* I. i. 35. Perhaps it also accounts for Cleopatra's words beside the dying Antony:

Shall I abide
In this dull world, which in thy absence is
No better than a sty? (IV. xv. 60-62)

Since Palingenius elsewhere speaks of the "stable" of the earth as a place for "swine" (204*b*), it seems likely that his two uses of "stable" have resulted in Cleopatra's "sty" as an image of the world. Googe uses "stable" to translate Latin *stabulum,* a shelter for beasts.

Palingenius' discussion of earth in Q. 183 is continued in these lines:

185 But now the Earth vnweldy thing, of nature euer stayes, (p. 112)
And more, is cause that sundry things can moue no kinde of wayes.
For wher most earth abounds, most waight is found, such things appeere

Lesse apt to moue, the light more quick, and vnto life more neere.
For Lyfe in euery thing is cause whereby they moue alone:
It needes no profe, the senslesse Corse, doth stirre as doth a stone.

Earth's lack of motion is reflected in Juliet's words just before her death:

Vile earth, to earth resign, end motion here,
And thou and Romeo press one heavy bier. (III. ii. 59-60)

The "vile earth" is her body, which will now return to its native element, earth, and will cease all motion because deprived of life, the causer of its motion. Her double use of "earth" echoes the last two lines of Q. 178:

186 O *earth to earth returning* soone, that in a smallest while (p. 201)
In tumbe shalt freshly feede the wormes, with foode of *carcasse vile.*

The first "earth" is the body, the same as the "carcasse vile." The second "earth" is the element of earth to which the body is returning. This could account for Juliet's image, including the "vile" earth of the body. Earth's lack of motion may come from Q. 185, which also draws a comparison to "the senselesse Corse." The same idea of the motion of life being stilled when the body returns to earth is evident in Claudio's words:

This sensible, warm motion to become
A kneaded clod. (*Measure for Measure,* III. i. 120-121)

Without employing the "motion," Antony uses the image of the dead body as "earth" in his words to Julius Caesar's corpse: "O pardon me, thou bleeding piece of earth" (III. i. 254).

Just as the element of earth lacks motion, so does the globe of the earth, a fixed body in the midst of a moving universe. This assumption of Ptolemaic astronomy is thus expressed by Palingenius:

187 Thus now the almighty Lord, by whome the world created was, (p. 215)
All things he made, diuided in these two, Mouing and Rest.
But in the Centre, rest vpon the earth hir place possest:
In all the others motion dwelles.

This stability and fixed quality of the earth is used metaphorically by Shakespeare. In *King John,* Constance exclaims, as she seats herself on the ground:

My grief's so great
That no supporter but the *huge firm earth*
Can hold it up. (III. i. 71-73)

Macbeth uses the same image as he goes to Duncan's room:

Thou sure and *firm set earth,*
Hear not my steps. (II. i. 56-57)

Shakespeare's various uses of the word "centre" as applied to the earth are determined by the *Zodiake.* In several instances he uses the word alone, apparently in reference to the whole earth, not merely to its central point. In *Troilus and Cressida,* Ulysses says in his speech on degree:

The heavens themselves, the planets, and *this centre*
Observe degree, priority, and place. (I. iii. 85-86)

In *The Winter's Tale,* Leontes says of his wife's supposed guilt:

If I mistake
In those foundations which I build upon,
The *centre* is not big enough to bear
A schoolboy's top. Away with her, to prison. (II. i. 100-103)

In *Hamlet,* Polonius says:

If circumstances lead me, I will find
Where truth is hid, though it were hid indeed
Within the *centre.* (II. ii. 157-159)

Polonius' reference could be either to the earth itself or to the center of the earth. The other two references are clearly to the earth as a whole.

In Q. 182 the earth is defined as "the Centre of the vniuersal world." Googe repeats this definition in another marginal note explaining Palingenius' phrase "of all the worlde":

188 Of all the worlde. He meneth not *Centrum* this terrestriall (p. 232) tabernacle: but that which the Grecians cal Cosmus, the Latines Mundus, or Totum vniuersum.

Here is made an important distinction for the reader of Shakespeare. "World" is often used as an equivalent of "earth," but not always. It is more properly used to refer to the visible universe. Googe's note tells us that, astronomically, "Centrum" indicates the earth, just as "Cosmus" and "Mundus" indicate the world or universe. Used alone, "centrum" or "centre" does not indicate the center of the earth, but the whole earth as the center of the universe.

In *Troilus and Cressida,* we twice have the center of the earth—distinct from the earth as the world's center—used as a simile for faithful love. Among other similes is Troilus' declaration that he is "as true . . . as earth to th' centre" (III. ii. 186). In the next act, Cressida says:

> Time, force, and death,
> Do to this body what extremes you can;
> But the strong base and building of my love
> Is as the very *centre of the earth,*
> *Drawing all things to it.* (IV. ii. 107-111)

In modern terms, this is equivalent to saying that her love is as strong as the law of gravitation. The basis of the simile could have stemmed from these lines in the *Zodiake:*

189 *a* Amyd this earth a Centre lies, wherby it is sustainde, (p. 225)
For thither falles eche waighty thing, as God at first ordainde,
That neuer of their propre force, can from this Centre flye,
b And therfore fixed stands the earth, and in the midst doth lye
Sustained with hir heauy waight, that fast on euery side,
To Centre runnes and frames a *ball,* both darke and thick, and wide:
c About the which with Crimson horse, the Sunne is alwaies led
And on the parte contrary still, the darkesome night is spred.

Googe supplies a marginal note:

190 All ponderous & weitie things fall to the Centre.

The use of the earth's center as a simile for the drawing power of love comes from another source, possibly from Ficino's commentary on Plato's *Symposium;*[1] but the physical basis of the image is in Palingenius' lines. He envisions the earth's center as a focal point ordained by God in space. To this point from all sides all weighty matter "fell" until a massive ball of earth had accumulated about the focal point. Since the earth itself is the center of the universal world, its center or focal point is also the central point of the

[191] [1] "Amor autem simile ad simile trahit. Terrae partes singulae amore mutuo copulante, ad partes alias terrae sui similes sese conferunt. Tota etiam terra ad simile sibi mundi centrum illius aviditate descendit." (*Commentarium in Convivium,* III. ii)

whole universe. God is the ultimate highest point of the universe, the center of the earth is the ultimate lowest point, and between them stretches a chain of causes, each dependent upon the one above it (*Zodiake,* pp. 133-134). All parts of the earth are drawn toward its center, and it is balanced in space by the weight pressing equally from all sides. As earth by its weight is irresistibly drawn toward the center, so fire by its lack of weight seeks to fly upward from the center (*Zodiake,* p. 217). As the point farthest from God, hell is popularly believed to be at the center of the earth:

192 Declare to me good guide quoth I, if Hell beneath doth lye, (p. 161)
In deepest dungeon of the earth, and to the Centre nye.

While these lines repeat a familiar tradition, they may have furnished the suggestion for lines in *Titus Andronicus:*

> No; Publius and Sempronius, you must do it;
> 'Tis you must dig with mattock and with spade,
> And pierce the inmost *centre of the earth;*
> Then, when you come to *Pluto's region,*
> I pray you, deliver him this petition. (IV. iii. 10-14)

Palingenius also supplies the verbal link for using the "Centre" as a metaphor for the soul within the body. We have already noticed references to the body as made up of the element of earth, and it is sometimes compared to the globe of the earth. Palingenius attempts to refute Lucretius' Epicurean dogma of the material, atomic nature of the soul:

193 *a* We neede not doubt but Soule proceeds, & doth from Ioue descend, (p. 127)
And neuer dies, whom he permits, the world to comprehend.
b What if so be the Atomies,[2] which some wise men do faine,
The Soule is rather thought to be, then body to maintaine,
All Bodies be of quantity, and may diuided bee,
c But *Soule* is indiuisible and of no grosse degree,
And *as a Centre* doth she seeme, where many lines do meete,
Which Senses do conuey to her, as flouds to seas do fleete.
d Wherefore I maruell much at such, as thinke a like decay,
And iudge the Soule no more to be, when body fades away.

The analogy is clear. Floods fleeting to the sea are being drawn by the attracting power of the earth's center. Likewise the soul is a cen-

[2] "Atomies" is the form regularly used by Shakespeare.

tre to which the senses bring impressions from all directions. In living men, she is necessarily a center within the fleshly body, which is thus made analogous to the earth.

This image appears several times in Shakespeare. The first line of Sonnet 146 reads: "Poor soul, the centre of my sinful earth." The body is the earth; the soul is its center. The "earth" is sinful because of the taint of original sin that accompanies the soul in its covering of flesh. The implied use of the soul as the "centre" occurs again in *The Winter's Tale,* when Leontes analyzes the awakening of his jealousy: "Affection, thy intention stabs the *centre* (I. ii. 138). The "affection" of jealousy presents to his imagination a picture which pierces him to the soul, figuratively speaking. This picture is based upon impressions brought by the senses to their "centre," his soul (cf. 193*c*). These impressions were first received by the senses when he saw Polixenes kiss his wife.

Romeo's use of the image is more complicated still. Leaving the Capulets' ball, he exclaims:

> Can I go forward when my heart is here?
> Turn back, *dull earth,* and find thy *centre* out. (II. i. 1-2)

Here two images are involved. The "dull earth" is his body. Its "centre" is his soul. But, according to the contemporary version of Platonic love, lovers exchanged souls; each soul lived anew in the body of the beloved. Hence Romeo's soul or "centre" now lives in Juliet, and there he must seek it.

This fancy was very popular in love poetry of the Renaissance. The terms "heart" and "soul" are used indiscriminately in this connection. For instance, Shakespeare thus addresses his friend in Sonnet 22:

> For all that beauty that doth cover thee
> Is but the seemly raiment of my heart,
> Which in thy breast doth live, as thine in me.

Professor Fernand Baldensperger's edition, *Les Sonnets de Shakespeare* (1943), quotes parallels to this image from Ronsard and Sidney (p. 151). We should also observe its use in Chaucer's *Troilus and Criseyde,* II. 925-931. Ficino's commentary on the *Symposium* explains the exchange of souls at some length (II. viii) and doubtless enhanced its popularity as a poetic image.[3]

Another image found in Shakespeare is that of the earth as mother. This image occurs frequently in literature, most notably in the work of Lucretius (*De Rerum Natura,* V. 259, 783- 815), where Shakespeare may possibly have read it. Nevertheless, his immediate source seems to be *The French Academie.* La Primaudaye writes:

> 194 If we consider how *our common mother the earth,* being prodigal in giuing vnto vs all things necessary for the life of man, hath notwithstanding cast all of vs naked out of her bowels, and must receiue vs so againe into her *wombe,* I see no great reason wee haue to call some rich, and others poore; seeing the beginning, being, and ende of the temporall life of all men are vnlike in nothing, but that some during this *little moment* of life haue that in abundance and superfluitie, which others haue onely according to their necessitie. (Pt. I, ch. 34)

The "little moment" of life is echoed in Sonnet 15 (*infra,* p. 255). The reference to earth as the mother occurs twice in Shakespeare. Timon, digging in the earth, addresses her thus:

> *Common mother,* thou
> Whose *womb* unmeasurable and infinite breast
> Teems and feeds all. (IV. iii. 177-179)

Friar Laurence speaks while tending his garden:

> The *earth,* that's nature's *mother,* is her tomb;
> What is her burying grave, that is her *womb;*
> And from her womb children of divers kind
> We sucking on her natural bosom find. (*Romeo and Juliet,* II. iii. 9-12)

Timon uses exactly La Primaudaye's phrase "common mother."[4] He stresses the prodigality of the earth-mother in feeding all creatures born of her. Friar Laurence also uses this image in the sucking children, adding the reference to the earth's "womb" as both the birthplace and the grave of all living things. The presence in La Primaudaye's words of several significant images used by Shakespeare makes this probably his immediate source. The last two lines

---

[3] For discussions of this and like images, see L. J. Mills, *One Soul in Bodies Twain,* Bloomington, Ind., 1937; John D. Rea, "A Note on *Romeo and Juliet,*" *Modern Philology,* XVIII (1921), 675-676.

[195] [4] Cf. Marlowe's *Edward II,* III. ii. 129: "By earth, the common mother of us all."

quoted from Friar Laurence also show some resemblance to another passage from *The French Academie,* occurring in close proximity to the "rain from heaven" and the garden of the world (cf. pp. 101, 189):

> 196 For I pray you what difference is there in euery herbe, or in euery seuerall tree, I meane between the root and the stalke, the body and the branches, the boughes and the leaues, the flowers, seeds and fruits? And yet all these sundry parts receiue nourishment from one Mother, and from one and the same substance and liquor. (Pt. II, ch. 64)

Here we have the image of the various plants taking nourishment from the earth their mother, or "sucking on her natural bosom," as Friar Laurence has expressed it. Shakespeare may well have associated the two passages from La Primaudaye to secure his image.

Chapter 12

The Misanthrope

THE EXAMPLES THUS FAR taken from the *Zodiake* will show how congenial to Palingenius' taste is the denunciation of this world and its vices. He achieves real eloquence in portraying the earth and the human body as vile, contemptible objects. His picture of the generality of mankind is distinctly unfavorable. Only a few choice spirits regulate their lives according to reason; the rest are either knaves or fools, shortsightedly pursuing earthly goals instead of laying up treasures in heaven. This attitude, not unfamiliar in moralists of all eras, finds its reflection in Shakespeare. Sometimes it emerges in single phrases, such as Hamlet's reference to "the fatness of these pursy times" (III. iv. 153); sometimes in settled states of mind, as with Jaques and Thersites; sometimes in violent emotional upheavals, as with Timon and Lear. I have discussed elsewhere Shakespeare's handling of this mental attitude;[1] here I shall consider it only in terms of its sources.

Palingenius is particularly violent in his denunciations of gold and the power which it exercises in human affairs. The general desire for it is the cause of most evil deeds that are done. It sets relatives at variance with each other, causes priests to abuse their holy office, perverts feminine modesty, and makes a travesty of law and justice:

197 *a* O mischiefe great, O beastlinesse, and vile desire to get, (p. 73)
O piteous plague eche where disperst, on profit all be set:
The vertue left. Who seketh now the righteous thing to vse?
What man is he that will not now all goodnesse cleane refuse
b If any hope of gayne he haue? *GOLD guides the lawes wee see,*
c And might of Gold than strength of bloud of greater force to be.
d For Gold both shamefastnesse and faith are set abrode to sell,
e For Gold the Gods aboue be serude and wee set free from Hell.

The final line refers to priests who sell pardons and masses for the dead. With the phrase, "Gold guides the lawes," compare another passage on the same theme:

[1] "Misanthropy in Shakespeare," in *The Character of Hamlet.*

198 *a* But thou wilt say, such vertuousnesse doe Lawes and Kings
defend. (p. 95)
O would to God that this were so, but now in euery place
b *With money lawes corrupted are,* and eke the Princes grace
c Is pleasde with precious gifts and sute, the Lawes set them on rack
That eyther haue no pence to pay or frendship els do lack: (p. 96)
The other scape as innocents howsoeuer iudgment trye.

The two images of gold corrupting the law seem to be reflected in Claudius' lines from *Hamlet:*

In the *corrupted* currents of this world,
Offence's *gilded* hand may shove by justice,
And oft *'tis seen* the wicked prize itself
Buys out the law. (III. iii. 57-60)

The inequality of the law in its treatment of rich and poor (198*c*) occurs several times in Shakespeare. In *Cymbeline,* Cloten cynically observes:

'Tis gold
Which makes the true man kill'd and saves the thief. (II. iii. 75-76)

Lear cries in his madness:

Through tatter'd clothes great vices do appear;
Robes and furr'd gowns hide all. Plate sins with gold,
And the strong lance of justice hurtless breaks;
Arm it in rags, a pigmy's straw does pierce it. (IV. vi. 168-171)

The "lance of justice" is the law, which will not harm the "gold-plated" armour of the rich but will seize upon the slightest offense of the ragged poor. The same theme is evident in Romeo's words to the Apothecary:

Famine is in thy cheeks,
Need and oppression starveth in thy eyes,
Contempt and beggary hangs upon thy back;
The world is not thy friend nor the world's law. (V. i. 69-72)

Timon denounces the effect of gold upon society in the following words:

Thus much of this will make black white, foul fair,
Wrong right, base noble, old young, coward valiant . . . .
This yellow slave
Will knit and break religions, bless th' accurs'd,
Make the hoar leprosy ador'd, *place thieves*
And give them title, knee, and approbation
With senators on the bench. (IV. iii. 28-37)

The italicized words apparently reflect Palingenius' attempt to define nobility. The common people think of it as resulting from the possession of wealth. If so, every successful tradesman, farmer, bawd, thief, etc., must be thought noble, for Fortune may exalt the lowest born to the possession of wealth and may likewise reduce the noblest to poverty. Therefore wealth is not the proper basis for judging nobility:

199 *a* Nobilitie therefore, as dooe the common people say, (p. 89)
In heapes of Riches doth consist, or in the Golden sway . . . .
b If he should be a Gentleman that riches doth obtayne,
Why then good Gentlemen may be Jhon Frankling and his feares,
The Butcher, Barbar, Fishmonger, and he that horses reares,
The Shepheard, and the Baker, and the Tanner with his hide,
The Baud, *the Thefe,* the Grasyer, and other all beside
Of fylthy sorte, for them among full many riches haue,
c And many may, for Fortune ofte *extolles the wretched slaue,*
And often she doth throwe a downe with her vnequal hand,
Such as of late she did permit aloft on wheele to stand.

"Jhon Frankling" is a stock nickname for a farmer; "feares" or "feres" is the Chaucerian word for companions. The farmer's companions are various kinds of tradesmen, bawds, thieves, and others of "fylthy sorte," all of whom may obtain wealth in following their professions. The inclusion of "the Thefe" among those ennobled by riches has given Timon his image. Again, the fact that through gold Fortune "ofte extolles the wretched slaue" has furnished Timon with the central image of another speech:

What a god's gold
That he is worshipp'd in a baser temple
Than where swine feed!
'Tis thou that rigg'st the bark and plough'st the foam,
Settlest admired reverence in a slave.
To thee be worship, and thy saints for aye
Be crown'd with plagues, that thee alone obey. (V. i. 50-56)

This passage includes several other echoes from the *Zodiake*. The fact that gold is the reason for maritime commerce—" 'Tis thou that rigg'st the bark and plough'st the foam"—is taken from the following passage:

200 *a* Golde is the thing that all men seeke, in golde their hope doth dwell. (p. 233)
b For this, runnes into raging warres the Captaine stout of minde.
c For this, his Children, wife, and house, and countrey left behinde,
The Merchaunt *cutting foming seas, in ship with sailes set out,*
Assaies the blewe and dreadfull gulfes, and coastes the worlde about.
d Eche man doth practise craft and thefte, this golde to keepe in sight,
Golde euery man desires and loues, golde pleaseth euery wight.
e Ne feare they any kinde of paines, that after death is due.
O altogither earthly men, that onely in the viewe,
From beasts are knowen.

The setting out the ship with sails is equivalent to rigging the bark, and cutting foaming seas is equivalent to ploughing the foam.

It should be observed that the ultimate source of this image is Ovid's *Metamorphoses*. Ovid pictures the Golden Age as one of primeval simplicity, with no desire for individual wealth and no maritime commerce:

201 Nondum caesa suis, peregrinum ut viseret orbem,
Montibus, in liquidas pinus descenderat undas:
Nullaque mortales, praeter sua, littora norant. (I. 94-96)

In other words, no pines were as yet cut to be the masts of merchant ships. But with the development of private property and the consequent struggle for wealth in the Iron Age, maritime commerce began:

202 Vela dabat ventis (nec adhuc bene noverat illos)
Navita: quaeque diu steterant in montibus altis,
Fluctibus ignotis insultavere carinae. (I. 132-134)

Now the pines were brought down from the mountains to construct merchant ships that would travel unknown seas. Ovid pictures this as an evil resulting from the thirst for gold. Palingenius has adapted the image in his picture of the merchant risking his life in dangerous voyages in order to increase his wealth, and from this source Shakespeare has borrowed it.

Returning to Timon's speech, we find gold pictured as a god who is worshiped by his own "saints" or devotees in a "baser" temple than a pig sty. Timon's servant Flaminius uses a similar image when he hurls back at Lucullus the trivial coins offered as a loan to Timon:

Fly, damned *baseness,*
To him that *worships* thee! (III. i. 50-51)

This image of gold as a god worshiped by the miserly and covetous man is probably based on yet another passage from the *Zodiake:*

203 *a* Beside, the wicked thirst of wealth, and *vile desire of golde* (p. 177)
Must thou eschew: for where a place this couetousnesse doth holde,
b There reigne almost eche other vice: as shamefull Periuries,
Vngodlines, theft, and deceyt, with open Robberies,
Guiles, Treasons, and Conspiracies, with frayes and *Murders* vile.
c What needs it for to shew them all? nothing beside more *vile,*
Nor worse than is the couetous man, that drownd in earth below,
d Doth like the Mole no kind of thing desire, loue, or knowe
Saue only riches of the earth, for which he doth not feare
e Eche yll to worke, *nor other God he doth acknowledge here,*
f But purse and pence his chiefe delight: nor sees the vnhappy beast,
How short the life of man is here, how fraile, how sone deceast.

Timon's "baser temple" in which gold is worshiped is a figurative expression for the earth. We have seen in the preceding chapter the repeated emphasis upon the earth's "baseness," and we have noticed Cleopatra's comparison of the world to a sty (*supra,* p. 151). The image of the earth as a temple was perhaps suggested by Googe's phrase for the earth, "this terrestriall tabernacle" (Q. 188). Palingenius' earlier reference to the earth as the "stable" of the world is repeated on the page following Q. 200, and this time in connection with swine:

204 *a* Leaue *earthly things, to earthly mindes.* Let *swine* in durt delight. (p. 234)
And let your onely traueile be, to gaine the heauens bright. . . .
b For so the earth may called bee which is the *Stable* sure
Of all the world, the Mother and the nource of vice vnpure.

The "earthly men" of 200*e* are repeated on the next page in the "earthly mindes" of 204*a*. This resemblance has apparently caused the association of the two passages, the "swine" and the "Stable" of the second passage suggesting the form of Timon's contemptuous reference to the earth.

Palingenius' many denunciations of the greedy clergy who sell pardons (cf. 197*e*), together with the contempt for gold, appear in

King John's words to Philip of France and the papal legate Pandulph:

> Though you and all the kings of Christendom
> Are led so grossly by this meddling priest,
> Dreading the curse that *money may buy out;*
> And by the merit of *vile gold,* dross, dust,
> Purchase *corrupted* pardon of a man
> Who in that sale *sells pardon from himself,*
> Though you and all the rest so grossly led
> This juggling witchcraft with revenue cherish. . . . (III. i. 162-169)

The "corrupted" rule of the Church, which "money may buy out," recalls the "buying out" of the law, already noted. The phrase "sells pardon from himself" means that such corruption condemns to hell the priest who practices it. It seems to be drawn from Palingenius' line on friars, priests, and monks

205 That pardon others, and can not their owne misdeedes forgiue. (p. 183)

Such clerics are condemned to hell, Palingenius concludes.

John's phrase "vile gold" suggests an indebtedness to 203*a, c,* on the worship of gold as a god. There is perhaps a general suggestion that honoring the papacy constitutes such vain worship, that the papal pardon is a mere commodity to be sold for a price. Palingenius stresses the word "vile." There is nothing more "vile" than the covetous man who is moved by the "vile desire for gold." It is the cause of all vices and crimes, including "Murders vile." This use of gold as a procurer of murder is reflected in Romeo's words as he pays the Apothecary for the poison:

> There is thy *gold,* worse poison to men's souls,
> Doing more *murders* in this loathsome world,
> Than these poor compounds that thou mayst not sell.
> I sell thee poison; thou hast sold me none. (V. i. 80-83)

Gold as a murderer appears again in Timon's address to his newly found gold:

> O thou sweet king-killer, and dear divorce
> 'Twixt natural son and sire! Thou bright defiler
> Of Hymen's purest bed; thou valiant Mars!
> Thou ever young, fresh, lov'd, and delicate wooer,
> Whose blush doth thaw the consecrated snow

> That lies on Dian's lap! thou visible god,
> That sold'rest close impossibilities,
> And makest them kiss! that speak'st with every tongue
> To every purpose! O thou touch of hearts!
> Think, thy slave man rebels, and by thy virtue
> Set them into confounding odds, that beasts
> May have the world in empire! (IV. iii. 382-393)

Gold as a "king-killer" and a "divorce" between son and father repeats a theme used in the death scene of Henry IV. Thinking his father already dead, Prince Hal takes the golden crown from his pillow into the next room. When the King awakes, he reproaches Hal with having wished him dead in order to hasten possession of the golden crown. His speech suggests gold as the "divorce" between son and sire:

> See, sons, what things you are!
> How quickly nature falls into revolt
> When gold becomes her object! (*2 Henry IV*, IV. v. 65-67)

This image may have been suggested by a line from the *Zodiake,* already quoted, on the evil effects of gold (197*c*):

206 And might of Gold than strength of bloud of greater force to be.

This means that the desire for gold is stronger than the natural loyalty of relatives to each other. The next line of the *Zodiake* reads:

207 For Gold both shamefastnesse and faith are set abrode to sell.

"Shamefastnesse" was a term for womanly modesty and virtue, the opposite of the bold effrontery of the strumpet. Its use here indicates that women will sell their virtue for gold. The two lines together recall a couplet in Palingenius' indictment of the world:

208 Where brother seekes the brothers blud, *where sonne the father hates,* (p. 106)
Where Discorde euermore doth raigne, and *Guile in married mates.*

If Shakespeare made this association, we can see why his two images for gold as a "divorce" between son and father and as the defiler of Hymen's bed occur in such close conjunction. Since Hymen is the god of marriage, Timon's reference indicates infidelity of wives to their husbands, or "Guile in married mates." Mars appears here as the seducer of Venus from her husband Vulcan; the word "valiant" is used ironically. As the reference to Hymen indicates the seduction of wives, so the reference to Diana indicates the seduction of virgins, for Diana was a virgin goddess. "Thou visible god" recalls Timon's other reference to gold as a god, but here it seems to be a reference to Jupiter's seduction of the virgin Danaë in the form of a shower of gold (Ovid, *Metamorphoses,* IV. 611).

The "snow . . . on Dian's lap" is the purity and "coldness" of unassailable chastity, as instanced in Hamlet's words to Ophelia: "as chaste as ice, as pure as snow" (III. i. 140). Yet gold, like a wooer, whose charm is irresistible, can overcome this "coldness" and successfully assail this chastity. The imagery of Diana's lap is again suggested in Romeo's description of Rosaline, who rebuffs his advances:

She'll not be hit
With Cupid's arrow; she hath *Dian's* wit;
And, in strong proof of chastity well arm'd,
From Love's weak childish bow she lives unharm'd.
She will not stay the siege of loving terms,
Nor bide th' encounter of assailing eyes,
Nor ope her lap to saint-seducing gold. (I. i. 214-220)

Here the snow is present only by implication, but the image is apparently the same as Timon's description of the gold which thaws the snow of chastity on Dian's lap, once it gains admittance there. Lear places this snow "between her forks," i.e., legs, in describing the cold but secretly lustful woman (IV. vi. 121).

Such thinly veiled references to the female genitals are fairly common in Shakespeare. Mercutio summons Romeo in these words:

I conjure thee by Rosaline's bright eyes,
By her high forehead and her scarlet lip,
By her fine foot, straight leg, and quivering *thigh,*
And the demesnes that there adjacent lie. (II. i. 17-20)

This example is borrowed directly from the *Zodiake.* The speaker is praising the beauty of Mellina, a shepherd lass:

209 More sweete than are the withred Figges, or Wines that new be made: (p.45)

> Such lippes, such brests, or eyes I thinke, dame Venus neuer had.
> What should I here commende her *thighes, or places there that lie?*
> Such partes in practise put, than speake, with better will would I.

Not only the phrasing but also the jocular spirit of this passage has been caught in Mercutio's speech.

Certain elements of Timon's railing are indebted to the *Zodiake*. His long ironical admonition to the thieves (IV. iii. 427-453) has several echoes of Palingenius' lines. We have already observed one echo of "boyling wines" (*supra,* p. 125). Palingenius de-
[210] clares that "this world may now be calde of theeues a gaping den" (p. 106), adapting Christ's image of the degradation of the Temple into a "den of thieves" (Matt. 21:13) (B). Timon ingeniously expands the image, picturing the earth as a thief and a den of thieves. He exclaims:

> The earth's a thief,
> That feeds and breeds by a composture stol'n
> From gen'ral excrement; each thing's a thief. . . .
> All that you meet are thieves. To Athens go,
> Break open shops; nothing can you steal,
> But thieves do lose it. (IV. iii. 443-451)

The "gen'ral excrement" may be the sweepings of the elements left over from the creation of the stars; these sweepings fell downward and formed earth (Q. 183). The image also draws from that of the earth as the "stable" of the world, full of filth and dung, items which suggest the terms "composture" and "excrement" (QQ. 184, 204). Timon has adapted these to his image of universal thievery.

In a later general denunciation of the world's vices, Palingenius writes as follows:

> 211 *a* Then many filthy things I sawe, there done, and full of shame, (p. 194)
> And nothing else of iustice left but vaine and ydle name.
> *b* Th' vnguilty to be punished, the guilty scaping free,
> The Vertue hydde in vice, and Vice in vertue hid to bee,
> *c* The poore in euery place opprest, and fauour more to get
> Than iust deserts, the law a bribing craft, for golde a fishing net:
> *d* Eche kinde of handy craft corrupt by guile of *workmens* will,
> The *theefe* to fee the Inkeper his guests therby to *kyll*.

Here are repeated many of the images already noted: the punishment of the innocent and the escape of the guilty, the buying out of the law for gold and its unequal treatment of rich and poor, stupidity and beastliness in high places. In 211*d* we have one definite verbal image used in Timon's speech to the thieves:

Take *wealth and lives* together;
Do villany, do, since you protest to do't,
Like *workmen.* (IV. iii. 436-438)

Here Palingenius' suggestion that "guile of workmens will" causes them to cheat and corrupt their crafts has combined with the next line, on the thief who conspires to rob and slay guests at an inn. It is not necessary to kill the victims in order to rob them, but Timon urges the thieves to do both, to do a thorough *workmanlike* job of it.

In this same speech, Timon says:

Trust not the physician;
His antidotes are poison, and he slays
Moe than you rob. (IV. iii. 434-436)

This seems to reflect Palingenius' bitter indictment of physicians, who have little knowledge of their profession:

212 But Leache (whom we *Physitian* name) while he the water shakes (p. 80)
Wherby he doth his iudgement giue, and feeles the beating vayne
And rakes the dung, he is deceaude, and doth deceaue agayne . . . .
But these among whereof we talke, among a hundred yll,
There scarce is one whom they can saue: or whome they do not kyll. . . .
Hereby they stipendes do require, and thinke inough the same: (p. 81)
(Nor are they here deceiude) for this, that with an honest name
They may be murderers of men. . . . By these same murdring knaues,
How many men both night and day haue found their fatall graues?

In seeking to justify their calling, the thieves plead necessity:

Bandit. We cannot live on grass, on berries, water,
As beasts and birds and fishes.
Timon. Nor on the beasts themselves, the birds and fishes;
You must *eat men.* (IV. iii. 425-428)

This repeats an image earlier used by Apemantus:

O you gods, what a number of men *eats* Timon, and he sees 'em not!
It grieves me to see so many dip their meat in *one man's blood.*
(I. ii. 39-42)

This image echoes Palingenius' personification of Avarice:

213 Her greedy iawes with *bloud of men,* coulde neuer haue their
fill. (p. 21)

To produce Timon's comment, this line seems to have been associated with Palingenius' description of the brawling youth who grows up to become a thief, like those whom Timon is addressing:

214 Now one, now others shall he harme, and mischiefe euerie
howre: (p. 153)
Most commonly a warfare goes, or else becomes a *thiefe,*
That Tigre like *by others bloud* he may receiue reliefe.

The account of Timon's thoughtless generosity before the loss of his wealth is also indebted to the *Zodiake*. Palingenius thus warns of the dangers of prodigality:

215 *a* An other vice contrary now to this, doth yet remaine: (p. 22)
This same from thee to banish quite, thy senses looke thou straine.
b If thou dost *spende without respect,*[2] in vaine thou shalt beholde
An hungred eft anothers spitte, with deinties manifolde.
When all thy liuing quite is spent, by ryot cleane destroyde:
c Betwene them both the vertue lyes, the vice therefore auoyde.
As reason doth require, so geue, and euermore take heede:
Be not to bolde to vse excesse, within thy tether feede . . . .
d All godlinesse is clean extinct, to no man geues doubtlesse
The welthy wretche, although he hath wherewith to giue excesse.
Of no man tho[3] *he pitie hath, all heartes doe yron seeme:*
Who geues the *begger* now a myte? their teares they nought esteeme.
e If ought they giue to scoffers now, or else to rake hell knaues:
They do it deale to Colmon birds, and eke to baudy *slaues.*

In 215*b* we find an accurate picture of Timon's excessive spending. Its phraseology is echoed in the words of his steward Flavius:

No care, no stop! so senseless of expense,
That he will neither know how to maintain it,
Nor cease his flow of *riot;* takes no account
How things go from him, nor resumes no care
Of what is to continue. (II. ii. 1-5)

Again he describes Timon's generosity:

When all our offices have been oppress'd
With *riotous* feeders . . . .

[2] *respect.* Reason, caution.
[3] *tho.* Then.

> How many prodigal bits have *slaves* and peasants
> This night englutted! (II. ii. 167-168, 174-175)

These lines perhaps reflect the "ryot" of 215*b* and the "slaues" of 215*e*. Flavius' earlier phrase "When all's spent" (I. ii. 168) echoes "When all thy liuing quite is spent" (215*b*). In yet other lines he reflects the cautious advice of 215*c*, to give within reason and no more than the occasion requires:

> When, for some trifling present, you have bid me
> Return so much, I have shook my head and wept;
> Yea, 'gainst th' authority of manners, pray'd you
> To hold your hand more close. (II. ii. 145-148)

The language of 215*d* is employed by Timon and others to describe his wealthy "friends" who refuse to help him. The First Stranger observes that Lucius owes everything to Timon's generosity:

> And yet—O, see the monstrousness of man
> When he looks out in an ungrateful shape!—
> He does deny him, in respect of his,
> What charitable men afford to *beggars.*
> . . . But I perceive
> Men must learn now *with pity to dispense,*
> For policy sits above conscience. (III. ii. 79-94)

The phrase "all heartes doe yron seeme" emerges later in Timon's lines:

> What, are my doors oppos'd against my passage?
> Have I been ever free, and must my house
> Be my retentive enemy, my gaol?
> The place which I have feasted, does it now,
> Like *all* mankind, *show me an iron heart?* (III. iv. 80-84)

The first part of the speech refers to the fact that his servants had locked the doors to keep out the creditors (cf. III. iii. 38-42), a situation familiar enough in Elizabethan England. The sentiments of 215*d* seem also to be echoed in Timon's later phrase, "Flinty mankind . . . Pity's sleeping" (IV. iii. 491-492).

Timon's basic error lies in his misjudgment of his supposed friends. Apemantus and Flavius take a more disillusioned view of his friends and of friendship itself. The sources for both points of view are to be found in the *Zodiake*. Palingenius writes:

216 *a* And if so be that loue should knitte, the heartes of men in one, (p. 52)
This would not be, for euery man his frend would tend vpon.
And all men for their partes would ayde, the frend that they hold deare:
b Assuredly, nothing more good, nor sweeter doth appeare,
Than truly while we here do liue, of many loued to be:
c A safe defence are alwayes frends, agaynst aduersitie,
The mynd in doubtfull things they ease and helpers seke to bee.
Thy cares and losse they lighten much, they wepe and wayle with thee.
But seldome perisheth the man, that thus is *rich in frends.*
d When fortune laughes vpon thy lucke, and happy chaunce thee sends:
Wyth thee thy profyts they embrace, with thee they *ioyfull* bee:
Wyth frendship they thy haps increase, and feast in mirth wyth thee.
e Who list therefore to leade his life, in safety, and in ioy,
Great store of frends for to retayne, let him his care employ.

Timon's sharing of fortunes reflects 216*d,* the benefit of friends to the rich man. They increase his joy by sharing his "profyts" and by "feasting in mirth" with him. The assurance that his fortunes are safe while he has friends (216*c*) appears in his words to Flavius:

Canst thou the conscience lack
To think I shall lack friends? Secure thy heart;
If I would broach the vessels of my love,
And try the argument of hearts by borrowing,
Men and men's fortunes could I frankly use
As I can bid thee speak. . . .
And, in some sort, these wants of mine are crown'd,
That I account them blessings; for by these
Shall I try friends. You shall perceive how you
Mistake my fortunes; I am *wealthy in my friends.* . . .
Never speak or think
That Timon's fortunes 'mong his friends can sink.
(II. ii. 184-193, 239-240)

Timon's belief that he is "wealthy in my friends" repeats Palingenius' assurance that the man "rich in frends" will seldom perish for lack of help.

The skeptical attitude toward friendship also appears in the *Zodiake:*

217 *a* The hand and toung declares the heart, such things as pleaseth than (p. 55)
Who seketh frendes let him perfourme, for *fawning* loue doth get.
b But most men yet dooe gape for gayne, and all mens hearts are set
On gold, and giftes, and many frendes by gyftes obtayned be.
c But sure such loue endureth not, for when that gayne doth flee:

Then fayleth frendship, chiefly then when hope to haue, is gone:
d But som there be (though fewe of them) that styll remayne as one,
And mindfull eke of frendship shewed, do neuer cease to loue.
e But graunt th' vnthankfuls frendship fayle, it doth not yet behoue
The good and frendly man to leaue, (who may as rare be found, (p. 56)
As Phoenix bird in all the world, that breedes in Arabs ground)
To profit many men, and ayde, with all his power the same.

The first six lines are admirably reflected in the manners and motives of Timon's friends. The true friend, he who is both "good and frendly," is as rare in the world as the Phoenix (217*e*), of whom only one exists in the world at any given time. This may be reflected in Timon's insistence that only one honest man, his steward Flavius, lives in the world (IV. iii. 502-505).

The language of 217*c* is recalled in Apemantus' bitter question after Timon's loss:

> What man didst thou ever know unthrift that was beloved after his means? (IV. iii. 311)

In 217*b* we may have the suggestion for Timon's bitter response:

> Who, without those means thou talk'st of, didst thou ever know belov'd? (IV. iii. 313)

The remark that "fawning" gets love (217*a*) may be reflected in Flavius' comment upon Timon's rich creditors who could "smile and fawn" upon him while they ate up his substance (III. iv. 51).

Apemantus' other speeches are also largely indebted to the *Zodiake*. Palingenius thus warns against too great a trust in one's friends:

218 *a* No trust there is at all in man, deceipts are vsed vile, (p. 50)
Now euery man doth practise how his fellow to beguile.
b If any man vnto his frende his secretes doth disclose,
Then must he stande in feare of him least he his frendship lose:
Least he in angry moode reueale that earst in harte he hydes.
c If free, therefore thou seekst to be, and safe to liue besydes,
Let no man knowe thy secrete deedes: *thy frende* haue alwayes so
d While frendship lasts, that thou foresee he once *may be thy foe*.
Which thing in profe hath eft ben knowen, for fewe such frends we see
e That alwayes loue: and much herein ought *enuy* fearde to be,
Which euer striues, the happy chaunce with *poyson* fell to stayne.

Apemantus speaks in these words:

We make ourselves fools to disport ourselves,
And spend our flatteries to drink those men
Upon whose age we void it up again
With *poisonous* spite and *envy.*
Who lives that's not depraved or depraves?
Who dies that bears not one spurn to their graves
Of their *friends'* gift?
I should fear those that dance before me now
Would one day stamp upon me; 't has been done;
Men shut their doors against a setting sun. (I. ii. 141-150)

The poison of envy which sunders friends is apparently recalled in these lines. The theme of 218*d,* that friends may become foes, is recalled by Coriolanus as he enters Antium to seek Aufidius:

O world, thy slippery turns! Friends now fast sworn,
Whose double bosoms seem to wear one heart,
Whose hours, whose bed, whose meal and exercise
Are still together, who twin, as 'twere, in love
Unseparable, shall within this hour,
On a dissension of a doit, break out
To bitterest enmity. (IV. iv. 12-18)

All of these observations on friendship are summed up in the final lines of *The Passionate Pilgrim:*

Whilst as fickle Fortune smil'd,
Thou and I were both beguil'd.
Every one that flatters thee
Is no friend in misery.
Words are easy, like the wind;
Faithful friends are hard to find:
Every man will be thy friend
Whilst thou hast wherewith to spend;
But if store of crowns be scant,
No man will supply thy want.
If that one be prodigal,
Bountiful they will him call,
And with such-like flattering,
"Pity but he were a king!"
If he be addict to vice,
Quickly him they will entice;
If to women he be bent,
They have at commandement;
But if Fortune once do frown,
Then farewell his great renown;
They that *fawn'd* on him before

> Use his company no more.
> He that is thy friend indeed,
> He will help thee in thy need:
> If thou sorrow, he will weep;
> If thou wake, he cannot sleep;
> Thus of every grief in heart
> He with thee doth bear a part.
> These are certain signs to know
> Faithful friend from flatt'ring foe.

These lines read almost like an "argument" for *Timon of Athens.* They restate at greater length the theme of Q. 217. Here are the warning against prodigality, the fair-weather friends, the fawning and flattery. The particular aid of the faithful friend rather closely parallels 216*c*:

> If thou sorrow, he will weep;
> If thou wake, he cannot sleep.

> Thy cares and losse they lighten much, they wepe and wayle with thee.

The "friend and foe" phraseology of the final line recalls 218*d*.

Returning to *Timon,* we find Apemantus expressing disgust with the ceremonious manners and pretended gentility of Timon's flatterers:

> That there should be small love 'mongst these sweet *knaves,*
> And all this *courtesy!* The strain of man's bred out
> Into baboon and monkey. (I. i. 258-260)

Apemantus is disgusted with the elaborate ceremony with which the guests address each other; they are like monkeys acting men's parts. This passage reflects a lengthy discussion of gentility by Palingenius, who expresses disgust with the "Knauish sorte" of his time who seek to be called gentlemen for superficial appearances rather than for integrity of character. He uses for a comparison the Romans, who forsook the honorable virtues of their ancestors and allowed their empire to decay. The passage is here quoted in part:

219 *a* Who would not now be calde, and thought, a Gentleman by
name, (p. 90)
O *Knauish* sorte, O creatures vile, beyond all kinde of shame:
Triumphing names do thee delight, and fame abrode to yell,
Thee glory likes, then why not payne, and vertuousnesse as well

Contents thy minde, that worthily thou mayst be named than
A Gentleman, lykes it thee more a wise and sobre man,
Deseruing not, than of desert accompted for to be?
b Why is not Chalke for Cheese as well delighting vnto thee,
As lying name of Noblenesse? O vile disguised spright,
c O *Monkey,* learne to brydle wyll, to guyde thy minde aright, (p. 91)
Reason to vse, to flye the things that shamefull are and vayne,
Haunt righteousnesse, & know thy selfe, and labour hard sustayne.
Fly slouthfulnesse, wherby thou mayst attaine to vertue hy
Then mayst thou well a Gentleman be calde, and worthily . . . .
d It is not kinred thoe, nor bloud, nor spechelesse Imagrie,[4]
Nor heapes of Golde that can thee make a Gentleman to be.

In the succeeding lines he declares that an unworthy son born to a noble father is like an "Ape" born to an elephant, or an ass born to a lion. His merit lies not in his blood, but in himself. It seems likely that the monkey and the ape of this passage have suggested the monkey and the baboon of Apemantus' lines, and that the false gentility of the "Knauish sorte" has suggested the false courtesy of the "sweet knaves" who are Timon's friends.

In debating the relative merits of their condition after Timon's fall, Apemantus considers his own lot superior because he is contented with it:

Willing misery
Outlives incertain pomp, is crown'd before;
The one is filling still, never complete;
The other at high wish. Best state, contentless,
Hath a distracted and most wretched being,
Worse than the worst, content. (IV. iii. 242-247)

"The one" is incertain pomp, which is more discontented the greater it grows; "The other" is willing misery, vowed to poverty, and therefore finding in the "worst" state contentment and the height of its wishes. Here "misery" refers to poverty, not to sadness.

Among several passages of this general tenor in the *Zodiake,* the following most nearly explains Apemantus' lines:

220 *a* The rich man now will suffer nought, but allwayes doth abound (p. 18)
With deynties, so that lothsomnesse in him may eft be found.
b Sometime he doth desire and wishe on earthy rootes to crash,
Sometyme on pescods fast he feedes, sometime on other trash.
c And royall fare wyth deinty dish abhorring, nought esteemes.

---

[4] *Imagrie.* Imagery; coats-of-arms and heraldic devices.

Nothing so sweete he then receiues but bytter, loe, it seemes,
And lykes him not, if any tyme it chaunceth to endure.
d But chaunges new doth him delight, and for to haue in vre
Forbidden things, as sweeter much, such things be nought and yll
e That alwayes are at hand to haue, so not the thing, but *wyll*
And iudgement of the minde, doth cause a man to be *content*. . . .
f For best it is to couet least, and liue within the lystes (p. 19)
Of counsayle good, nor vexed be with vaine and fonde desyre.
g For who the things, he cannot haue, doth earnestly require,
Tormented is with frustrate hope and loseth time in vaine:
h Wherefore desyre thou nothing els but that thou maist obtaine,
And rule thy minde with bridling bitt. But he that doth abounde
i With riches, alwayes couets more then lawfull may be founde.
With little and *content* to liue, he knowes not yet: therefore
j *Whom least of all doth full suffise, him happier iudge I more.*
k For lofty landes doe cause a man, to swell in *pompe* and pride.

Here are the probable explanations for the phrases "incertain pomp" and "'willing misery." The pomp is like that of 220*k*, the pomp of the rich man. "Incertain" may be explained by 220*a, b, c, d*. The rich man is so uncertain of his mind that he never knows what he wants. He always wishes something new, but as soon as he has it he no longer wants it. This restlessness causes him to seek forbidden things. At times he rejects the daintiest food in favor of coarse fare, out of mere caprice. Since he is never contented with what he has, he cannot be happy. "Willing misery" may be explained by 220*e*. Happiness results from the will and the judgment of the mind. The person who wills to be satisfied with what he has can be happy. Thus "willing misery" means poverty that one wills to bear contentedly. It is at "high wish" in the person "whom least of all doth full suffise" and who is therefore happier because he has the extent of his wishes (220*j*.) I take it that Apemantus does not mean that all rich men are "incertain" and that all poor men are "willing"; but, when they do have such states of mind, the poor man is the happier of the two. The dissatisfaction of the rich man who always wants something different from what he has seems to have suggested the Duke's words to Claudio in *Measure for Measure:*

Happy thou art not;
For what thou hast not, still thou striv'st to get,
And what thou hast, forget'st. (III. i. 21-23)

Timon replies to the above argument with the statement that Apemantus can easily be contented with poverty because he has never known anything else, but that it is harder for Timon, who has plunged from great fortune into misery:

> Thou art a slave, whom Fortune's tender arm
> With favour never clasp'd. . . . But myself,
> Who had the world as my confectionary,
> The mouths, the tongues, the eyes, and hearts of men
> At duty, more than I could frame employment,
> That numberless upon me stuck as leaves
> Do on the oak, have with one winter's brush
> Fell from the boughs and left me open, bare
> For every storm that blows; I to bear this,
> That never knew but better, is some burden.
> Thy nature did commence in sufferance, time
> Hath made thee hard in't. (IV. iii. 250-269)

The germ of this speech seems to be found in Palingenius' statement that those of poor estate may be happier, for those of high estate suffer more when overthrown by Fortune:

> 221 But if of poore estate thou arte, then beare it paciently, (p. 178)
> And in good part sustayne the lotte, of this thy pouerty:
> For greater ouerthrowes hath he, and greater griefe and care,
> Whome Fortune most enriched hath, and giuen the greater share.

Timon's fatuous love for the society of his admirers, his desire to have great numbers of people about him, turns into an extreme hatred of human society, a distaste for the company of men. As Apemantus tells him, he goes from one extreme to the other. His hatred of all mankind is as unreasonable as his former undiscriminating good opinion of his flatterers. He is so stricken with his sense of injury that he would escape from all human beings and from his own human nature, if he could:

> There's nothing level in our cursed natures
> But direct villainy. Therefore, be abhorr'd
> All feasts, societies, and throngs of men!
> His semblable, yea, himself, Timon disdains.
> Destruction fang mankind. (IV. iii. 19-23)

This hatred of his own human nature appears again in his statement to the painter and the poet that, though each should travel alone, he would be accompanied by a villain, himself:

> You that way and you this, but two in company,
> Each man apart, all single and alone,
> Yet an arch-villain keeps him company. (V. i. 109-111)

Even Timon's steward Flavius is sent away. And in his epitaph Timon repeats his craving for solitude:

> Here lie I, Timon; who, alive, all living men did hate.
> Pass by and curse thy fill, but pass and stay not here thy gait.
> (V. iv. 72-73)

Timon's feeling partakes of an unbearable humiliation that he could have been so deceived in human nature, and for that reason he cannot bear to see people who know of his folly and downfall. Other misanthropes, such as Jaques and Thersites, enjoy having an audience for their vaporings and therefore seek human society, but Timon wishes to avoid the whole race of men and drives them from him with his violent denunciations.

Timon first announces his intent to abandon human society in these words:

> Timon will to the *woods,* where he shall find
> Th' unkindest beast more kinder than mankind. (IV. i. 35-36)

These lines have a verbal echo of the *Zodiake.* After a description of the world in which Fortune exalts villains to high places and wisdom is held in contempt, Palingenius comments that great patience is required to hold one's anger in check:

222 Who naught canne beare, let him absent himselfe from company, (p. 180)
And *leade his life alone in woodes,* or else on mountaines hy.

Timon, who cannot bear the slights put upon him nor control his wrath at mankind, chooses to live alone in the "woods" in the way that Palingenius advises.

In the quotations in this chapter, we can see how pervasive is the influence of the *Zodiake* upon *Timon of Athens.* I have given the passages at some length, since their mood and tone are as important as specific verbal reminiscences. They are the mood and tone used by Shakespeare whenever he wishes to portray misanthropy and hatred of the world.

Chapter 13

The Uses of Adversity

THE THEMES WHICH ARE stressed in *Timon*—the ingratitude of friends, the exile to the woods, the need of resignation to poverty—occur elsewhere in Shakespeare and provide some of his most effective images. Apemantus taunts Timon with the statement that here in the woods he will find no flatterers among the objects of nature or the beasts of the field who live naked and exposed to all the elements:

Thou hast cast away thyself, being like thyself;
A madman so long, now a fool. What, think'st
That the bleak air, thy boisterous chamberlain,
Will put thy shirt on warm? Will these moss'd trees,
That have outliv'd the eagle, page thy heels
And skip when thou point'st out? Will the cold brook,
Candied with ice, caudle thy morning taste
To cure thy o'er-night's surfeit? Call the creatures
Whose naked natures live in all the spite
Of wreakful heaven, whose bare unhoused trunks,
To the conflicting elements expos'd,
Answer mere nature; bid them flatter thee. (IV. iii. 220-231)

The latter part of the speech, on the naked creatures exposed to the elements, recalls Lear's words on the heath:

Poor naked wretches, wheresoe'er you are,
That bide the pelting of this pitiless storm,
How shall your houseless heads and unfed sides,
Your loop'd and window'd raggedness, defend you
From seasons such as these? O, I have ta'en
Too little care of this! Take physic, pomp;
Expose thyself to feel what wretches feel.
That thou mayst shake the superflux to them,
And show the heavens more just. (III. iv. 28-36)

In Lear's anguish, he is able to submerge, momentarily at least, his personal sufferings in a feeling for the sufferings of all humanity; he develops a greater, not a lesser, sense of kinship with the human race. It is just this experience that Timon cannot undergo. He does not feel the purifying power of suffering. He generalizes the ingratitude of his friends into a quality of the entire human race and cannot perceive that others suffer also, that his experience is part of the tragedy of man. From a too optimistic view of humanity he swings to a too pessimistic one; action and reaction are equal (cf. *supra,* p. 30). Apemantus reasons more clearly because more calmly, but he too lacks the emotional feeling of kinship with humanity which might place his experiences in a juster perspective.

Before his disillusionment, Timon remarks:

> And, in some sort, these wants of mine are crown'd
> That I account them blessings; for by these
> Shall I try friends. (II. ii. 190-192)

This sentiment, that misfortune separates the true friends from the false, together with Apemantus' reference to the objects of nature that are no flatterers, is the subject of the exiled Duke's opening speech in *As You Like It.* Like Lear and Timon, he has just occasion for resentment at the ingratitude of his friends, particularly of his brother who has usurped the throne. Yet he is able to view his situation philosophically, to see its advantages, and not to extend his resentment to all humanity. He speaks as follows:

> Now, my co-mates and brothers in exile,
> Hath not old custom made this life more sweet
> Than that of painted pomp? Are not these woods
> More free from peril than the envious court?
> Here feel we not the penalty of Adam,
> The seasons' difference, as the icy fang
> And churlish chiding of the winter's wind,
> Which, when it bites and blows upon my body
> Even till I shrink with cold, I smile and say,
> 'This is no flattery: these are counsellors
> That feelingly persuade me what I am.'
> Sweet are the uses of adversity,
> Which, like the toad, ugly and venomous,
> Wears yet a precious jewel in his head;
> And this our life, exempt from public haunt,
> Finds tongues in trees, books in running brooks,
> Sermons in stones, and good in everything. (II. i. 1-17)

The cold and the wind are honest; they will not flatter him as would his admirers at court. The image is repeated in Apemantus' lines on the cold brook and other natural objects which will not flatter Timon. The Duke values the honesty of these counsellors "that feelingly persuade me what I am," that through his sense of feeling let him know that he is only a mortal human being subject to extremes of heat and cold, and thus induce a proper sense of humility and a proper evaluation of the "painted pomp" of his former office. This is the same sentiment found in Lear's words already quoted:

> Take physic, pomp,
> Expose thyself to feel what wretches feel.

Later in the same scene Lear illustrates "what I am" in his words to the naked madman:

> Thou wert better in a grave than to answer with thy uncover'd body this extremity of the skies. Is man no more than this? . . . Thou art the thing itself; unaccommodated man is no more but such a poor, bare, forked animal as thou art. (III. iv. 105-113)

These later repetitions of the theme help us to visualize the exact form of the image in the Duke's mind.

The significant line from the Duke's speech states its general theme, "Sweet are the uses of adversity." Here again Shakespeare has produced a memorable phrase probably recalled from several sources. In Psalms 94:12-13 we read:

223 Blessed is the man whom thou chastenest, O Lord, and teachest him in thy law;
That thou mayest give him patience in time of *adversity,* until the pit be digged up for the ungodly.

In another connection, Mr. Noble cites Ecclesiasticus 2:5:

224 For like as gold and silver are tried in the fire, even so are acceptable men in the furnace of *adversity.* (B)

We find in these quotations adversity as a test and a strengthener of men's spirits. In another we find it as a trier of friends:

225 He is a friend that alway loveth, and in *adversity* a man shall know who is his *brother.* (Prov. 17:17) (B)

This last usage is echoed by Palingenius in 216*c*: "A safe defence are alwayes frends, agaynst *aduersitie.*" It is perhaps echoed in the Duke's words to his companions, "my co-mates and *brothers* in exile," which open his speech on adversity. Of some interest is a passage of the same tenor from *The French Academie:*

226 As a pearle sheweth her beautie euen in the midst of a puddle:
so a patient man causeth his vertue to appeare in all *aduersities.*
(Pt. I, ch. 29)

Here at least is the general image of virtue as a jewel shining in the midst of adversity, though as images for adversity itself the puddle and the toad are so different that the parallel is not very significant. The connection may be there, but it is tenuous.

The biblical uses of adversity are echoed in the *Zodiake* in a passage whose language marks it as Shakespeare's primary source for the image. Palingenius explains why God allows good men to suffer harms:

227 But yet somtimes the Good man seemes to liue in misery, (p. 154)
To suffer Neede, and Sicknesses, and Great *aduersity.*

On the next page Googe has a marginal note, "The good that *aduersitie* brings to the godly," accompanying the following lines of text:

228 But here admit the Iust man feeles both Griefe and sicknesses, (p. 155)
And leades his life in Pouerty, and aye in Great distresse,
Exiled from his Countrey farre, or pent in Prison vile,
Or vexte with other Casualties, doth he take harme this while?
No: for in suffring of such thinges, more clerely shine he shall:
All to the best to Godly men as God commaundes doth fall.
And as Phisitians vse to giue the byttrest medcines oft
Vnto the sicke, to bring them health, and rayse them vp aloft:
So oftentymes God tries the iust, to stirre them vp thereby,
That so he may them more compell their vertue to apply.

The leading example of beneficial adversity, as here given, is to be "exiled from his Countrey farre," the precise adversity from which the Duke is suffering. The conjunction of these images has largely determined the Duke's speech on adversity's "sweet uses."

The use of "adversity" in connection with exile from one's country is repeated again and again by Shakespeare, showing that Q. 228 remained long in his mind. In *The Two Gentlemen of Verona,* on his way into exile from Milan, Valentine says to the outlaws: "A man I am cross'd with *adversity*" (IV. i. 12). King Henry VI, exiled in Scotland after his defeat, says as he slips over the border into England:

> Let me embrace thee, *sour Adversity,*
> For wise men say it is the wisest course. (*3 Henry VI,* III. i. 24-25)

Here "sour" suggests the "byttrest medcines" to which Palingenius compares adversity. The same suggestion appears in Friar Laurence's advice to Romeo upon announcing the latter's banishment from Verona:

> I'll give thee armour to keep off that word;
> *Adversity's* sweet milk, philosophy,
> To comfort thee, though thou art banished. (III. iii. 54-56)

Here the bitterness of adversity is to be overcome by the "sweet milk" which it may produce, philosophy. We have seen that philosophical reflections were among the "sweet uses" which the banished Duke found in adversity. It is interesting to see the word "adversity" repeated so often in connection with exile throughout Shakespeare's plays.

Though Coriolanus does not use the word "adversity," he apparently reflects the same theme in his farewell before going into exile:

> Nay, mother,
> Where is your ancient courage? You were us'd
> To say *extremity was the trier of spirits.* (IV. i. 2-4)

One passage from the *Zodiake* which has contributed to Timon's denunciatory images of the world (Q. 211) is attributed by Palingenius to the wise man of Mt. Soractis, a hermit who has withdrawn from mankind to devote himself to solitary contemplation. In the lines connected with this man we find the imagery of the "woods" that is echoed in Shakespeare. Palingenius first advises such retirement for contemplative men who wish to study upon God's wisdom and give up the ambitious pursuits of the world. An humble dwelling and few companions are best:

229 *a* Then shall the Gods appeare, thoughe he in valley low doe ly, (p. 191)
Or on the hilles, or *shadowed woodes,* or in the mountaines hie,
In cottage small do place himselfe. It is not safe nor well

b With many for to liue, or in the *tounes* of fooles to dwell,
And in the company of theeues, of slaues, and couetous,
And cutthrote brauling swearing mates, or men ambitious.

He then tells of his visit to the hermit of Mt. Soractis:

230 He had his dwelling place (p. 193)
In *wildernesse,* where round about the *woods* did him embrace.

The old hermit is living in a cave. He explains to his visitor that as a young man he had delighted in riches, pleasure, and "to leade my life with great and much resort," i.e., to have a great many companions. As he grew older, he saw the evils of the world more clearly and determined to abandon it:

231 *a* By this occasion left I all, and from the *townes* I went (p. 194)
Accompting it more safe for me to liue in *desert place,*
And in this hill to runne the rest, of all my raunging race. . . .
b But hard perchaunce it seemes to thee, and straunge it doth appere, (p. 195)
That I can liue in *desart* such, and stony places here,
Where seldome any man doth come, where wanting seemes to be,
Moste thinges that should sustaine the life, of man at libertie . . .
c Yet neuer lackt I meate, nor clothes vpon this lofty spyre,
As much as nature doth content, not wanton fonde desyre.
d A litle thing doth nature serue, a small thing doth content,
Such one as loues none ouerplus, a man to vertue bent.

These images are reflected in *The Two Gentlemen of Verona.* After joining the band of outlaws, Valentine develops a fondness for the solitude of the woods:

How use doth breed a habit in a man!
This *shadowy desert, unfrequented woods,*
I better brook than flourishing peopled *towns.* (V. iv. 1-3)

Both Q. 229 and Q. 231 contrast the solitude of the country with the bustle of the "townes" and express a preference for the former. Valentine uses the same contrast. His descriptive phrase "shadowy desert, unfrequented woods" represents a combination of "shadowed woodes" and "desart . . . where seldome any man doth come," the last phrase being the equivalent of "unfrequented." Shakespeare's memory has transposed the two modifiers. To follow Palingenius accurately, he would have written "unfrequented desert, shadowy woods," which in truth would be more a logical form for the image. Valentine's "woods" are termed a "wilderness" when the outlaws elect him their leader:

> Are you content to be our general?
> To make a virtue of necessity
> And live, as we do, in this *wilderness?* (IV. i. 61-63)

This reflects Palingenius' description of the hermit's dwelling "in *wildernesse,* where round about the *woods* did him embrace" (Q. 230).

The theme of false friendship as exemplified by Proteus' conduct toward Valentine is also reminiscent of the *Zodiake.* On seeing Proteus' attempt upon Silvia's chastity, Valentine exclaims:

> Thou common friend, that's without faith or love,
> For such is a friend now! . . . O time most accurst,
> 'Mongst all *foes* that a *friend* should be the worst! (V. iv. 62-72)

Here is reflected 218*d,* the statement that a friend may become a foe. The lines immediately following this quotation advise a man to trust not even his friends with the secrets of his love affairs:

> 232 Take heede therefore of enuy Syrs I warne you louers playne. (p. 50)
> Let no man know thy minde in loue, but hide this loue of thine,
> (If witte thou hast) and let not thou thy fyer forth to shine.

These lines should be read in connection with another couplet from the *Zodiake:*

> 233 Thou art deceaud, if thou dost thinke that any kinde of man (p. 75)
> Wyll faythfull be in Venus case; No man is faithfull than.

"In Venus' case" means "in matters of lovemaking." In that no man can be trusted. Proteus may reflect this thought in his words, "In love who respects friend?" (V. iv. 54). We should remember that Valentine's difficulties arose because he trusted Proteus with the secret of his love for Silvia, showed him her picture, and told him their plans for escape. It is possible that this element of the plot was suggested in part by Q. 218 and Q. 232.

Valentine's line, "How *use* doth breed a habit in a man," is a reflection of Palingenius' discussion of use and custom as formers of habits (QQ. 116, 117, 118). We have already shown the occurrence of the image in Hamlet's advice to his mother (*supra,* p. 105), where he employs both "use" and "custom." Valentine employs "use," but in *As You Like It* the Duke employs "custom" in exactly the same connection:

> Hath not old *custom* made this life more sweet
> Than that of painted pomp? (II. i. 2-3)

The two words come from the same sources in the *Zodiake* and afford evidence that the same background of imagery in Valentine's speech was in Shakespeare's mind when he wrote the Duke's speech.

Further evidence of this fact appears in the Duke's reference to life in the "woods" as "exempt from public haunt." His phrase conveys the same image as Valentine's "unfrequented" and stems from the same source in 231*b,* "where seldome any man doth come." This protean phrase emerges again in Orlando's description of the forest as "this desert *inaccessible*" (II. vii. 110). Rosalind also describes the forest as a desert, using the exact phrase of 231*a:*

> I prithee, shepherd, if that love or gold
> Can in this *desert place* buy entertainment,
> Bring us where we may rest ourselves and feed. (II. iv. 71-73)

In *As You Like It* the theme of the forest outlaws has been combined with that of pastoral simplicity, following the source in Lodge's *Rosalynde.* The shepherd life is used to illustrate the theme of contented poverty which we have observed so often in the *Zodiake.* Corin the shepherd describes his life thus:

> Sir, I am a true labourer. I earn that I eat, get that I wear, owe no man hate, envy no man's happiness, glad of other men's good, content with my harm, and the greatest of my pride is to see my ewes graze and my lambs suck. (III. ii. 77-81)

This same theme is again exemplified in *The Winter's Tale,* when the child Perdita is cast ashore in the "deserts" of Bohemia (III. iii. 2) and finds herself among shepherds, whose life is idyllically described in Act IV. What is perhaps Shakespeare's earliest use of the theme appears in a speech by King Henry VI deploring the war in which he is engaged:

> Would I were dead! If God's good will were so;
> For what is in this world but grief and woe?
> O God! methinks it were a happy life
> To be no better than a homely swain;
> To sit upon a hill, as I do now,
> To carve out dials quaintly, point by point. . . .
> So minutes, hours, days, months, and years,
> Pass'd over to the end they were created,
> Would bring white hairs unto a quiet grave.
> Ah, what a life were this! how sweet! how lovely!
> Gives not the hawthorn bush a sweeter shade
> To shepherds looking on their silly sheep
> Than doth a rich embroider'd canopy
> To kings that fear their subjects' treachery?
> O, yes, it doth, a thousand-fold it doth.
> And to conclude, the shepherd's homely curds,
> His cold thin drink out of his leather bottle,
> His wonted sleep under a fresh tree's shade,
> All which secure and sweetly he enjoys,
> Is far beyond the prince's delicates,
> His viands sparkling in a golden cup,
> His body couched in a curious bed,
> When Care, Mistrust, and Treason waits on him.
>
> (*3 Henry VI,* II. v. 19-54)

This speech has very obvious affinities with the speeches on sleep by Henry IV and Henry V (*supra,* pp. 114-15), each of whom describes the laborer as happier than the king, because of the cares and worries attendant upon high estate. The probable source in Q. 120 has already been noted, but the greater enjoyment of the laborer's plain food than the king's dainty fare may have been indebted to another passage from the *Zodiake:*

234 The minde, and not the thing therefore, doth cause a
quietnesse: (p. 19)
Wherby the poore no lesse their ioyes, then rich men doe possesse.
Excesse the riche man doth desire, fewe things the poor suffise,
To him doth greater charge of house, but lesser ioyes arise.
The shipman, or the labouring wight, much pleasure more doe take,
With egges, and leekes, and homely foode, his hungred mawe to slake:
Than kyngs & Queenes with deinty dishe of seas and land to dine.

Henry's desire for a humble life and his recognition of his own incapacity are shown when he offers to resign his government to Warwick,

> that I may conquer Fortune's spite
> By living low, where Fortune cannot hurt me. (IV. vi. 19-20)

These lines may have been suggested by the *Zodiake:*

> O famous worthy pouertye, O giftes of God vnkende,[1] (p. 19)
> Of vertues aye the safe defence, to shamefastnes a frende.
> The brydle tryde of wantones, and patron of the lyfe:
> Thou onely canst, and wel despise the shamelesse *fortunde* ryfe,
> The raging of the Seas and wyndes, whilste in thy little bote
> Thou kepst the safe assured foordes, and rydste by shore a flote.
> The lofty hylles on hye, full oft, the flashing lightnings smite:
> And s[o]ring Ash trees long be bette by northren Boreas
> might. (p. 20)
> *Low things do lie vnknowen to harmes,* the tempestes neuer greues
> The lowly shrouded Iunipers, nor shakes the Myrice[2] leues.

In this chapter, we have traced some of the ways in which Shakespeare has handled the theme of adversity. Ill fortune or low fortune has its compensations to the philosophic mind. Through slight but significant verbal parallels we are able to determine what passages from the *Zodiake* he had in view and to watch the development of the theme in several plays. We have seen that similar situations, such as exile and forest refuges, are likely to recall the same fund of imagery to his mind and to result in a repetition of earlier themes. We are enabled to see a little farther into the processes of his artistic imagination.

---

[1] *vnkende.* Unknown; unrecognized.
[2] *Myrice.* Tamarisk.

Chapter 14

The Unweeded Garden

SOMEWHERE BETWEEN the calm acceptance of adversity by the Duke in *As You Like It* and the violent hatred of the world by Timon lies the melancholy disillusionment of Hamlet. This is at once evident in his first soliloquy:

> O, that this too too solid flesh would melt,
> Thaw, and resolve itself into a dew!
> Or that the Everlasting had not fix'd
> His canon 'gainst self-slaughter. O God! God!
> How weary, stale, flat, and unprofitable,
> Seem to me all the uses of this world!
> Fie on't! oh fie, fie! 'Tis an *unweeded garden,*
> That grows to seed; things rank and gross in nature
> Possess it merely. (I. ii. 129-137)

The "unweeded garden" is one of Shakespeare's most vivid images and appears in various forms throughout his works. I think we can trace the image to its source in *The French Academie*. La Primaudaye draws an elaborate parallel between the "garden" of the great world, the universe or macrocosm, and the "garden" of the little world, the microcosm or body of man; the ocean corresponds to the liver, the streams to the veins, etc. He writes:

236 Euen so doth nature, or rather the prince thereof worke in a *mans body,* which is as it were *a garden* that hath a soule. Wherein the Creator of this whole frame sheweth himselfe no lesse wonderfull, nay rather much more then in this great *garden of the whole earth,* & *of the great world,* of both which he is the Gardener that watereth them, to nourish all the fruits they bring forth, & to cause them to grow. (Pt. II, ch. 64)

Here it will be observed that there are three "gardens": the body of man, the earth, and the great world or universe. The last two are more or less identified with each other, since God is the gardener for them both.

Hamlet's "garden" is the world, yet by metonymy he may be expressing his disgust with the other two "gardens" as well. Certainly his disgust is not directed at the solar system or other constellations of the macrocosm; it is disgust with a world of men and women, and with the vices that characterize those men and women. In particular, as his next lines show, he is disgusted with one woman, his mother, and with her "frailty," a disgust which extends itself to include the rest of creation.

We have already quoted Iago's comparison of the human body to a garden (*supra*, p. 81) and shall repeat only part of his speech here:

> *Our bodies are our gardens,* to the which our wills are gardeners, so that if we will plant *nettles* or sow lettuce, set hyssop and *weed up* thyme, supply it with one gender of herbs or distract it with many, either to have it sterile with idleness or manured with industry, why, the power and corrigible authority of this lies in our wills.
>
> (I. iii. 323-329)

The figurative implication is clearly that we should plant virtues and weed out vices in order to tend our "garden" properly. The imagery of this passage seems to have resulted from a combination of La Primaudaye's words with a passage from the *Zodiake*. On p. 172 Googe has a marginal note:

237 An apt similitude or resemblance betweene *a weedy plot of land,* and the minde of man.

The accompanying text reads:

238 And first, as nature so disposing it the rude and Countrie
fielde, (p. 172)
Vile *nettles, weedes* and brembles sharpe continually doth yelde,
Except it oftentimes be tild, and eke with labour sore,
The hurtfull *weedes* with Plough and rakes be causd to grow no more.
Nor this enoughe, it needefull is good seedes therein to cast,
And dayly for to husband it till daunger all be past.
Euen so the minde whilst it is bounde *within the body* here, (p. 173)
Is ouergrowne with *Briers* sharp, and wilde it doth appeare:
Except it ayded be with helpe of one that tilleth well,
And aptly vertues therin plantes, and vices doth expell.

We can now see how Iago probably derives his image from the two sources. From La Primaudaye he derives the image of the body as a garden. From Palingenius he derives the "weeds," or vices, which overrun the mind within the body unless the "garden" is well tended. The will ultimately makes the decision for or against these vices (*supra,* p. 63) and is therefore pictured as the gardener.

This interpretation of the "unweeded garden" is confirmed by Hamlet's advice to his mother, urging her not to seek self-justification for her guilty love of Claudius:

> Confess yourself to heaven;
> Repent what's past, avoid what is to come,
> And do not spread the compost on the *weeds*
> To make them *rank*. (III. iv. 149-152)

Here the "weeds" are very clearly the vices of human nature; if they are encouraged to grow, they will become "rank," like the "things rank and gross in nature" of Hamlet's earlier speech. The garden or field is obviously the mind and body of the Queen; she should root out the weeds or vices before fertilizing the field to cause the good seed to sprout and grow, or else she will merely make the weeds grow faster.

The use of "weeds" for vices occurs several other times in Shakespeare. Henry IV says of Prince Hal, in *2 Henry IV*:

> Most subject is the fattest soil to *weeds,*
> And he, the noble image of my youth,
> Is overspread with them. (IV. iv. 54-56)

Antony has in mind the same image in his self-reproach:

> O, then we bring forth *weeds*
> When our quick minds lie still. (I. ii. 113-114)

In *Measure for Measure,* the Duke comments upon Angelo's conduct:

> Shame to him whose cruel striking
> Kills for faults of his own liking!
> Twice treble shame on Angelo
> To *weed* my vice and let his grow. (III. ii. 281-284)

"My" is used in a general sense, meaning "of others than himself."

In *Lucrece* the image occurs in connection with the struggle between reason and affection in Tarquin's mind:

> *As corn o'ergrown by weeds,* so heedful fear
> Is almost chok'd by unresisted lust. (281-282)

Here unmistakably is Palingenius' image of the mind of man as a weedy field. Lucrece uses a similar image to describe the taint proceeding from her violation by Tarquin: "Unwholesome *weeds* take root with precious flowers" (870).

In these examples, the "weeds" are vices within an individual man, whose body and mind constitute the "garden." La Primaudaye has stated that the whole earth is also a "garden"; in such a case the "weeds" would be vicious individuals upon the earth. Shakespeare frequently uses the term in this sense also. Its ultimate source is undoubtedly Christ's parable of the wheat and the tares (Matt. 13), sown in the same field:

239 The field is the world. And the children of the kingdom, they are the good seed: the tares are the children of the wicked. (verse 38) (C)

Thus the field is a figurative term for humanity: the world is a world of men, the good seed are the good men, the tares or weeds are wicked men. When the sower's servants ask if they shall pull up the tares, he answers:

240 Nay; lest while ye gather up the tares, ye *pluck* up also the wheat with them. (verse 29) (C)

The separation must await the harvest. Christ's words are reflected in *2 Henry IV,* when the Archbishop of York reasons concerning the King:

Full well he knows
He cannot so precisely *weed* this land
As his misdoubts present occasions.
His foes are so enrooted with his friends
That, *plucking* to unfix an enemy,
He doth unfasten so and shake a friend. (IV. i. 204-209)

The comparison of vicious people to weeds occurs twice in the *Zodiake.* Palingenius says:

241 Of fooles the greatest number is: who doth not plainly know? (p. 170)
Dame nature ioyes in making Fooles, as she doth oft to sowe
Both *Nettles, Docks & filthy weedes.* Dul wit and doultish braine (p. 171)
These idiotes haue, they seeke not for the ioyes of soule to gaine:
And only of their life, and panche,[1] like beastes their God they make.

[1] *panche.* Paunch.

Again he writes:

242 Now last of all, in number not a fewe there is a kinde (p. 190)
Both voide of learning, wealth, & Art, of lasey slouthfull minde,
To mischiefe giuen, prone to vice, and stoute, and full of crime:
Such men, or rather shadowes vaine, at one appointed time
Doth God a warfare send, with death of cruell kinde to dye:
And thus he purgeth mortall state, whereby liue merily
Long time the rest that doe remaine, this mischiefe ouerthrowne:
Tyll that againe suche wicked *weedes* a newe be sprong and growne,
That must be *rooted out* with warres, and cut with weapon grimme.

In both these passages the "weedes" are vicious people within a commonwealth. Shakespeare uses the unweeded garden with this connotation in an elaborate analogy from *Richard II*. The head gardener of the royal palace is talking with his assistant servant:

Gard. You thus employ'd, I will go root away
The noisome weeds, which without profit suck
The soil's fertility from wholesome flowers.
Serv. Why should we in the compass of a pale
Keep law and form and due proportion,
Showing, as in a model, our firm estate,
When our sea-walled *garden,* the whole land,
Is full of *weeds,* her fairest flowers chok'd up,
Her fruit-trees all unprun'd, her hedges ruin'd,
Her knots disorder'd and her wholesome herbs
Swarming with caterpillars?
Gard. Hold thy peace.
He that hath suffer'd this disorder'd spring
Hath now himself met with the fall of leaf.
The *weeds,* which his broad-spreading leaves did shelter,
That seem'd in eating him to hold him up,
Are pluck'd up root and all by Bolingbroke,
I mean the Earl of Wiltshire, Bushy, Green.
Serv. What, are they dead?
Gard. They are; and Bolingbroke
Hath seiz'd the wasteful king. O, what a pity is it
That he had not so *trimm'd and dress'd his land*
As we this garden! (III. iv. 37-57)

In *2 Henry VI,* Queen Margaret urges the death of Duke Humphrey in these words:

Now 'tis the spring, and *weeds* are shallow-rooted;
Suffer them now, and they'll o'ergrow the *garden*
And choke the herbs for want of husbandry. (III. i. 31-33)

In *Henry VIII,* Bishop Gardiner speaks of Archbishop Cranmer:

He's a rank *weed,* Sir Thomas,
And we must *root him out.* (V. i. 52-53)

In *Macbeth,* the Scotch nobles express their willingness to overthrow Macbeth by shedding all their blood,

Or so much as it needs
To dew the sovereign flower and drown the *weeds.* (V. ii. 29-30)

The "sovereign flower" is Malcolm; the "weeds" are Macbeth and his followers.

Othello says to Desdemona:

O thou *weed,*
Who art so lovely fair and smell'st so sweet. (IV. ii. 67-68)

Because of Desdemona's supposedly vicious nature, he calls her a weed, though she gives the appearance of a beautiful and fragrant flower.

In *Henry V,* the Duke of Burgundy pictures France as an unweeded garden for lack of tillage and makes the figurative application to the minds of French citizens and their children:

Should not in this best *garden* of the world,
Our fertile France. . . . her fallow leas
The darnel, hemlock, and rank fumitory
Doth root upon, while that the coulter rusts
That should deracinate such savagery. . . .
Even so our houses and ourselves and children . . .
But grow like savages. (V. ii. 36-59)

The "Even so" is the same transitional phrase used in Q. 238, as Palingenius turns from his physical description of the weedy field to its figurative significance of the untaught mind overgrown with vices. Burgundy's speech shows the same sequence of ideas.

In *King Lear,* the image of the weedy field appears in Cordelia's description of her father's madness:

Alack, 'tis he! Why, he was met even now
As mad as the vex'd sea, singing aloud,
Crown'd with rank fumiter and furrow-weeds,
With *hardocks,* hemlock, *nettles,* cuckoo-flowers,

Darnel, and all the *idle weeds* that grow
In our sustaining *corn.* (IV. iv. 1-6)

Here she recalls, not weeds alone, but the image of the weedy field as well. Though the passage seems to have no figurative significance at first glance, we may wonder why the image of the corn and the weeds—or the wheat and the tares—occurred to Shakespeare's mind at this particular time.

A possible answer is found in another passage from the *Zodiake,* which makes use of the good seed and the weeds, this time applied to the inheritance of good and bad qualities by children from their parents. One cannot assume that the child of a nobleman will be noble in mind, since these matters are controlled by nature and the stars:

243 *a* The highest houses often fall and come to meere decay: (p. 92)
Oft comes the litle house aloft. Of man the state alway
Can not endure. The skyes aboue doe alter mortall things.
b But thou wilt say, what kinde of seede is sowne, such fruit it brings,
If I of noble stocke doe come, then shall I noble bee:
Not so, for oft a Squall is borne of Goodly men, wee see.
And faire and eke welfauourd men yll fauourd knaues haue got,
Of witty men haue Asses come. The mind ingendreth not
c As doth the corps of fathers seede, nor in the fathers sure
It lyes, to giue the children minde. This, nature doth procure.
d What fruite can noble seede vp bring if skyes doe not agree?
Most true it is that people say, The year, not husbandrie
Doth giue the *corne* a good increase. If seede amyd the grounde
Though best be cast, and therto starres agreeing not be founde,
e Therof will eyther *Darnell* spring or lost it els will be,
Thus noble children for to get the father not (we see)
Sufficient is, except the grace of Heauens him permit.

In this passage, the field or "grounde" into which the seed is cast figuratively represents the mother's womb. The father's "seed" may largely determine the physical qualities of his child, but the child's mental qualities are determined by the stars in the ascendant at the moment of its conception or birth. The image is used to explain how children can be so unlike their parents. The phrase "Of witty men haue Asses come" (243*b*) seems to be reflected in *Cymbeline,* in the Second Lord's comment upon Cloten:

> That such a crafty devil as his mother
> Should yield the world this *ass!* A woman that
> Bears all down with her brain; and this her son
> Cannot take two from twenty for his heart
> And leave eighteen. (II. i. 57-61)

In *King Lear,* Q. 243 is reflected in Kent's speculation on how Lear's children can be so different from each other:

> It is the stars,
> The stars above us, govern our conditions;
> Else one self mate and make could not beget
> Such different issues. (IV. iii. 34-37)

This reflects Palingenius' statement that the parents' "seede" is not the determining factor in a child's character. Since children may be unlike their parents through influence of the stars, it is clear that they may be unlike each other for the same reason. Kent's speech occurs just twenty lines before Cordelia's speech on the darnel and other weeds worn by Lear, involving her image of the unweeded field. I suggest that both her speech and Kent's speech were suggested by Q. 243 and therefore appear in close proximity to each other.

In its figurative significations, the unweeded garden is one of the most effective images used by Shakespeare. His familiarity with the details of gardening probably shows a personal interest in it, but his figurative uses of it were largely suggested by his reading and thus constitute a valuable part of his derived imagery.

Chapter 15

The Vanity of Human Wishes

Hamlet's view of the world as an "unweeded garden" reflects a mood somewhat like Timon's misanthropy, milder in degree but similar in kind. This is marked by a tendency to generalize his grievances into a condemnation af all mankind. His phrase "the drossy age" reflects this tendency, condemning the use of artificial and insincere speech (V. ii. 197). He scorns the pursuit of wealth in his phrase "these pursy times," already quoted. His words, "The time is out of joint," express a similar point of view (I. v. 189). His contempt for flatterers is expressed to Horatio:

> No, let the candied tongue lick absurd pomp,
> And crook the pregnant hinges of the knee
> Where thrift may follow fawning. (III. ii. 65-67)

Hamlet is ironically declaring that it is unnecessary to flatter Horatio, who is poor and has no money to give him. "Thrift" is used in a general sense as referring to one who "thrives" by securing wealth or advancement of any kind. Mercenary friendship of this kind, which uses "fawning" as its means of securing favor, is perhaps echoed from 217*a*. The other images of the lines represent a probable combination of two passages from the *Zodiake*. On p. 62 we have Palingenius' description of a ridiculous king, "a crowned Owle, an Asse of stature faire," who rejoices in ceremonious flattery,

> 244 And to be duckd and *knelde vnto,* and haue them *kisse his feete,* (p. 62)
> Nor seeth the *mad man* what he is, how *vaine* and apt to fleete,
> Like water bleb,[1] and thistle doune, that flieth in euery place.

This accounts for the "kneeling" and "licking" of Hamlet's speech. His image of flattery is the same as that implied in our modern term "bootlicking" and reflects the foot-kissing of Palingenius' line.

The description of a king who is an "Asse" seems to have caused Shakespeare to recall another passage which provides the "absurd pomp":

[1] *bleb.* Bubble.

245 Wherfore if Lecherers on earth, beare al the rule and sway, (p. 148)
If *Asses* sit in seate as Kings, in *pompe* of proud aray,
If charge of sheepe committed is, to wolues of rauening kinde,
If Harlots in the Churches dwell, and men of monstrous minde. . . .

The "pomp" in Hamlet's speech may be echoed from this passage; the absurdity of such pomp proceeds from the incongruity of an ass on the throne. Such a sense of incongruous absurdity seems to be present in Hamlet's opinion of his uncle as king: "a paddock, a bat, a gib" (III. iv. 190), or in other words "a toad, a bat, a tom-cat." These words imply contempt as well as resentment and show Hamlet's opinion that his uncle was a ridiculous choice for the kingship.

From the second passage above, the "Lecherers" who bear the rule and sway may be reflected in Thersites' comments upon the Greek leaders:

> Nothing but lechery! All incontinent varlets!. . . . Lechery, lechery; still wars and lechery; nothing else holds fashion.
> (*Troilus and Cressida,* V. i. 106, ii. 195)

The two passages from Palingenius appear to be combined in one of Apemantus' speeches:

> Like madness is the glory of this life,
> As this pomp shows to a little oil and root.
> (*Timon of Athens,* I. ii. 139-140)

The "pomp" of the stupid, conceited king may be echoed in this line and contrasted with "a little oil and root," i.e., the meager fare of the very poor. The "madness" of such pomp seemingly proceeds from the "madman" of Q. 244, who cannot realize the transiency of his mortal nature and of all the glory which surrounds him. A few lines later Apemantus asks:

> What needs these feasts, *pomps,* and *vain glories?* (I. ii. 248)

Here the key words echo the baptismal service of the Prayer
[246] Book, in which one vows to renounce "the vain pomp and
glory of the world," a phrase quoted literally in *Henry VIII,*
III. ii. 365. They also recall the hermit of Mt. Soractis in the *Zodiake,* who describes two kinds of men:

247 This life he liues (though nought) that doth for stately honours proule (p. 198)
And seekes with all his force the fruite of praise and *glory vaine,*
Desiring only men to please, with fonde *vain glorious* braine. . . .
But now on the other side: (p. 199)
He that doth praise of men despise, and *pomp of worldly pride* . . . .

Here Googe's translation obviously echoes the words of the Prayer Book and would almost certainly have been recalled by Shakespeare. The combined sources have resulted in Apemantus' lines, which have much the same sources of imagery as Hamlet's words to Horatio.

On analyzing his own state of mind, Hamlet explains that to him the earth seems but "a sterile promontory" and the air "a foul and pestilent congregation of vapours" (II. ii. 310, 315). This bears at least a general resemblance to Palingenius' lines:

248 O worthy life, O goodly gift of God: man in this world is bredde[;] (p. 198)
Among the brutishe beastes, and fooles and knaues his life is ledde,
Where stormes, and flakie snowes and yse and durt and dust, & night,
And harmefull *ayre, & cloudes* and *mistes & windes,* with hellishe sight,
And griefe and wayling reignes, where death beside doth worke his feat.

In the *Zodiake,* disillusionment with the world is accompanied by a sense of its transiency. Glory and wealth soon fly away like mist or smoke. One is a fool to fix all his hopes upon such fleeting things. Earthly goods are not a gift but a loan, to be returned at death. This note of transiency is evident in Shakespeare, particularly in the Sonnets. In other instances a single significant word or phrase is recalled from such passages in the *Zodiake.* Here is an example:

249 *a* If ought there be here in this life, both fayre and good beside, (p. 200)
Like smoke and mist it flyes away, and doth no time abide.
b Time suffers nothing long on earth, death maketh al things vaine,
And turnes and tumbles vnder foote, of man the proud disdaine.
c Alas how al this worldly pompe, doth quickly passe away,
d How wauering is *renoume* of man, how soone doth it decay:
Much like the *bubble* swelling great amyd the waters cleere,
e Is sone destroyed, and with a puffe, of winde doth not appeere.
For in a moment al the ioyes, of man are fetcht away.

In this passage appears the image of renown as a bubble. In Jaques' speech on the Seven Ages, from *As You Like It,* there appears the image of reputation as a bubble:

> Then a soldier,
> Full of strange oaths, and bearded like the pard,
> Jealous in honour, sudden, and quick in quarrel,
> Seeking the *bubble reputation*
> Even in the cannon's *mouth.* (II. vii. 149-153)

The two final lines of the speech repeat an image from *King John,* in Lewis' description of his soldiers:

> Before I drew this gallant head of war,
> And cull'd these fiery spirits from the world,
> To outlook conquest and to win *renown*
> Even in the *jaws* of danger and of death. (V. ii. 113-116)

The soldier seeking "reputation" in the cannon's "mouth" and the soldier seeking "renown" in the "jaws" of danger and death apparently stem from the same image in Shakespeare's mind; in each case the visualized situation of the soldier is the same. "Reputation" and "renown" are synonyms, to be employed as metrical considerations may dictate.

Jaques' words are part of his speech to the effect that "all the world's a stage." We have already seen how this stems from Palingenius' image of the world-stage in Q. 13. The next line following this quotation reads:

> 250 Fame, Glorie, Praise, and eke Renowne are dreames, and profitlesse. (p. 99)

The transiency of renown in this line has immediately recalled the same image on p. 200, where renown is compared to a bubble. Hence, the "bubble reputation" emerges in the context of Jaques' speech on the world-stage because the bubble of renown was associated with the world-stage in the *Zodiake.*

In Q. 250, fame, praise, glory, and renown are called "dreames." The image appears again and again in Shakespeare. In *3 Henry VI,* Warwick calls to the princes: "Stay we no longer, *dreaming of renown* (II. i. 199)." In *Richard III,* Queen Margaret tells the fallen Queen Elizabeth how she has changed from the height of her glory:

> I call'd thee then poor *shadow,* painted queen . . .
> A *dream* of what thou wast . . . a breath, a *bubble.* (IV. iv. 83-90)

Elizabeth's grandeur had been merely a dream, a deceptive appearance of greatness. It was only a "bubble." Here the bubble of renown may well have combined with the "water bleb," or water bubble, of Q. 244, where the term is applied to a sovereign who takes excessive pride in the pomp of his office. The words "painted queen" mean that she had been like a portrait painted on canvas, the appearance but not the reality (cf. 280*c, infra*). The "shadow" recalls the various uses of the shadow-image as applied to life; its particular association with royalty and regal display may reflect Palingenius' usage in his contrast of this world with the next:

251 For creatures doth the Skies containe, and euery Starre beside (p. 218)
Be heauenly townes & seates of saincts, where Kings & Commons bide,
But perfect *Kings* and people eke, all things are perfect there:
Not shapes and *shadowes vaine* of things, (as we haue present here,)
Which death soone takes, and time destroyes, defiles, and driues away.

In that world kings are perfect; in this world they are "shadowes vaine." The application to Elizabeth, a queen, may have been suggested by this description of royalty. The passage has several verbal parallels to Q. 249.

The dreamlike quality of glory and renown accounts for Henry V's comment on Ceremony, knee-bending, and the adulation given to a king. He addresses Ceremony thus:

> No, thou proud *dream,*
> That play'st so subtly with a king's repose. (IV. i. 274-275)

He is not referring to a dream experienced in sleep but to the pomp and glory of kingship, of which the attendant cares cause insomnia. This unusual use of "dream" is the same as that in Q. 250.

In the *Zodiake,* Q. 250 is the sequel to a discussion of ambition on the preceding page. Palingenius introduces the subject by considering the meaning of fame, praise, and glory. After giving examples of Phaeton, Icarus, and the frog who sought to be as big as an ox, he writes:

252 The Godly wyse containes himselfe within Dame Natures wall, (p. 97)
Nor more he dare than hym becomes, except that God him moues:
Let mortall men such things regarde as mortall men behoues.
Let them not search beyond their powre, *least if they clyme to hy,*
They hedlong fall, and proue themselues a laughing stocke thereby.

The second and third lines are the source of Macbeth's reply to his wife:

I *dare* do all that may *become a man.*
Who dares do *more* is none. (I. vii. 46-47)

The fourth and fifth lines are echoed as he reasons with himself before the murder of Duncan:

I have no *spur*
To *prick* the sides of my intent, but only
Vaulting *ambition, which o'erleaps itself*
And falls on th'other. (I. vii. 25-28)

This reflects Palingenius' comment on those who climb too high and fall headlong; the comment itself comes in the midst of a warning against ambition. (In line 26 I read "but" as meaning "except.") The image was reinforced by Palingenius' description, on the next page, of ambition as a spur. Such a spur can be valuable in urging sluggish persons on to deeds of virtue and glory. Yet ambition is also a vice because of the pride which it instills. Googe supplies a marginal note: "Ambition Cause of vainglory." The text reads:

253 *a* *Ambition* many doth enforce, and driue to Glories gaine (p. 98)
Much like a *spurre,* and many brings to toppes of *Vertue* hye
With *prickes,* prouoking sluggish folk *by force of sworde* to try
Some worthy thing, and if they nill by force perfourme the same,
That then by wyt they take in hande some thing of worthy fame.
b Yet is Ambition sure a vice, and no man will, wee see
Be called so, and they that are ambitious, counted bee
Both vaine, and proude, of naughty mind, as once the Romans war,
c Requested of the common sort (reiecting shame afar)
As oft as they their voices sought, with humble suite did pray
Good will of Rascalles for to get, that they might beare the sway
In Common wealth, their owne things left, whereby they might go iet[2]
Amid the stretes with traine of men, and stately countnaunce set.

[2] *iet.* Jet; walk proudly.

d For her own self is vertue sought, and not for honors sake, (p. 99)
Though shee of right deserueth sure chiefe honors for to take.

In 253*a*, ambition is pictured as a spur stirring men to virtuous exploits, particularly to exploits with the sword. This sentiment occurs in *Antony and Cleopatra,* in Ventidius' reference to "ambition, the soldier's virtue" (III. i. 22-23). It occurs again in Othello's reference to "the big wars That make ambition virtue" (III. iii. 349-350). Othello's comment seems to imply that in other circumstances ambition might not be a virtue. This probably reflects the double usage of ambition in Palingenius' speech: in deeds of war ambition may be a spur to noble virtue, but in politics and other activities of peace it may be a vice conducive to pompous pride.

In *1 Henry VI,* Richard Plantagenet's remark that his uncle Mortimer had been "chok'd with ambition of the meaner sort" (II. v. 123) indicates that there are two kinds of ambition, that of true nobility and that of meaner persons, the latter presumably being more selfish. In *2 Henry VI,* Duke Humphrey says: "Virtue is chok'd with foul ambition" (III. i. 143). Such ambition is selfish and therefore vicious. It is further described in *The Tempest* by Prospero in referring to his brother "that entertain'd ambition, Expell'd remorse and nature" (V. i. 75-76). The basis of the distinction between the two kinds of ambition is found in 253*d*. Good ambition causes one to pursue virtue for its own sake and therefore to deserve honor. The other causes one to seek for honor or fame without deserving it. This distinction is evident in the Princess' lines from *Love's Labour's Lost*:

Glory grows guilty of detested crimes,
When, for fame's sake, for praise, an outward part,
We bend to that the working of the heart. (IV. i. 31-33)

When the desire for honor or glory among men becomes one's primary motive, then ambition becomes evil. Macbeth's "vaulting ambition" carried him too far. In so far as it animated him to fight for his country, it was good, but when it became a selfish desire for the crown it was bad. The same idea is in Prince Hal's mind as he views Hotspur's corpse:[3]

[3] A likely source for Hal's speech is Juvenal's *Saturae,* X. 168-173 (Baldwin, II. 539).

Fare thee well, great heart!
Ill-weav'd ambition, how much art thou shrunk! (V. iv. 87-88)

The same image of shrunken greatness occurs in Antony's words beside Julius Caesar's corpse:

O mighty Caesar! dost thou lie so low?
Are all thy conquests, glories, triumphs, spoils,
Shrunk to this little measure? (III. i. 148-150)

It is likely that Shakespeare had Palingenius' words in mind while writing the debate about Caesar's "ambition" found in the speeches of Brutus and Antony, but any resemblances are general in nature.

It seems likely that Q. 253*c* finds some reflection in *Coriolanus.* Palingenius' ironic description of the custom in Rome of having candidates for high office appeal to the populace for their "voices... with humble suite" reflects the temper of Coriolanus' own comments upon the custom, which he tries to observe. While events and actions of the play are derived from Plutarch, it is possible that these lines had a supplementary effect upon the manner of Coriolanus' speeches.

The theme of ambition plays a great part in *Henry VIII,* particularly in the characters of Wolsey and Gardiner. Here there seems to be more indebtedness to another passage in the *Zodiake:*

254 *a* No proude man loues the Gods aboue, nor is beloued of them: (p. 179)
For God esteemes the humble sort and lowly minded men.
b And well he likes the gentle mindes where no *ambition* lyes,
Thrustes downe the proude, & suffers not to dwell with him in skies.
c Wherfore you proude disdainful swarme what doth your pride you gain?
What helpes your great renoumed names & Princely titles vaine?
d Which death in shortest time doth spoyle, & in the *streame* hath drounde
Of *Lethes* flouds, where sinking lowe they neuer can be found.

The pride and ambition of Wolsey are much stressed early in the play. After his fall he exclaims to Cromwell:

Cromwell, I charge thee, fling away ambition!
By that sin fell the angels; how can man, then,
The image of his Maker, hope to win by it? . . .
Had I but serv'd my God with half the zeal
I serv'd my king, he would not in mine age
Have left me naked to mine enemies. (III. ii. 440-457)

The rhetorical question of the second sentence may reflect 254*c*. The final sentence reflects in a general way God's rejection of the ambitious man (254*a,b*). The theme of these lines is more clearly pictured in Cranmer's goodness and humility (V. iii. 166) and in his words to Gardiner:

> Love and meekness, lord,
> Become a churchman better than ambition. (V. iii. 62-63)

Earlier Wolsey soliloquizes:

> I have ventur'd,
> Like little wanton boys that swim on bladders,
> This many summers in a sea of glory,
> But far beyond my depth. My high-blown pride
> At length broke under me, and now has left me,
> Weary and old with service, to the mercy
> Of a rude *stream that must forever hide me*. (III. ii. 358-364)

The final line is suggested by 254*d,* the "streame" of Lethe in which proud renown sinks and can never be found. Googe has a marginal note to "Lethe":

255 The flouds of forgetfulnes: Meaning, that death destroyeth the memorie of their Noblenesse.

Wolsey's figure of the boys swimming on bladders in a sea of glory may have been derived from or suggested by Q. 254 as given in the original Latin:

256 Nemo superbus amat superos, nec amatur ab illis.
Vult humiles Deus ac mites, habitatque libenter
Mansuetos animos procul ambitione remotos:
Inflatos vero ac *ventosos* deprimit idem,
Nec patitur secum puro consistere Olympo.
Ergo, *utres tumidi,* quid vestra superbia vobis?
Quid tituli illustres, praeclaraque nomina prosunt?
Quae cito mors rapit, et lethaeas mergit in undas? (IX. 901-908)

Wolsey's "high-blown pride" may have been suggested by Palingenius' characterization of the proud as "swollen bladders . . . blown-up . . .full of wind." (It seems likely that Cordelia's phrase "blown ambition" in *King Lear,* IV. iv. 27, is intended to convey a similar image.) Wolsey does not describe himself as a bladder but compares himself to boys riding upon inflated bladders, yet this image in this context may well have been suggested by the "utres tumidi" of Palingenius' line. Since Googe does not translate literally at this point and omits all reference to bladders, we must assume that the Latin and English texts were associated in Shakespeare's memory if we grant the parallel any significance.

We have already discussed Lethe as a cause of dullness (*supra*, p. 121). Shakespeare also has several other uses of it as the stream of forgetfulness. Henry V, newly crowned, says to the Chief Justice who had formerly punished him:

> What! rate, rebuke, and roughly send to prison
> The immediate heir of England! Was this easy?
> May this be wash'd in *Lethe,* and forgotten?
> (*2 Henry IV,* V. ii. 70-72)

Richard III says to Queen Elizabeth:

> So in the *Lethe* of thy angry soul
> Thou drown the sad remembrance of those wrongs
> Which thou supposest I have done to thee. (IV. iv. 250-252)

In these two instances Lethe signifies forgetfulness but not death. In Palingenius' lines, the drowning in Lethe signifies the world's forgetfulness of one's glories immediately after one's death. Since we have just observed this general theme in Antony's words by Caesar's corpse, it seems likely that this curious use of "lethe" on the same occasion may be traceable to the *Zodiake:*

> Here didst thou fall; and here thy hunters stand,
> Sign'd in thy spoil, and crimson'd in thy *lethe.* (III. i. 205-206)

The term is used for Caesar's blood, which shows on the conspirators' hands. Five lines earlier Antony had said:

> Had I as many eyes as thou hast *wounds,*
> Weeping as fast as they *stream forth thy blood.* . . .

He visualizes the blood flowing from Caesar's wounds as a stream of death. This stream becomes the stream of forgetfulness, in which one's glories are quickly drowned and forgot by the world after one's death. Hence Caesar's blood is referred to as "lethe"; its flowing causes his death, and in its stream both he and his glories are drowned.

Perhaps we cannot end this chapter on a better note than this. Caesar's name is a symbol of earthly greatness and grandeur, of glory, fame, and successful ambition. Yet he was but mortal as we are and came to the same end. The vanity of earthly pomp which is but transient and fleeting should be avoided and one's attention fixed upon truer and better thoughts of an eternal life. Palingenius stresses this theme over and over again, and his statements of it made a lasting impression upon the mind of Shakespeare.

Chapter 16

The Painted Walls

THE FIGURATIVE USE of "dreams" for the unreality of earthly appearances is found in *Timon,* in Flavius' words concerning his master's fall:

O the fierce wretchedness that glory brings us!
Who would not wish to be from wealth exempt,
Since riches point to misery and contempt?
Who'd be so *mock'd with glory,* or to live
But in a *dream* of friendship?
To have his *pomp* and all what state compounds
But only *painted,* like his varnish'd friends? (IV. ii. 30-36)

Here the mockery of "glory" and the "dream" of friendship are closely associated, suggesting a possible verbal echo of Q. 250. Their association with "pomp" recalls the "vain pomp and glory of the world," already cited (*supra,* p. 198). Timon's pomp is "painted" and promptly recalls the "painted pomp" of the Duke's speech in *As You Like It* (II. i. 3). The "painted" image occurs again in Mowbray's speech from *Richard II*:

The purest treasure mortal times afford
Is spotless reputation; that away,
Men are but *gilded loam* or *painted clay.* (I. i. 177-179)

Here the image seems indebted to another passage from the *Zodiake,* on what makes a gentleman. Not wealth or birth, but true merit:

257 *a* But yet we count not this ynough, though all therefore thee call (p. 93)
A Gentleman, and thou art fayre, and framed well withall,
Of pleasaunt face, and farest well, and goest in proud aray,
b And thereby shewst thy noble stocke, for this no man can say
Thou art a Gentleman, but that dame Fortunes grace is thine,
c And thou full like a *Gilded* puffe, and like a Marble signe.
d But who regardes, for now ynough it is, to haue the name
Of vertues, and of gentlemen, eche man to seeme the same
Desyreth more than it to be. O Gods aboue that guide,
e Now names of great magnificence and titles high besyde
All men desire and arrogate, they hunt and it possesse,
f The Asse a Libarde calles himselfe, the Ant a Lionesse.
g Who will not Gentle, Just, and Wyse, well Learnd, and Honest now

Be counted here? contented well with barke alone of bow
h And outward shadowes of the thing: that vnder such a cloke
His wicked maners he may hide. Now name beares all the stroke
And not the thing: well take therefore this noble name to thee
i As Pasquill is at Rome, and as both Theeues and Harlots bee [;]
To marble signe, and *painted poste* in noblenes agree.

The significant images for Mowbray's speech occur in 257*c* and 257*i*. The "marble signe" occurring in both lines brings together in Shakespeare's mind the "Gilded puffe"[1] and "painted poste" as figures for the false gentleman. Mowbray's theme of "spotless reputation" may reflect to some degree Palingenius' emphasis on true gentility. In his speech, the "marble signe" has dropped out after bringing the two adjectives together, but it may have been verbally recalled in Sonnet 55:

Not *marble* nor the *gilded monuments*[2]
Of princes shall outlive this pow'rful rhyme.

Palingenius' "marble signe" apparently refers either to statues or to the splendid tombs that conceal corruption within, the "whited sepulchres" of Matt. 23:27. Cranmer's Great Bible renders this verse as "painted sepulchres"; the Geneva Bible, "painted tombs." In Mowbray's speech, the "gilded" and "painted" are attached to loam and clay, the native earth of which man's substance is made. They represent the splendor of the living man instead of the splendor of the dead.

This is a very useful quotation, for it guides us back to Hamlet's speech in the churchyard, where the "loam" and "clay" occur again in conjunction:

Alexander died, Alexander was buried, Alexander returneth into dust, the dust is earth, of earth we make *loam*, and why of that *loam* whereto he was converted might they not stop a beer-barrel?

Imperial Caesar, dead and turn'd to *clay*,
Might stop a hole to keep the wind away.
O, that that earth which kept the world in awe
Should patch a wall t'expel the winter's flaw. (V. i. 231-239)

We may reasonably suppose that the "gilded loam" and "painted clay" of his earlier line were in Shakespeare's mind. Thus the

[1] *puffe*. Bladder. The Latin reads "Utri Aurato similis" (VI. 411-12).
[2] Malone suggests an indebtedness to Horace, *Carmina*, III. xxx.

"painted pomp" of the Duke's speech may be part of the same imagery which suggested the Gravediggers' scene (cf. *supra,* p. 140). This is further confirmed by Hamlet's words a moment earlier:

> Now get you to my lady's chamber, and tell her, let her *paint* an inch thick, to this favour she must come. Make her laugh at that.
> (V. i. 212-214)

Here the literal "paint" of the cosmetics is symbolic of the "painted pomp" which shall likewise vanish. Earlier, in King Claudius' speech, the cosmetic "paint" is used with a different symbolism, representing deceptive speech, or language which covers up the truth:

> How smart a lash that speech doth give my conscience!
> The harlot's cheek, beautied with plast'ring art,
> Is not more ugly to the thing that helps it
> Than is my deed to my most *painted* word. (III. i. 50-53)

This association of the image with the "harlot" may result in part from the conjunction of "Harlots" and "painted poste" in *257i*. The "painted word" of Claudius' speech repeats the phrases "painted flourish of your praise" and "painted rhetoric" from *Love's Labour's Lost* (II. i. 14, IV. iii. 239). In this entire sequence of images, "painted" and "painting" are used for outward ornament that conceals inner reality.

A most interesting use of "painting" for outward ornament occurs in Sonnet 146:

> Poor soul, the centre of my sinful earth,
> . . . these rebel powers that thee array!
> Why dost thou pine within and suffer dearth,
> *Painting thy outward walls* so costly gay?
> Why so large cost, having so short a lease,
> Dost thou upon thy fading mansion spend?
> Shall worms, inheritors of this excess,
> Eat up thy charge? Is this thy body's end?
> Then, soul, live thou upon thy servant's loss,
> And let that pine to aggravate thy store;
> Buy terms divine in selling hours of dross:
> Within be fed, without be rich no more.
> So shalt thou feed on Death that feeds on men,
> And Death once dead, there's no more dying then.

The imagery of the first line has already been discussed (*supra,* p. 156). In line 2, the "rebel powers" are the affections that war against the soul (cf. ch. 6). The particular affection discussed is the inordinate love of fine clothing. Since the line concerns the war of the affections against the soul, the missing word at the beginning should carry the sense of "subdue," restoring the "rebel powers" to their proper state of obedience to the soul. I suggest that the proper word is "control," which Shakespeare uses repeatedly in *Lucrece* when describing the attempts of Tarquin's rational soul to subdue or restrain his affections (189, 500, 645, 727).

The subject of the sonnet is essentially the theme of *Love's Labour's Lost,* as we have already discussed it (*supra,* p. 123), the eschewing of vain affections in order to enrich the mind through study. Lines 9-12 are a restatement of Longaville's line, "The mind shall banquet, though the body *pine*" (I. i. 25). The phrase "Buy terms divine" and the final couplet repeat the substance of the King's opening lines:

> Let fame, that all hunt after in their lives,
> Live regist'red upon our brazen tombs
> And then grace us in the disgrace of death;
> When, spite of cormorant, devouring Time,
> Th' endeavour of this present breath may buy
> That honour which shall bate his scythe's keen edge
> And make us heirs of all eternity. (I. i. 1-7)

In the third line, "death" is personified and should perhaps be capitalized, as in the sonnet.

The "outward walls so costly gay" and the "fading mansion" soon to be eaten by worms, recall Q. 95:

> 258 Doe not the *gorgeous Hangings* hyde the dusty mouldred *Wall,*
> Where gaping Riftes vnsemely syt and *Wormes consuming* crall?

As already observed, the "Wall" is the wall of flesh constituting man's body. Accordingly, the "gorgeous Hangings" correspond to the clothing with which the body is adorned. Shakespeare has associated this passage with another in which the "walls" are "painted." After describing the rich man decked with silks and jewels, Palingenius writes:

259 And yet these Princely *painted walles do nought within contayne,* (p. 5)
A blather[3] ful implete with winde they may be termed playne.

Here the walls of flesh decked with rich clothing are painted walls hiding the emptiness within. The sonnet echoes the phrases:

Why dost thou pine *within* and *suffer dearth,*
Painting thy outward walls so costly gay?

The "dearth" refers to poverty of mental resources and reflects Palingenius' statement that such painted walls "do nought within contayne." The two passages have combined in Shakespeare's mind, one furnishing the "fading mansion" that will be the inheritance of worms, the other furnishing the "painting" and the dearth of mental resources. The walls of flesh are common to both passages and perhaps caused their association with each other.

The use of "gorgeous Hangings" for rich clothing recalls another passage from the *Zodiake:*

260 *a* With purple faire, and cloth of golde, the riche man is arayd, (p. 14)
His *gorgeous* shirt doth cast a shewe with silke all ouerlayde,
About his head he weareth aye, the fleece of Scythian bow:
And Iewels fayre about his necke of price he weares. But now
b *Are these of greater force, for to expell the bitter colde,*
Than if in garments made of wooll, thy body were infolde?
c Or doth the wouen webbe of flaxe, not so repulse the heate,
When as the Sunne doth feruent flame amid the Lion great?
Or when the rageing Dog[4] the fieldes, of greene doth quite defeate[,]
As if the fine and tender silke, enclosde thee round about?
d But thou wilt say, he is estemde whom *gorgeous* geare settes out,
Vnto him passing by the way, the people ducke and ryse:
And onely he is counted then, both noble, good, and wyse,
And worthy worship to receiue, and frendship for to haue.

These lines appear to be reflected in Lear's words when his daughters insist that he has no "need" of his own retainers:

O, reason not the need! Our basest beggars
Are in the poorest thing superfluous.
Allow not nature more than nature needs,
Man's life is cheap as beast's. Thou art a *lady;*
If only to go warm were gorgeous,

[3] *blather*. Bladder.
[4] *rageing Dog*. The Dog-Star.

Why, nature needs not what thou *gorgeous* wear'st,
Which scarcely keeps thee warm. But, for true need. . . .
(II. iv. 267-273)

Here the "gorgeous" clothing is recognized as the badge of wealth or rank, not a necessity for comfort. The similarity to Palingenius' lines is apparent, both in particular phrases and in the general theme.

Palingenius' image of the "Princely painted walles" comes eight lines after his description of rich men dressed in silk and gold as "twolegd Asses." While this is a favorite epithet of Palingenius, its use in this manner recalls another passage, on p. 72, in which the ass is used to characterize those who will act, for the sake of greater riches, as servants or henchmen of men in high place. The author has contempt for their subservience:

261 *a* A fond and filthy thing it is, when thou maist leade thy life (p. 72)
With little liuing safe and free and voyd of all such strife
b To beare the yoke of bondage vile, for hope of greater gayne,
And freedome sell, the chiefe of all, and stately checke sustaine.
c O mindes of men degenerate why seeke ye greate mens halls,
To be an honour vnto them and make your selues as thralls?
d Wo worth you all that shepherdes neede like beastes of brutish sorte,
That of your selues not able be to keepe an honest porte.
e For who so serues by any meanes can no wayes happy be,
It is *an Asses parte to beare the saddle* styll wee see. . . .

f And when that aged haires shall hap & sicknesse shall thee hent, (p. 73)
Who shall thy wearied age relieue? who shall thy hurts lament?
g Thy brother or thy kinsman nere, or will doe this thy frende?
No sure, for to be heyre to thee they rather wish thine ende.
On thee aliue they wayt and fawne thy goods at graue to take,
And eche man loues and feares thy good, of thee no force they make.

The two parts of this passage are reflected in the Duke's speech in *Measure for Measure,* as he seeks to comfort Claudio:

If thou art rich, thou'rt poor;
For, like an ass whose back with ingots bows,
Thou bear'st thy heavy riches but a journey,
And Death unloads thee. Friend hast thou none;
For thine own bowels, which do call thee sire,
The mere effusion of thy proper loins,
Do curse the gout, serpigo, and the rheum,
For ending thee no sooner. (III. i. 25-32)

The second sentence of this speech reflects the second part of Palingenius' speech. The "kinsman nere" of 261*g* becomes a son in the Duke's lines, who with the "frende" desires the death of one from whom they will inherit wealth. The first sentence, comparing the riches to a burden borne by an ass, reflects 261*e,* the rich sycophant who bears the saddle willingly for gold. Here the close conjunction of a similar sequence of images in both works suggests the *Zodiake* as a source. It is probably not the only source, however. The Arden Shakespeare cites a parallel from *The French Academie:*

262 They [couetous men] are like Mules that carry great burthens of gold and siluer on their backs, and yet eate but hay. (Pt. I, ch. 42)

It seems highly probable that this is a contributory source of the Duke's image of the ass. It also seems to be reflected in *Julius Caesar,* in Antony's contemptuous description of Lepidus:

And though we lay these honours on this man
To ease ourselves of divers sland'rous loads,
He shall but bear them *as the ass bears gold,*
To groan and sweat under the business,
Either led or driven, as we point the way;
And having brought our treasure where we will,
Then take we down his load, and turn him off,
Like to the empty ass, to shake his ears
And graze in commons. (IV. i. 19-27)

Lepidus is an "ass" who bears gold and whose only reward will be to "graze in commons." La Primaudaye's covetous man is a "mule" who bears gold and whose only reward is to eat hay. The mule probably becomes identified as an ass through the use of that term in the *Zodiake* for a similar subservient bearer of wealth for others.

Mr. Noble finds that the Duke's words to Claudio ,"If thou'rt rich, thou'rt poor," are an echo of Revelation 3:17:

263 Because thou sayest: I am rich, and increased with goods, and have need of nothing, and knowest not, how thou art wretched and miserable, and poor, and blind, and naked. (C)

He also finds suggestions for "death unloads thee" in Psalms 49:17 and 1 Timothy 6:7, but these resemblances are not at all close. This phrase involves the proverbial idea that riches are not a permanent gift but a loan which we must return at death. Its ultimate source is probably Christ's parable of the rich man who laid up great stores of wealth and died immediately afterward (Luke 12:16-20). It appears several times in Shakespeare's sonnets (*infra,* pp. 247, 248, 252) and seems to be reflected again in *Measure for Measure,* in the Duke's speech to Angelo:

Nature never *lends*
The smallest scruple of her excellence
But, like a thrifty goddess, she determines
Herself the glory of a creditor,
Both thanks and use. (I. i. 37-41)

Here Nature is pictured as the creditor, though no mention is made of death in this instance. Among the several appearances of this image in the *Zodiake,* the following seems most likely to be a source for Shakespeare:

264 *a* Well whatsoeuer that it is, death yll I may not call, (p. 105)
Bycause it riches takes away and pleasaunt ioyes wythall.
b For vnto vs these are but lent, *the vse doth nature giue,*
And not the thing it selfe shee deales to mortall men that liue.
c Sith nothing then to me belongs, to death I will resigne
All other things that here I haue, as nothing sure of mine.
d What if I others goods doe leaue? wherfore should I lament
If *nature* nowe do aske agayne the things that shee mee *lent?*
e I naked came into this world and naked will I out.
f For this world is an Inne where hostes of men a wondrous route:
g Who for a time doe vse the foode that layes before their face
Their hoste, and therewithall doth say, Syrs take and eate apace,
Not for desertes of you we geue these things, but of good wyll
These pleasant dishes here wee set therewith your selues to fyll,
h Vntill such time as I thinke good to byd you hence departe
And say From vp my table rise. Now eate with ioyfull harte,
But when the houre last shal come wherin I byd you go,
With willing minde obey me then, and place resigne you tho[5]
To other guests that here shall syt, let them reioyce a while
i With dishes these. Who will repyne (except he bee to vile,
Lack wyt, or else vnthankfull bee) hearing these wordes to go
From others dores, or else wyll syt while he commaundeth so?
But he shall cry com forth you Knaue and thrust him out by th' eares:
Than yll appayd he forwardes goes, with wofull weping teares.

Beside the two parts of this quotation Googe has successive marginal notes:

[5] *tho.* Then.

265 *a* Ryches are but lent vs to vse, and not giuen vs to possesse.

b Theworld Compared to an Inn, Nature to a liberall hostess, and mortall men to guests or Trauaylers, &c.

The text beside the first note pictures Nature as the creditor who reclaims her goods at death; the image is similar to those in the Duke's speeches. The second note may have influenced Macbeth's description of sleep as "great *nature's* second course, Chief nourisher in *life's feast*" (II. ii. 39-40), in addition to the primary sources mentioned earlier (*supra,* p. 118). The "feast" of life may result from 264*g,* beside the second note.[6]

The image of the host (so in the text, but "hostess" in Googe's note) who bids some guests farewell while welcoming others and the regret of the guest who has to leave (264*h, i*) provide Ulysses with a simile in *Troilus and Cressida.* Instead of Nature, Time is the host in his lines:

> For Time is like a fashionable host
> That lightly shakes his parting guest by th' hand,
> And with his arms outstretch'd as he would fly
> Grasps in the comer. Welcome ever smiles,
> And Farewell goes out sighing. (III. iii. 165-169)

A more complicated borrowing occurs in the Queen's farewell to Richard II:

> Ah, thou, the *model* where *old Troy* did stand,
> The *map* of honour, thou King Richard's *tomb,*
> And not King Richard; thou most beauteous *inn,*
> Why should hard-favour'd Grief be lodg'd in thee,
> When Triumph is become an alehouse guest? (V. i. 11-15)

The intent of all these metaphors is to describe Richard's body, from which the essence of kingship has vanished, leaving the mere outline or shell of a king, the appearance but not the reality. Thus, his still living body is but the tomb or monument memorializing his kingship that has ceased to exist. This image may have been sug-

[6] The various figures here discussed were not uncommon. In Lucretius' *De Rerum Natura,* bk. III, the advice to withdraw willingly from the banquet of life or else be forced to retire by Nature occurs in lines 938-9, 961-2. Life as a loan, not a gift, is mentioned in line 971. It is also mentioned in Seneca's *Ad Polybium de Consolatione,* x. 4, and in the pseudo-Platonic *Axiochus.* For life as a sojourn at an inn, see Seneca's *Ad Marciam de Consolatione,* xxi. 1.

gested by the "marble signe" and the "painted tombs" in the complex of imagery already discussed, for these images were also used as metaphors for the body.

The "map" is perhaps reminiscent of 280*c, infra.* As a painted map is to the world which it represents, so is our world to the heavenly world; ours is only an appearance, a "figure plaine," a shadow without the "true" substance. The Queen uses this figure for honor. Richard is a "map," an appearance of kingly honor or rank, but the substance is no longer there. Here again Shakespeare may be thinking in terms of the microcosm, implying an analogy between the map of the "great world" and the map of the "little world of man."[7]

The same analogy is implicit in the comparison of Richard to an inn. Triumph now resides in the common alehouse; i.e., in Bolingbroke, and Grief has come to dwell in Richard. The inn of the world (264*f*) has become the inn of the "little world." A joyful heart, not grief, is proper for such an inn (264*h*). The "beauteous" outward show belies the ugly or "hard-favour'd" substance within.

In the first line, the "model" is usually assumed to be a ground plan of Troy, comparing Richard's present state with the ambitious outline of a city which is nothing but ruins. This comparison of one man to a ruined city may have its basis in Prov. 25:28:

266 He that cannot rule himself, is like a city which is broken down and hath no walls. (B)

The description aptly fits Richard, whose woes resulted from his lack of judgment and self-control.

The choice of "old Troy" for the image of the ruined city may have had a special significance. In the late sixteenth century it was a common practice to refer to London as Troynovant or New Troy. Both Peele and Greene casually use the term in their plays as an allusion which the audience would readily understand.[8] English kings traced their ancestry through Brutus and Aeneas to Dar-

[7] Cf. "'the map of my microcosm" (*Coriolanus,* II. i. 68).

[8] "A second Troy," Peele's *Arraignment of Paris,* V. i; "Troynovant," Greene's *Friar Bacon and Friar Bungay,* Bacon's last speech.

danus, the founder of Troy. Rome had been a second Troy, and London was another. The fall of the British sovereign was comparable to the fall of Troy's King Priam, and the remains of "old Troy" a fitting symbol for the low estate of Richard.[9] In each case the "walls" had fallen to ruin.

[9] Cf. Isabella E. Rathborne, *The Meaning of Spenser's Fairyland*, 1937, ch. 2.

Chapter 17

Life is a Dream

THE CLOSE ASSOCIATION of "ambition" with the "dreames" which constitute fame, praise, glory, and renown (Q. 250) is reflected in Guildenstern's reply to Hamlet:

> Which *dreams* indeed are *ambition,* for the very substance of the ambitious is merely *the shadow of a dream.* (II. ii. 263-265)

Here the identification of dreams with ambition seems to reflect the imagery discussed in the last chapter but one.

The comparison of life to a shadow is one of the images occurring most frequently in the *Zodiake,* which has almost certainly contributed to Shakespeare's uses of the image. Another contributory source, direct or indirect, is Plato's allegory of the Cave (*Republic,* VII. 514). We are in this world as in a dark cave, seeing only reflected images; the bodies and objects which we see are not real things, for they are perishable. They are but shadows of the invisible and permanent realities of the ideal world, which we cannot at present see. Our visible bodies are shadows of the ideas existent in the Divine Mind. Shakespeare toys with this idea in Guildenstern's speech. The "ambitious" are ambitious men, their substance is their bodies, and these bodies are but the shadows of a dream. Since, as Hamlet replies, a dream itself is only a shadow, the substance would then seem to be the shadows of a shadow. His friends' humorous confusion of the quality of ambition with the substance of the ambitious leads Hamlet into dialectic difficulties when he tries to apply their reasoning to actual people such as kings and beggars.

We may ask, however, what is Guildenstern's "dream" of which the human body is only a shadow? The answer is again Platonic and seems to be set forth in the first lines of Sonnet 107:

> Not mine own fears, nor the prophetic soul
> Of the wide world, dreaming on things to come.

Here there seems to be a reference to the World-Soul, which, in the Platonic Triad, contemplates the ideas in the Divine Mind, then reproduces them at the proper time in the world of material forms (cf. Ficino, *Commentarium in Convivium,* VI. vii). The World-Soul is the agent of creation, but it creates from models perceived in the Divine Mind. The "idea" is the reality; its perception by the contemplating World-Soul is the "dream" or first shadow; from this dream the World-Soul will later fashion the material forms of "things to come," the physical substances which are thus the shadows of its dream and hence the shadows of a shadow. Such seems to be the process of ratiocination involved in Guildenstern's speech. Yet the language in which this line of reasoning is couched, particularly the description of man's bodily substance as "the shadow of a dream," seems to be a verbal echo of *The French Academie,* Pt. I, ch. 1:

267 What other thing (saith Pindarus) is *man,* than *the shadow of a dreame* in ones sleepe? Whereby he sheweth the vanitie of man by an excellent manner of speaking, verie significantlie vttering his meaning. For what thing is lesse than a dreame, yea than *the shadow of a dreame?*

The further use of the "shadow" as a figure for earthly goods occurs in the *Zodiake,* between Q. 229 and Q. 230:

268 *a* Goe then O blinded mortall men, goe heape vp mony than, (p. 192)
And fill your caskets full of Golde, by all the meanes you can,
Beset with Ringes your fingers thick, and let the Iewels round,
In gorgeous lincks of golde, about your gracelesse necks be wound,
b Now rufle in your silks abroad, and brag it through the streete,
c Go, go I say, you blinded fooles, both crownes and Scepter sweete,
And all that Fortune rash can geue, to you with all your power,
d Go seeke: yet all these goodly things shall vanish in an hower,
All these thinges are but *dreames and toyes,* and haue but little stay,
Which quickly Chance doth from you take, or Death doth snatch away,
e Which soone do vanish hence lyke smoke, and neuer turne againe.
Go, go O wretches seeke to get these mistes, and *shadowes vaine.* . . .
f O mischiefous vntoward soules, O heartes of cankred kinde,
Why gaze you still vpon the earth like beastes of brutish minde?

Palingenius declares that one should fix his hopes on a future life and lay up treasures in heaven, where "churlish death" has no power and "fretting time" cannot overthrow his estate.

The "dreames and toyes" of 268*d* may be reflected in Tarquin's debate with himself before his violation of Lucrece:

> What win I, if I gain the thing I seek?
> A *dream,* a *breath,* a *froth* of fleeting joy.
> Who buys a minute's mirth to wail a week,
> Or sells eternity to get a *toy.* (211-214)

Here is an image parallel to Queen Margaret's "a dream . . . a breath, a bubble" (*supra,* p. 201). The "bubble" in one speech and the "froth" in the other may be essentially the same, since froth is made up of bubbles. Tarquin uses the figure for the evanescence of pleasure, as Queen Margaret uses it for the evanescence of worldly pomp.

In Q. 268, the vanity of earthly desires is powerfully expressed. The excessive love of gold and of gorgeous clothing, the fools who sit as kings, the inequalities of Fortune, the beastly quality of materialistic minds, are combined with the transiency and speedy disappearance of earthly possessions. The passage recalls another from the *Zodiake,* on the same page as Q. 254. Those who think only of earthly pomp are blind asses, Palingenius declares. They may deceive mortals but not the gods. They pay little thought to gods and a future life:

> 269 But you *O blinded Asses* thinke no Gods at all to bee, (p. 179)
> Nor yet beleeue the Corse in graue, the soule shall rise to dome,
> And therefore seeke these present ioyes, and scorne the life to come.
> A number great of Beastes aliue in shape of men doe stray,
> Hence springeth vp your errour great and cause of your *decay,*
> That with your *grosse* capacitie, none other thing you see,
> But *bodies grosse,* nor true things knowe, but such as *shadowes* bee.
> The greatest sort delight in smoke, and full with smoke they flowe?
> O fooles what lighter thing than smoke, what thing doth vainer
> showe?

Here the familiar images are repeated. It is interesting to observe, however, that the "shadowes" in many of the earlier quotations refer to wealth and earthly pomp, while they here refer to "bodies grosse," suggesting human bodies or at least including human bodies. The passage is therefore a useful link in the images which provided the "shadow and substance" speech in *Hamlet.*

The use of "Asses" to describe materialistic atheists appears again in the *Zodiake,* in a similar context:

270 And thinkes there is no other lyfe than this, that here we
holde. (p. 201)
A foolishe Asse, forgetfull of himselfe, and country olde,
From whence into this darksome dale, and dolfull place he went,
That so a wretche he should become, in wretched carcasse pent.
For euery *soule* that is *inclosde with fleshe* and members here,
Hath wretched life, till losde from thence, it flye to heauens clere.

Through this particular use of "Asse" Shakespeare associates the two passages with each other. Q. 270 follows immediately after Q. 178, with its many metaphors to express the vileness of the human body,

271 Al flowing ful with dregges vncleane . . .
O *heauie garment,* pryson strong, O quick and liuely graue:
That chokest here both minde, and sense, and them in darknesse hide.

To the association of these lines, we may trace an image used by Shakespeare. In *The Merchant of Venice,* Lorenzo, after describing the music of the spheres, says:

Such harmony is in immortal *souls;*
But whilst this *muddy vesture* of *decay*
Doth *grossly close it in,* we cannot hear it. (V. i. 63-65)

The italicized words will show the verbal links. The "muddy vesture" corresponds to the "heauie garment . . . flowing ful with dregges." Its inclosing the soul comes from Q. 270, "euery soule that is inclosde with fleshe." The "decay" may stem from Q. 269. The "grosse capacitie" which can perceive only "bodies grosse" is echoed in Lorenzo's "grossly," a word which suggests both of Palingenius' meanings, for Lorenzo refers both to gross bodies of flesh and to grosse perception which cannot hear the immortal harmony. The failure to hear is further suggested by the fleshly garment "that chokest here both minde, and sense";[1] to choke the sense is to impair the hearing and other means of perception.

---

[1] The body as garment of the soul is not an unusual figure; it occurs, for instance, in Seneca's *Epistulae Morales,* xcii. 13.

Shakespeare's "vesture" has replaced the *Zodiake's* "garment," possibly from his recollection of the Latin original, "O vestis gravis" (X. 746). A probable contributing factor is their use as synonyms in Psalms 102:25-27:

> 272 Thou, Lord, in the beginning hast laid the foundations of the earth, and the heavens are the work of thy hand. They shall perish, but thou shalt endure: they shall wax old as doth a *garment.* And as a *vesture* shalt thou change them, and they shall be changed; but thou art the same, and thy years shall not fail.

The fact that Lorenzo has just been speaking of the heavens may have caused Shakespeare to recall the language of the psalm and to substitute "vesture" for "garment" in describing man's fleshly body.

The image of the soul in a garment of gross flesh is repeated several times by Shakespeare. In *Twelfth Night,* Sebastian answers Viola:

> A *spirit* I am indeed;
> But am in that dimension *grossly clad*
> Which from the womb I did participate. (V. i. 243-245)

In *A Midsummer Night's Dream,* Titania says to Bottom:

> And I will purge thy *mortal grossness* so
> That thou shalt like an airy *spirit* go. (III. i. 163-164)

Dying, Richard II exclaims:

> Mount, mount, my *soul!* Thy seat is up on high;
> Whilst my *gross flesh* sinks downward, here to die. (V. v. 112-113)

Sonnet 151 reflects the "bodies grosse" of Q. 269:

> For, thou betraying me, I do betray
> My *nobler part* to my *gross body's* treason.

Lucrece reasons, after her violation by Tarquin:

> Though my *gross blood* be stain'd with this abuse,
> Immaculate and spotless is my *mind.* (1655-1656)

All these instances envision the human soul clothed with the "grossness" of the human body. Basically, they are all the same image as that in Lorenzo's lines.

The transiency of the universe appears in another passage from the *Zodiake:*

273 *a* O noble powre, O princely reigne, companions fine and braue, (p. 115)
What wants ther now (O God) to the? what sekest thou more to haue?
b Alone thou doste not now remaine: it well became thy Grace,
To frame so fayre a worlde as thys, to make such creatures place.
Let heauen serue their only vse the Starres, the Moone, the Sunne,
The Ayre, the Earth, the surging seas; what else? it shall be done.
c But straight they shall consumed be, and vanishe cleane away
As Snowe doth fade in summers heate, or flowre in frosty day.
d What state haue they that doe consist, of body weake and frayle?
What state haue they that in the space of so small tyme do fayle?

The theme of the Eighth Psalm is evident in *273b:* "thou hast put all things in subjection under his feet." From the grammatical structure of *273c* it is not clear whether "they" who shall vanish suddenly refers to men alone or includes earth and the heavenly bodies. Googe clarifies this point in a marginal note:

274 All thinges shall perish & consume.

The transiency of earthly glory and earthly possessions is accompanied by the transiency of man himself and of the whole universe which he inhabits. He is like his glory and his wealth, which are only "dreames" (250, 268*d*). In these lines we find a likely source, though not the only one, of Prospero's lines from *The Tempest:*

Our revels now are ended. These our actors,
As I foretold you, were all spirits, and
Are melted into air, into thin air;
And, like the baseless fabric of this vision,
The cloud-capp'd towers, the gorgeous palaces,
The solemn temples, the great globe itself,
Yea, all which it inherit, shall dissolve
And, like this insubstantial pageant faded,
Leave not a rack behind. We are such stuff
As dreams are made on, and our little life
Is rounded with a sleep. (IV. i. 148-158)

In these lines Prospero seems to attain the level of inspired prophecy, as Shakespeare himself felt, for he immediately has Prospero profess exhaustion from his troubled brain and take a walk to still his "beating mind" (159-163). Yet, like others of Shakespeare's finest passages, this one represents a fusion of several derived images.

George Steevens first noted a significant parallel from an earlier play, *The Tragedy of Darius,* by Sir William Alexander, later Earl of Stirling:

275 Let greatness of her glassy sceptres vaunt—
Not sceptres, no—but reeds, soon bruised, soon broken;
And let this worldly pomp our wits enchant.
All fades, and scarcely leaves behind a token.
Those golden palaces, those gorgeous halls,
With furniture superfluously fair:
Those stately courts, those sky-encountering walls
Evanish all like vapours in the air.

These lines may themselves be indebted to Palingenius. At least, they have verbal parallels which would have caused Shakespeare to link them promptly with Q. 268. "Sceptres" recalls 268*c*. "Evanish all like vapours" recalls "vanish hence lyke smoke" and "mistes" (268*e*), which occurs also in 249*a*. In Alexander's lines the objects that shall vanish are palaces, halls, courts, and "sky-encountering walls"; i.e., tall buildings or "skyscrapers." His lines have supplied Shakespeare with "the cloud-capp'd towers, the gorgeous palaces, The solemn temples." The vanishing of "the great globe itself" recalls the *Zodiake* (273*c*), as does the comparison to "dreams"
[276] (268*d*).[2] "All which it inherit" is biblical in phraseology,
probably from Psalms 37:9, 11, 22, 29, where "possess the land" and "inherit the earth" are used interchangeably in the several English versions.

The dreamlike quality of earthly existence may also be recalled in part from *The French Academie:*

277 The body onely is compounded earthly and mortal. But the generation of the soule is heauenly, being sent here below as a passenger, and stranger, or as one that is banished and sent out of his countrey. Whereupon she continually sigheth, groneth, and as it were drieth away, (like to a good plant translated out of a good plot of ground into a bad) vntill in the end shee returne, and be receiued into her immortall habitation, after she hath changed *her present life, which is vnto her but as a vaine illusion of some dreame;* in respect of a true, certaine, and permanent life. (Pt. I, ch. 8)

---

[2] Professor Baldwin (*op cit.,* I. 673-677) quotes from Watson a parallel to the *Zodiacus Vitae* less close than the one here given.

It is difficult to assign an image of such general currency to a particular source, but we can say that those present here are highly probable sources. To them we may add Job's lines on the wicked man:

278 He shall vanish *as a dream,* so that he can no more be found, and shall pass away as a vision in the night. (20:8) (B)

The dreamlike character of human life appears again in *Measure for Measure,* in the Duke's speech to Claudio:

> Thou hast nor youth nor age,
> But, as it were, an after-dinner's sleep,
> *Dreaming* on both. (III. i. 32-34)

He then explains that the pleasures of youth are illusory, since one has not the money with which to enjoy them, and that the wealth of age brings no happiness in the absence of health and youthful desires. Life is a "sleep" between two waking existences; its qualities, events, and possessions are unreal "dreams."

The theme appears again in Richard's farewell to his queen:

> Learn, good soul,
> To think our former state a happy *dream,*
> From which awak'd, the truth of what we are
> Shows us but this. (*Richard II,* V. i. 17-20)

Referring to her past state as Florizel's betrothed, Perdita compares it to a dream:

> Of your own state take care. This *dream* of mine,—
> Being now awake, I'll queen it no inch farther.
> (*Winter's Tale,* IV. iv. 458-459)

In another instance, Palingenius uses dreams to represent the former life of one who has changed from vice to virtue. The "slouthful sluggish man" will one day regretfully use such words as these:

279 *a* But me vnhappy wretch, alas, did pleasure swete deceaue, (p. 176)
And fled away, doth me in briers and many mischiefes leaue.
b For whilest that I in youthful yeares *the stewes* doe oft frequent,
And while to feeding, sleepe, and play, my doltish mind was bent,
c Nought would I learne, and hating bookes, did study much despise,
And learning scorne: but now, alas, I see before myne eyes,

My selfe vnlearnde, of yll report, in begerly aray,
My strength decayde, my minde appalde, my senses worne away:
d All this time haue I liued, as he that lyes a sleepe in *dreames,* (p. 177)
Doth thinke him selfe awake to be deceiued by such meanes.

This image is employed by the newly crowned king, Henry V, in his forceful dismissal of Falstaff:

How ill white hairs become a fool and jester!
I long have *dreamt* of such a kind of man,
So surfeit-swell'd, so old, and so profane;
But, being awak'd, I do despise my *dream.* (*2 Henry IV,* V. v. 52-55)

He identifies Falstaff with his own former riotous existence (line 66), which now assumes the unreality of a dream. His earlier statement that he would visit "the stews" (*Richard II,* V. iii. 16) and the accompanying account of his youthful conduct may reflect 279*b,* above.

Perhaps Palingenius' lines have had some influence on the Induction to *The Taming of the Shrew,* where Christopher Sly is made uncertain whether his past life of drunkenness has not been a dream. With 279*d,* compare his words:

Am I a lord? And have I such a lady?
Or do I dream? *Or have I dream'd till now?* (ii. 70-71)

The noble lord urges him to "banish hence these abject, lowly dreams" and the servant assures him, "These fifteen years you have been in a dream." The situation has obvious resemblances to that in the lines of the *Zodiake,* which may have supplemented the sources of the Induction.

The "shadowes" occur again in Palingenius' exposition of the universe. The visible heaven of stars is the real world, of which ours is but a copy:

280 *a* True worlde, and true estate is there, true ioyes and treasures dwell: (p. 117)
We onely haue the *shadowes* here and *counterfeits* retaine,
b Which lasting but a litle space *lyke waxe do melt* againe.
c Our World is but a *figure* plaine, of those so princely powrs,
And as our Worlde the *painted Map,* so it surmounteth ours.

The italicized words are terms for the transient objects of this world, and all seem to be reflected in Shakespeare. Most of them are fairly common, but their various conjunctions and the contexts in which they occur point to the *Zodiake* as at least a contributory source. The image of the melting wax seems to have combined in Shakespeare's mind with Psalms 68:2:

281 *As wax melteth at the fire,* so let the ungodly perish at the presence of God.

In *King John,* the dying Melun speaks:

> Have I not hideous death within my view,
> Retaining but a quantity of life,
> Which bleeds away even as *a form of wax*
> *Resolveth from his figure 'gainst the fire?* (V. iv. 22-25)

Apparently the Psalmist provides the "fire" and Palingenius the "figure" in this use of the melting wax. Three scenes later the dying King John uses an associated image:

> I am a scribbled form, drawn with a pen
> Upon a parchment, and against this fire
> Do I shrink up. (V. vii. 32-34)

The shrinking before the fire associates the two images. The second one may also have associated itself with the image of human lives as fleeting figures drawn by the pen of Genius, the high priest of the goddess Nature. The image occurs in Alanus de Insulis' *De Planctu Naturae,* Prose IX, but was probably known more widely from its use in Cebes' *Tabula,* a short allegorical work in Greek frequently read by English schoolboys (Baldwin, *op. cit.,* II. 649). The exposure to the fire is not found in these sources and may result from the image's association with the melting wax, as just indicated.

The use of melting wax as a figure for fickle and changing minds occurs in Shakespeare. In *3 Henry VI,* Warwick declares that the Queen and her friends "have wrought the *easy-melting* king like *wax*" (II. i. 171). The "melting" occurs again, this time in connection with "counterfeit," in the plan to expose the blustering Parolles, in *All's Well:* "When your lordship sees . . . to what metal this *counterfeit* lump of ore will be *melted*" (III. vi. 37-40). Here Q. 280 seems to be recalled, though the melting is applied to a substance other than wax. "Ore" is Theobald's emendation for "ours," the Folio reading, and seems called for by the reference to metal; but, whichever reading is adopted, the conjunction of "counterfeit" with the image of "melting" suggests a verbal reminiscence of the *Zodiake.*

In *The Two Gentlemen of Verona*, as Proteus falls in love with Silvia's picture, he says:

> She is fair; and so is Julia that I love—
> That I did love, for now my love is thaw'd;
> Which, *like a waxen image 'gainst a fire,*
> Bears no impression of the thing it was. (II. iv. 199-202)

The "shadowes" emerge when Proteus asks for Silvia's picture in Julia's presence:

> *Pro.* Madam, if your heart be so obdurate,
> Vouchsafe me yet your picture for my love. . . .
> For since the *substance* of your perfect self
> Is else devoted, I am *but a shadow;*
> And to your shadow will I make true love.
> *Jul.* (*Aside*) If 'twere a *substance,* you would, sure, deceive it,
> And make it but a *shadow,* as I am.
> *Sil.* I am very loath to be your idol, sir;
> But since your falsehood shall become you well
> *To worship shadows and adore false shapes,*
> Send to me in the morning and I'll send it. (IV. ii. 120-132)

Silvia's lines contain the relevant image. Her application of "shadows" to a picture may have been suggested by the conjunction with the "painted Map" of 280*c*. In another exchange on the same subject, she calls Proteus "Thou *counterfeit* to thy *true* friend" (V. iv. 53), perhaps borrowing the image from 280*a*. Shakespeare apparently envisions the love of Valentine and Silvia as corresponding to the "true world" of the heavens, while the love of Proteus corresponds to the mutable, shifting region of earth.

In the speeches of Proteus and Julia just given, we have another instance of the word-play on "shadow" and "substance." The meaning is difficult but seems to run as follows: The body is the shadow of the soul. When one loves, his soul enters and dwells in the body of the beloved (*supra,* p. 156). If the beloved fails to return his love, so that her soul may dwell in the lover, then the lover's body is without a soul and he is but a shadow. Hence Proteus professes himself to be a shadow because he is not loved by Silvia, and Julia calls herself a shadow because she is not loved by Proteus. If Silvia should love Proteus and he should then cease to love her, she would also become a shadow because her soul would still dwell in him while his soul would no longer dwell in her.

The image of human greatness as mutable and shifting is used in *Antony and Cleopatra,* when Antony says to Eros:

Ant. Sometime we see a *cloud* that's dragonish;
A *vapour* sometime like a bear or lion,
A tower'd citadel, a pendent rock,
A forked mountain, or blue promontory
With trees upon't that nod unto the world
And mock our eyes with air. Thou hast seen these signs;
They are black vesper's pageants.
Eros. Aye, my lord.
Ant. That which is now a horse, even with a thought
The *rack* dislimns, and makes it indistinct
As water is in water.
Eros. It does, my lord.
Ant. My good knave Eros, now thy captain is
Even such a body. Here I am Antony;
Yet cannot hold this *visible shape,* my knave. (IV. xiv. 2-14)

Antony's "visible shape" involves not only the idea of his physical existence but also his state as a great ruler, lord of half the world, the "shape" in which he had appeared to men. This state will quickly change, as a cloud changes in its shape and cannot be fixed in any single position or form. While the descriptive details of Antony's clouds are probably taken from other sources,[3] the figurative image involved in his comparison may well have been taken from the *Zodiake.* Palingenius regularly associates earthly pomp with riches, which pass away like smoke, vapor, or mist; but twice he employs the cloud for his image:

282 These earthly goods that as the cloudes away doe swiftly flye. (p. 234)

[3] Cf. Lucretius' *De Rerum Natura,* IV. 129-142. The Arden Shakespeare cites several other parallels.

Again the image occurs:

283 For what is riches, but a thing which aptest we may like (p. 12)
Vnto a *cloude,* which Boreas if descending happe to strike[,]
Thou shalt beholde whereof it came, to smoke resolued than.

These lines may have caused Shakespeare to recall the shifting, vanishing cloud as a figure for Antony's vanishing grandeur.
[284] There may also be a reminiscence of Job 30:15, "My health
[285] passeth away as a cloud" (B), or of Isaiah 60:8, "What are
these that flee here like the clouds?" (B). Antony's words
have affinities with Prospero's words on the transient dreamlike nature of life and of the universe, for Prospero's use of the word "rack" shows that he also had the image of the vanishing cloud in mind.

In Cleopatra's memory of Antony's greatness, we find again the confusion of past reality with illusion, expressed in terms of a dream:

I *dream'd* there was an Emperor Antony.
O, such another sleep, that I might see
But such another man. . . .
Think you there was or might be such a man
As this I *dream'd* of?—Gentle madam, no.—
You lie, up to the hearing of the gods!
But, if there be or ever were one such,
It's past the size of *dreaming*. Nature wants stuff
To vie strange forms with fancy; yet t'imagine
An Antony were nature's piece 'gainst fancy,
Condemning *shadows* quite. (V. ii. 76-100)

Cleopatra first declares that her memory of Antony is a dream, then denies this, since no dream could match the reality.

In the examples quoted in this chapter, the dreams referred to are not actual dreams. They are figurative expressions to convey a sense of reality as actually an illusion, to describe the transiency of earthly things as compared with the "true" or "real" things. Palingenius strikes this note repeatedly. Shakespeare echoes his words and to a great extent his thought. The dreamlike quality of earthly life beside the greater reality of eternity is often in the background of his thought, even when the verbal echoes are not employed.

Chapter 18

Love the Preserver

THE TRANSIENCY OF EARTHLY things naturally involves the im-[286] age of Time and its changes. Ovid's "Tempus edax" (*Metamorphoses,* XV. 234) is quoted by Shakespeare in Sonnet 19 and in *Love's Labour's Lost,* I. i. 4. Mortal beings can defeat Time only by generating new births and continuing themselves through their offspring. Hence marriage and the begetting of children become a natural duty and a means of eternizing one's memory. This theme is immediately recognizable in *Venus and Adonis* and in the first seventeen of the Sonnets.

Any study of this question must begin with Professor T. W. Baldwin's scholarly work, *On the Literary Genetics of Shakspere's Poems and Sonnets* (1950), which traces in minute detail various sources that entered into Shakespeare's non-dramatic works. Ovid emerges as the principal source for the themes of Time and Love, though numerous parallels are quoted from other authors. Among these, Professor Baldwin briefly mentions Palingenius, whom he definitely thinks Shakespeare had read but whose work is not stressed as a source for these particular themes. In my opinion, Professor Baldwin has concentrated too exclusively on the Latin of Palingenius without sufficiently studying the English version by Googe; for in Googe's English words one can perceive a number of verbal parallels to Shakespeare not evident in the Latin. In general, these supplement rather than conflict with the parallels noted by Professor Baldwin and supply a missing element in his picture of Shakespeare's composite imagery.

We find in the *Zodiake* the theme of mutability, introducing the idea of Time's ravages being defeated through the generation of new births:

287 For nothing can long time indure, but all things worse we fynde, (p. 92)
In *time* to be by natures rule, and law that still indures
Of destenies, till that againe another byrth procures (p. 93)

Restored state [;] this altering the worldes chiefe grace I take.
This is the highest workmans prayse, of little things to make
Great matters, and the ample things reduce to small estate,
To chaunge the face of euery thing, and still to renouate
Most prudently all things in *tyme.*

Since the law of nature allows the continuation of life only through new births, it is the duty of human beings to follow this natural law and to reproduce their kind. While Palingenius denounces unlawful lust, he vigorously espouses marriage and the rearing of children. He condemns those who are too self-centered to accept the responsibilities of a family. He makes exceptions for those who are hindered by sickness, extreme poverty, or the desire to lead saints' lives. Most priests, he believes, are not truly celibate and would do better to marry. All men and women, no matter how devoted to the ascetic life, are subject to erotic dreams, for it is natural to desire sexual love, which is good when not used excessively or unlawfully.

While these themes are not uncommon in literature, as Professor Baldwin's book sufficiently demonstrates, Shakespeare's verbal parallels with the *Zodiake* are such as to prove that it was definitely one of his sources. To illustrate the point, it is necessary to quote at some length. After describing Venus' birth, Palingenius writes:

288 *a* This Venus now Vranius got, and ioynde in wedlock life, (p. 47)
To one Pedogenes a God, *and bad they should encrease.*
b This is that Venus, wythout whome the vse of earth would *cease:*
And al the world wyth briers thick vnseemely should be thought.
c Hir God hath ordeynd, that she myght the losse which nature brought
Full recompence [;] which God appoynts that hurtfull cannot be.
d What then of them shall I reporte content with chastitie,
That *fayre encrease* do not esteeme: but voyd of issue die,
And leaue no signes of them behinde, they sinne assuredly.
e And if the truth may here be sayd, vnworthy byrth him giues
Nature, of whome not one is borne, vnworthy eke he liues
By whome another hath no life. . . .
f All ouer plus from out the corps doth nature cleane expell.
Hereof it commes that in night dreames sometimes doth Venus dwell,
In dreames that shew the ioyful acte and pleasant sporte in deede.
Let them more *chaste* than Sibyls be, or *Nunnes* of *Vestal* weede.
g Of two, which worthier is I aske, estemed for to be,
The *barreine* bows that *frutelesse* fade, or else the fertile tree?
The ground that giueth good encrease, or sand where nothing growes?
h O thoughts of men of none effect, O fond and foolish vowes,

Apply our selues not to despise the sacred *natures hest,* (p. 48)
Which would the bred should breede agayne [,] which made such ioyful rest
In wedlock bed, thee not to feare, but rather to allure.
i Why wilt thou nature thus withstand? no hurt in Venus sure
There is, if hir thou lawfull vse with meane, and not excesse.

After discussing the hazards of marriage, he writes:

289 *a* Although these things be so, (p. 72)
Yet think I sure with maried bed and nature for to go
More better farre, as shee to vs of birdes and beastes vntame
Example shewes, how both the kindes themselues togither frame,
And ioyne in one of *duty* must, and alwayes to remayne:
Encrease to get and nourish vp their yong wyth equall payne.
b Whereby the kinde[1] may styll endure and neuer more *decay,* (p. 73)
For wee as euery kinde of beast are moud[2] to Venus play
By natures will, a worser thing shall hap to thee be sure
c If thou thy selfe wilt neuer seeke this thing for to procure.
And voyd of issue shalt thou dye and yeld thy corps agayne,
A straunger then shall haue thy goodes for which thou tokest payne. . . .
d But now the wife her father leaues and mother deare besyde,
With al her house and houshold frends, with thee alone to byde
For euermore both night and day, and of thy seede shee beares
A sweete and goodly golpowlde[3] Boy of small and tender yeares . . . .
e She comfortes thee, shee helps thee then, shee neuer leaues thee there,
Shee watches thee and watching serues. Likewyse thy children dere
f With all the meanes they can they keepe, for both your blouds are one
And *Image* like: And when the day wherein thou must be gone
g Is come, thou art not cleane extinct but shalt aliue remayne
In them, who then shall represent their fathers face agayne.

In these passages Venus is pictured as the goddess who supervises the sexual act, by which the earth's population is constantly replenished. The general tenor of these lines is evident in Venus' amorous pleas to Adonis. With 288*e,* compare this speech:

Things growing to themselves are growth's abuse.
Seeds spring from seeds and beauty breedeth beauty;
Thou wast begot; *to get* it is thy *duty.* (166-168)

The theme in both passages is that the gift of life imposes an obligation to beget other lives. The "duty . . . to get" echoes the "duty . . . encrease to get" of 289*a.*

---

[1] *kinde.* Species.
[2] *moud.* Moved.
[3] *golpowlde.* Gold-polled; golden-haired.

Venus continues her plea in the following stanza:

> Upon the *earth's increase* why shouldst thou feed,
> Unless the earth with *thy increase* be fed?
> *By law of nature* thou art bound *to breed,*
> That thine may live when thou thyself art dead;
> And so, in spite of death, thou dost survive,
> In that thy likeness still is left alive. (169-174)

The line, "By law of nature thou art bound to breed," echoes "natures hest, Which would the bred should breede agayne" (288*h*). The last three lines recall 289*g,* the theme that one thwarts death when he lives in his children. The "earth's increase" recalls Psalms 67:6 and numerous other biblical uses. Increase as applied to offspring is also biblical (1 Sam. 2:33). These have probably combined in Shakespeare's mind with Palingenius' use of "encrease" for crops in 288*g* and for offspring in 288*d* and 289*a.* There is also perhaps an echo of God's injunction to man and woman to "increase and multiply" (Gen. 1:28), as the phrase was sometimes quoted. This injunction seems to be reproduced allegorically in the account of Venus and Pedogenes (288*a*).

Renewing her pleas later, Venus says:

> Therefore, despite of *fruitless chastity,*
> Love-lacking *vestals* and self-loving *nuns,*
> That on the earth would breed a scarcity
> And *barren* dearth of daughters and of sons,
> Be prodigal: the lamp that burns by night
> Dries up his oil to lend the world his light. (751-756)

We have already discussed the sources of the two final lines (*supra,* p. 47). The fruitless chastity of vestals and nuns is clearly recalled from 288*f, "chaste . . . Nunnes* of *Vestal* weede," and 288*g,* "The *barreine* bows that *frutelesse* fade." The analogy to earth's scarcity and dearth may proceed from "the sand where nothing growes," which is used with the same figurative meaning.

Palingenius' remark that Nature shows us through birds and beasts the duty of begetting offspring (289*a*) has perhaps suggested to Shakespeare the use of Adonis' stallion and the brood mare (259-408). Venus considers their yielding to desire an example of natural duty (385-386). Professor Baldwin suggests as sources several descriptions of horses in Virgil's *Georgics* and Ovid's *Ars Amatoria* (*Literary Genetics,* pp. 23-26). He also cites from Palingenius a passage in the Latin, which has more significance if reproduced in Googe's words. Palingenius is explaining the senses and the instincts. Beasts cannot fully appreciate the subtler pleasures of sight, hearing, and smell, but can fully enjoy taste and touch. The pleasure of taste urges them to seize food for the nourishment of the body. The pleasures of touch urge them on to sexual copulation for the reproduction of their kinds. Nature instills each urge and its accompanying pleasure for the practical purpose of continuing the species. Palingenius illustrates the urge to eat by a lion seizing a cow and illustrates the urge of sex desire by a stallion pursuing a mare:

290 *a* As when the Lion fierce doth spye, (p. 54)
In fieldes by chaunce a cowe, he leapes, & liftes his maine on hye.
And twines and twirls his twisting taile desirous of his pray:
b Or when *the fomey horse beholdes, the gadding mare astray.*
With hauty head vpheld he runnes, and here and there he kickes:
And leapeth hedge and ditch abrode, while lusty guts him prickes,
And causeth all the skies aboue, with hineying noyse to shrike:
c When meat therfore, and gendring act, the beastes do chiefest like. . . .

Since the horse pursuing the mare is here set forth as an example of natural instinct which desires the "gendring act," it seems very likely that 290*b* is a contributory source of Shakespeare's description and may have suggested its use in the first place.

Two pages before Q. 288, Palingenius has a passage which seems to be reflected in both *Venus and Adonis* and *A Midsummer Night's Dream.* The poet describes a shepherds' contest in singing. The first shepherd sings the praises of a beautiful young man, Philetus; the second sings of a fair and wanton maiden, Mellina. From the praise of Mellina comes Mercutio's jest about Rosaline's thighs (*supra,* p. 166). The singer describes her blandishments and passionate caresses in which she wooes him, much as Venus does Adonis:

291 How oft she beckes and byds me come, with eyes that rowling
moue. (p. 45)
And of her self she calles me thus, and fast begins to *twine*
Her armes so white about my necke, like *Iuey,* or the *Vine*
That wonted are their neighbor *trees with winding course to brace:*[4]
And fast the wanton bytes my necke, and softly on the face
With hand in sport she smites me oft, and by her trouth she sweares
That none on earth but me shee loues, nor none good will she beares,
But yet am I not such a foole, that I holde this for trewe.

The imagery of this passage seems to be present in another instance of feminine passion, Titania's infatuation for Bottom, in *A Midsummer Night's Dream:*

Sleep thou, and I will *wind thee in my arms.*
Fairies, be gone, and be always away.
So doth the woodbine the sweet honeysuckle
Gently *entwist;* the female *ivy* so
Enrings the barky fingers of the *elm.*
O, how I love thee, how I dote on thee! (IV. i. 42-48)

Palingenius' ivy and vine are repeated in Titania's ivy and woodbine. He does not specify what trees are embraced. The "elm" of Titania's speech may derive from a popular emblem book, Andreas
Alciatus' *Emblemata,* in which a dead elm embraced by the
[292] vine illustrates the motto "Amicitia etiam post mortem du-
rans" (Emblem 160). The manner in which the image is used in Titania's speech, however, seems to make the *Zodiake* the primary source. On the same page, Palingenius locates the singing match near a grass-bordered spring,

293 Wher Fayries sit in Summers rage, when Dogdayes heat doth glow.

This line associates itself with the "Midsummer" of Shakespeare's title and helps to explain why he connected Q. 291 with the Queen of the Fairies.

We have quoted from the second speech of the singing match, that in praise of Mellina. The first speech of the match is sung by an older shepherd who is enamored of Philetus, a lovely youth. It also has echoes in Shakespeare. Since it is long, only portions will be quoted. The speech opens with a comparison of Philetus to Gany-

[4] *brace.* Embrace.

mede, Jove's cupbearer. Then comes a reference to Philetus when he goes hunting:

294 *a* As oft as *him on horsbacke* swift, (the Gote, or Hart *to chace*) (p. 42)
The *Fayries* spie, *with loue they burne,* and wysh that louely face
Wyth *thousand kisses* for to meete, as many giftes wythall: (p. 43)
b And *floured garlands* trim him giue, contending best who shall.
And Apples fayre in baskets bring, and *Grapes* of pleasaunt tast:
c O that neglecting to be pleasd, in him were not so plast.
O that this liuelie Impe would shewe, himself alwayes at hand,
To ease the wretched louers griefe: then happiest should I stand.
d No man in al the world my mate, but he doth cleane despise
My plaints, and faithfull louers sutes, and hates my doleful cries:
And as the shaft from bowe departes, so from me fast he flies.
e But flye not from me thus, nor hate me so (Philetus deare)
I am no cruell *Cannibal* wherby thou shouldst me feare.
But worthy to be lou'd I am, perchaunce if thou me knowe.
f For though vppon my body rough, the hoary heares they growe,
And though from chin with locks vnkempt my griesly beard doth fall:
I am not yet yll fauoured sure, for beard and bristels all
Be decent eke, and meete they be, for fyghting folkes and strong:
Let maydly men haue tender skinnes the sheapheardes all among. . . .
g All mine is thine and I thine owne, though cruell thou deny.
If thou me loudst, and wouldest thy selfe sometyme come sit me by,
h I would thee pleasaunt Apples get, that hangs on braunches hy,
Wyth Golden sydes like yellow waxe, and red as Strawberies die.
I would thy lap wyth Fylbertes fyll, and Nuts of diuers kinde:
i How oft, how oft, *mine armes* should I, *about thy myddle winde?*
Two thousand kisses would I giue, those rosey lippes of thine:
Doubt not (swete boy) but walke with me by cleared spring so fine [.]
We both wyll rest, and grateful *sleepe, wyth hausing*[5] *armes* will take:
Allurde wyth shade of hushing trees, and noyse that riuers make,
j While Greshops[6] in the heat do chirp. Alas, and dost thou now
Despise both me and all my giftes, that here to thee I vow?
Do naught my *wofull teares* thee moue nor all that I can say?
k More fiercer far, than *Tigre* stout, (whose whelp is tane away.)
More deafe, than *pictures* which be made of Parus *Marble stone:*
And *harder* eke than are agayne, the Mountaynes euery chone[7]
Of Alpes high, and *Adamant* strong. What doth thy beauty
good? (p. 44)
l If all men so thou dost despise, with fierce and cruell moode?
And slayst the soules of woful wightes whose hearts thine own be tride?
m Thus wise her selfe in *floures fayre,* the dreadful *Snake* doth hide.
And thus with poyson hony myxt. Lay downe Disdaine asyde
A monster vile, and vnto God, the auncient enmy, Pryde.

---

[5] *hausing*. Neck-embracing.
[6] *Greshops*. Grasshoppers.
[7] *euery chone*. Every one (Mid. Eng. *everich oon*).

The reference to "Fayries" loving the mortal youth Philetus immediately suggests Titania's infatuation for Bottom. The kisses (294*a*) appear in IV. i. 4, "And kiss thy fair large ears." The "floured garlands" (294*b*) appear in Oberon's words:

> For she his hairy temples then had rounded
> With coronet of fresh and fragrant flowers. (IV. i. 54-55)

The gifts of apples and grapes (294*b*) suggest her instructions to the fairies:

> Feed him with apricocks and dewberries,
> With purple *grapes*, green figs, and mulberries. (III. i. 169-170)

In 294*i*, we have a source of Titania's line, already quoted: "*Sleep* thou, and I will *wind thee in my arms*." The "winding" immediately recalls Q. 291, which occurs two pages later, since the winding arms of the lover occur in both passages. One provides the sleep, the other the simile of the tree and the vine.

It is possible that some of the jesting about Bottom's "hairy face," "hairy temples," and "hairy scalp" may reflect 294*f*, the Shepherd's commendation of his own hairy face and body. The illusion itself, of a man seeming to have an ass's head, is mentioned by Reginald Scot as an enchantment commonly supposed to be performed by spirits.[8] It should not be confused with complete transformation to an ass, which is also mentioned by Scot.[9]

We find the influence of Q. 294 present also in *Venus and Adonis*. The opening of the poem may have been suggested by 294*a*. Adonis "hied him to the *chase*" on horseback, like young Philetus. Like the "Fayries," Venus sees him and promptly burns with love. Soliciting him, she says:

> A *thousand* honey secrets shalt thou know.—
> Here come and sit *where never serpent hisses*,
> And being set, I'll smother thee with *kisses*. (16-18)

Later Venus uses the exact phrase "thousand kisses" (517), possibly recalling Palingenius' use of the words. The place "where never serpent hisses" recalls 294*m*:

[8] *The Discoverie of Witchcraft* (1584), XIII. xix.
[9] *Ibid.*, V. iii.

295 Thus wise her selfe in floures fayre, the dreadfull Snake doth hide.

The snake is analogous to the youth who slays by refusing to return proffered love. If Adonis will return her love, there will be none of the serpent in him. He is the "field's chief flower," and the flower should not conceal a serpent.

The image is also indebted to Palingenius' description of the garden of Lady Voluptuousness, a garden in which Venus and Cupid appear (p. 31). The garden has the usual details of the medieval gardens of love: trees, flowers, singing birds, eternal spring. The significant lines follow:

296 *a* And waters flowes the flours vpon, from cleare continuall spring, (p. 30)
And here, and there, their courses runne, & moystes the hearbes so grene.
b No Dragon there, nor greedy wolfe, might euer yet be seene.
No Bore, no Beare, nor Tigre fierce, *nor Serpent* foule there dwels,
To harme with triple *hissing* toung, with poysen fierce that swels.

This garden has apparently contributed to the description of the spot "where never serpent hisses."

In her reproaches to Adonis, Venus echoes clearly the language of 294*k*:

Fie, *lifeless picture,* cold and senseless *stone,*
Well-painted idol, image dull and dead,
Statue contenting but the eye alone. (211-213)

The "picture of stone," or statue, has been borrowed to express the youth's unresponsiveness. We have already seen this image used in a different manner in *The Winter's Tale* when the Clown refers to Hermione's statue as "the Queen's picture" (*supra,* p. 128).

Venus' images for the hardness of Adonis' heart may have an indebtedness to the "mountaynes" and "Adamant" of 294*k,* which also illustrate the hardness of heart in the unresponsive youth. Venus mentions his "hard heart" in lines 375, 500, and asks in line 199: "Art thou *obdurate, flinty,* hard as steel?" The indebtedness is confirmed when her words appear in connection with other images from Q. 294 in *3 Henry VI.* York is reproaching Queen Margaret for murdering his young son, the Earl of Rutland:

> O *tiger's heart* wrapt in a woman's hide!
> How couldst thou drain the life-blood of the child,
> To bid the father wipe his eyes withal,
> And yet be seen to wear a woman's face?
> Women are soft, mild, pitiful, and flexible;
> Thou stern, *obdurate, flinty,* rough, remorseless. . . .
> That face of his the hungry *cannibals*
> Would not have touch'd, would not have stain'd with blood;
> But you are more inhuman, more inexorable,
> O, ten times more than *tigers of Hyrcania.* (I. iv. 137-155)

The reader will recognize in the first line of this quotation the words parodied in *Greenes Groats-worth of Wit,* a work containing Robert Greene's famous attack on Shakespeare as the "upstart crow . . . with his Tygers hart wrapt in a Players hyde."

In 294*k,* the unresponsive lover is described as "More fiercer far, than Tigre stout, (whose whelp is tane away.)" In the Latin, Palingenius' line reads, "Saevior Hyrcana sublato tigride foetu" (IV. 134). Googe has omitted the identifying term "Hyrcana," but Shakespeare has employed it when he repeats the image of the fierce tiger in the final line above. This fact suggests that the *Zodiake* was his source for the rather commonplace use of the tiger as a symbol of cruelty, and also suggests that he recalled both the Latin and the English versions. He quite probably associated them with the "Hyrcanae tigres" in Dido's reproach to Aeneas (*Aeneid,* IV. 367), where the phrase is likewise used to describe an unresponsive lover. York's use of the plural in "tigers of Hyrcania" may be following Virgil's plural form and suggests that it is a contributory source.

York's use of the cannibals as additional examples of cruelty probably stems from 294*e,* the shepherd's protest that he is not a "cruell Cannibal." The repetition of "obdurate, flinty" from *Venus and Adonis* suggests that in both passages Shakespeare is recalling 294*k,* where the tiger is associated with the "Adamant" and "picture of stone." It is difficult to be sure of this conclusion, since the tiger and the stone as symbols of hard-heartedness had become commonplaces of love poetry. In *A Midsummer Night's Dream,* however, there is repeated the situation of *Venus and Adonis,* a woman pursuing a reluctant lover. Helena says to Demetrius:

You draw me, you *hard-hearted adamant.* (II. i. 195)

Here the image is exactly that of 294*k,* and is employed in the same manner as Venus' "obdurate, flinty, hard as steel."[10] The image also involves the adamant as a loadstone drawing iron objects toward it. As symbolic of the drawing power of love, it appears twice in Ficino's *Commentarium in Convivium,* VI. ii, VII. iv, and may have become a commonplace from its use therein. The language of Helena's speech indicates a probable echo of the *Zodiake.*

It is now time to quote the remainder of the shepherd's speech to Philetus:

297 *a* Nor be not thou with Grace beguilde, or forme of fading hewe: (p. 44)
For Beauty lasts but little time, like flowre fresh and newe
Full fayre at first, is gone in tyme [;] while flouring age doth last,
b While tender skinne in face doth shine, let not in vaine be past
Such happy tymes, but vse the giftes, now graunted vnto thee
While tyme doth serue, for euery thing by vse commended be.
c The tyme shal come when this thy chin with bristled beard beset
Shall vggly seeme, and eke thy face shall *riueled wrinkles* fret.
And when thy golden lockes shal tourne to ghastly gresild heares,
d To late then shalt thou Foole bewayle, the losse of youthfull yeares.
And oft thy selfe shalt say, Where is my beauty olde now gone?
Where is my colour fresh become, both red and white in one?
e Vaine hope, (Alas) of this thy face, then shalt thou sore lament
Thy chaunged cheekes, and face so foule, thy selfe when represent
f Thou shalt thy glasse perceiue. But why thus waste I wind in vayne?
What meane I thus in barren soyle, to let my seedes remayne?
g Vnhappy wretch in vayne I toyle, my destnies will me so.
O cruell destenies, that now, so sore against me go.
And chiefly now, when wretched loue hath pearst my wofull hart:
h Of greater force is lucke in loue, than all the swelling part
Of richesse great, or noble bloud, to destnies vertue thrall:
By luck in loue the prince despisde, the Clowne obtaines the ball.
i But though more fiercer thou remainst, then *fearfull raging drake,*
Or doeste my loue no more esteme, than weedes in fenny lake[,]
j Yet thee (Sweete hart) I serue, and thee for euer shall I loue:
And nothing shall thee from my minde, (Philetus deare) remoue.

The passage reflects the familiar theme of "Carpe diem," particularly in 297*b.* The transiency of beauty and the enthrallment to hapless love are thoroughly conventional themes. Yet some of the images suggest that Shakespeare recalled these particular lines, as

[10] Mr. Noble cites Zech. 7:12: "They made their hearts as an adamant stone." (B)

we should expect, since he used the first part of the shepherd's speech so extensively.

In 297*i*, the youth disdainful of love is said to be fiercer than a dragon, or "drake." When Juliet thinks Romeo's slaying of Tybalt is a repudiation of her love, she exclaims:

> O serpent heart, hid with a flow'ring face!
> Did ever *dragon* keep so fair a cave?
> Beautiful tyrant! fiend angelical! . . .
> O nature, what hadst thou to do in hell,
> When thou didst bower the spirit of a fiend
> In mortal paradise of such sweet flesh? (III. ii. 73-82)

We have already discussed the origin of the "cave" (*supra,* p. 148). The "serpent heart" and "flowring face" may be indebted to 294*m*. On the same page of the *Zodiake* occurs the image of the dragon applied to a heartless lover (297*i*) and thus used in the same sense that Juliet uses it. This conjunction of images confirms their indebtedness to the same source. Since Q. 297 stresses the beauty of the cruel youth, it is possible that "Beautiful tyrant" stems from this passage also.

The fierceness of the dragon and of the "dreadfull Snake" (294*m*) may have suggested Rosalind's words to Silvius in *As You Like It,* IV. iii. 70: "I see love hath made thee a tame snake." If the unloving youth is a fierce snake, presumably when he loves too abjectly, he becomes a tame snake. Without some such recollected image, it is difficult to see why she should call Silvius a snake at all, for he has none of the subtlety and treachery conventionally associated with the serpent.

The two images of Juliet's lines are combined in *King John,* in Chatillon's account of the English soldiers,

> With *ladies' faces* and *fierce dragons'* spleens. (II. i. 68)

The sources already cited from the *Zodiake* do not account for the "faces" in the images quoted, though Palingenius has elsewhere a somewhat similar image of the wealthy man. Outwardly he presents a fair face of happiness, but the hinder parts are snakes; i.e., cares and sorrows that gnaw the heart (*Zodiake,* p. 12). This is in a quite different context and cannot fully account for the "flowering face" and "ladies' faces" which hide the serpent-like nature of man in the two Shakespearean quotations.

Several years ago, in an informal comment at a meeting of the Modern Language Association, Professor R. A. Law suggested that Juliet's image of the "serpent heart" concealed by a "flow'ring face" may have come from sixteenth century drawings of the temptation in Eden, which show the Serpent's face framed in flowers. He found confirmation for this in Juliet's further comparison of Romeo's body to a "mortal paradise," obviously suggesting the paradise of Eden. The "fiend" or devil in the paradise is thus the same as the "serpent heart." I have observed a similar tradition in Vincent de Beauvais' account of a curious monster called the Draconopede (*Speculum Naturale,* XX. 33). It is described as a great serpent having the fair face of a virgin on the body of a dragon. Vincent thinks that the devil entered into a serpent of this kind in order to tempt Eve, for Bede says that the serpent in Eden had a virgin face. It supposedly showed Eve only its face, hiding its body among the foliage. Some memory of these traditions may have combined in Shakespeare's mind with the images from the *Zodiake,* resulting in the "flow'ring face" and "ladies' faces" of young men with the natures of serpents and dragons.

Venus presents to Adonis a series of arguments on the injustice to posterity if one fails to produce children:

> O, had thy mother borne so hard a mind,
> She had not brought forth thee, but died *unkind.* (203-204)

> What is thy body but a swallowing grave,
> Seeming to bury that posterity
> Which by the rights of time thou needs must have,
> If thou destroy them not in dark obscurity. (757-760)

This theme appears again in Romeo's conversation with Benvolio concerning Rosaline, who will not love:

> *Rom.* O, she is rich in beauty, only poor
> That, when she dies, with beauty dies her store.
> *Ben.* Then she hath sworn that she will still live chaste?

Rom. She hath, and in that sparing makes huge waste;
For beauty starv'd with her severity
Cuts beauty off from all posterity. (I. i. 221-226)

Romeo applies to a woman the same images that Venus applies to a man. The failure to bear children and thus perpetuate her beauty means that her beauty will be wasted, for it will soon vanish away. While there is a resemblance to Q. 288 in these passages, there are closer parallels in Sidney's *Arcadia,* III. v, in Cecropia's advice to her niece concerning marriage and motherhood. This passage, quoted at length by Professor Baldwin (*Literary Genetics,* pp. 194-195), has long been recognized as a probable source for this theme in Shakespeare:

298 *a* No, no, my deere neece, *Nature,* when you were first borne, vowed you
a woman, & *as she made you child of a mother, so to do your best to be*
b *mother of a child:* she gaue you beautie to moue loue; she gaue you wit
to know loue, she gaue you an excellent body to reward loue: which
kind of liberall rewarding is crowned with vnspeakable felicitie. For
c this, as it bindeth the receiuer, so *it makes happy the bestower:* this
doth not impouerish, but enrich the giuer. O the sweet name of a
mother: O the comfort of comforts, to see your children grow vp, in
d whom you are (as it were) *eternized:* if you could conceiue what a
hart-tickling ioy it is to see your own litle ones, with awfull loue come
e running to your lap, and like *litle models of your selfe,* still cary you
f about them, you would thinke *vnkindnes in your own thoughts,* that
euer they did rebell against the mean vnto it. . . . Haue you euer seene
g a pure *Rosewater kept in a christal glas;* how fine it lokes, how sweet
it smels, while that beautifull glasse imprisons it? Breake the prison,
and let the water take his owne course, doth it not imbrace dust, and
loose all his former sweetnesse, and fairnesse? Truly so are we, if we
haue not the stay, rather then the restraint of Cristalline mariage. . . .
h And is a solitary life as good as this? *then can one string make as*
good musicke as a consort; then can one colour set forth a beautie.

Venus' reference to Adonis' mother who would have died "unkind" if she had not borne a child echoes 298*f* and perhaps also 298*a*. We shall find the other phrases emerging in various passages of the Sonnets.

In passages so much alike in meaning as the several sources quoted in this chapter, it is not always easy to tell which is the exact source or whether an image is limited to a single source. The following instances should show that in the first seventeen of the sonnets, also, the lines of the Googe translation are an important supplement for the sources put forward by Professor Baldwin and other scholars.

The first sonnet begins:

From *fairest* creatures we desire *increase,*
That thereby beauty's rose might never die,
But as the riper should by time decease,
His *tender heir* might bear his memory.

The general meaning of these lines is that found in the latter part of Plato's *Symposium,* when Socrates quotes Diotima's definition of love as a desire for birth in beauty and allies it to man's instinctive desire for immortality. The particular phrases are echoes of the *Zodiake.* Line 1 contains a verbal reminiscence of "fayre increase" (288*d*). Lines 3-4 have a general resemblance to 289*g,* the survival of a father in his children. The "tender heir" may be indebted to the golden-haired boy "of small and *tender* yeares" (289*d*). The remainder of the sonnet repeats the theme already noticed in *Venus and Adonis:* the childless man makes his own body the grave of his beauty.

In Sonnet 2 the begetting of a child is pictured as a renewal of oneself:

This were to be *new made* when thou art old,
And see thy blood warm when thou feel'st it cold.

This may reflect Q. 287, that new births are Nature's way "to renouate. . . all things in tyme."

Several images from the *Zodiake* appear in Sonnet 3:

Look in thy glass, and tell the face thou viewest
Now is the time that face should form another;
Whose fresh repair if now thou not *renewest,*
Thou dost beguile the world, unbless some mother.
For where is she so fair whose unear'd womb
Disdains the *tillage* of thy *husbandry?*
Or who is he so fond will be the tomb
Of his self-love, to stop posterity?
Thou art thy mother's glass, and she in thee
Calls back the lovely April of her prime;
So thou through windows of thine age shalt see,

> Despite of *wrinkles,* this thy golden time.
> But if thou live rememb'red not to be,
> Die single, and thine *image* dies with thee.

In line 1, the "glass" into which the unloving youth should look is perhaps reminiscent of 297*f,* while the "wrinkles" of line 12 may proceed from the "riueled wrinkles" which will "fret" the face of the youth grown old (297*c*). The "face" in line 2 recalls the "fathers face" which is re-formed in his children (289*g*). The renewal or renovation through new births appears again in line 3. Lines 7-8 repeat the image of the childless man who makes his own body his grave. The final couplet seems to associate 288*d,* on those who die void of issue and "leaue no signes of them behinde," with 289*f,* the children who are a surviving "Image" of the father. Lines 5-6, picturing the womb as a field or garden to be tilled, recall "the ground that giueth good encrease" (288*g*), an image which appears again in the "maiden gardens, yet unset" of Sonnet 16. In "husbandry" Shakespeare puns on the double signification of the word: the "husband" who has sexual relations with his wife, and the "husbandman" or farmer tilling the garden, which figuratively represents the womb. A contributory source of Shakespeare's words appear below in the quotation from Erasmus (301*d, e*), which seems to have combined in the poet's mind with the like quotations from Palingenius.

In Sonnet 4, "when Nature calls thee to be gone" is reminiscent of 289*f,* "the day wherein thou must be gone." This phrase has recalled the similar language of Nature's speech to her guests in 264*h,* "when the houre last shal come wherin I byd you go," and the two have combined to form Shakespeare's phrase. In 264*b* may be the source of line 3, "Nature's bequest gives nothing, but doth lend." The two passages from the *Zodiake* were further associated in Shakespeare's mind by another verbal link: "What if I others goods doe leaue?" (264*d*), and "A straunger then shall haue thy goodes" (289*c*). These resemblances brought the passages together in his mind, and the composite images appear in Sonnet 4.

Sonnet 8, which pictures marriage as a musical harmony of "strings," apparently was suggested by the *Arcadia* (298*h*), which prefers a "consort," or harmony of sounds, to music from a single string.

As a parallel to the "usury" of Sonnet 4, Professor Baldensperger cites Marlowe's *Hero and Leander,* I. 234-236:

299 Treasure is abused
When misers keep it; being put to loan,
In time it will return us two for one.

The theme appears again in Sonnet 6:

Make sweet some vial; treasure thou some place
With beauty's treasure, ere it be self-kill'd.
That use is not forbidden usury
Which happies those that pay the willing loan;
That's for thyself to breed another thee.

Here the riches of 264*a, b* are thought of as treasures of beauty. Nature but lends us the "use" of such riches temporarily. We may relend the treasure for interest or usury, which is allowable if repaying the loan will make the borrower happy. This seems to echo 298*c,* from the *Arcadia.* The "vial" repeats from Sonnet 5 the "walls of glass," an image which stems from 298*g*.

From the reproach for negligence in failing to reproduce oneself, Shakespeare passes to the charge of positive malice in those who conspire against or murder their posterity by not allowing them to enter into life. In Sonnets 3 and 4 we have these lines:

Or who is he so fond will be the tomb
Of his self-love, to stop posterity?

Thy unus'd beauty must be tomb'd with thee,
Which, used, lives th' executor to be.

But in Sonnet 9 the charge is more sinister:

But beauty's waste hath in the world an end,
And kept unus'd, the user so *destroys* it.
No love toward others in that bosom sits
That on himself such *murd'rous shame commits.*

Sonnet 10 repeats the same theme:

But that thou none lov'st is most evident;
For thou art so possess'd with *murd'rous hate*

That 'gainst thyself thou stick'st not to *conspire,*
Seeking that beauteous roof to ruinate
Which to repair should be thy chief desire.

This comparison of the non-lover to a suicide is repeated from *Venus and Adonis:*

So in thyself thyself art made away;
A mischief worse than civil home-bred strife,
Or theirs whose desperate hands themselves do slay,
Or butcher-sire that reaves his son of life.
  Foul cank'ring rust the hidden treasure frets,
  But gold that's put to use more gold begets. (763-768)

Repeatedly in these passages we also find the image of *264b*, the "use" of treasure to beget more treasure.

We may digress long enough to observe that the images of Sonnets 6 and 10 reappear in *All's Well,* in Parolles' humorous speech on virginity:

It is not politic in the commonwealth of nature to preserve virginity. Loss of virginity is rational increase, and there was never virgin got till virginity was first lost. That you were made of is metal to make virgins. Virginity by being once lost may be ten times found; by being ever kept, it is ever lost. . . . Virginity murders itself, and should be buried in highways out of all sanctified limit, as a desperate offendress against nature. . . . Besides, virginity is peevish, proud, idle, made of self-love, which is the most inhibited sin in the canon. Keep it not; you cannot choose but lose by't. Out with't! Within the year it will make itself two, which is a goodly increase, and the principal itself not much the worse. (I. i. 137-161)

It is amusing to notice that Parolles' argument has a theological precedent. Saint Jerome advanced it with entire seriousness as a justification of marriage. To praise virginity is not necessarily to condemn marriage, he said, since the loss of virginity in marriage is the means of producing more virgins:

300 Et ut scias virginitatem esse naturae, nuptias post delictum; virgo nascitur caro de nuptiis, et in fructu reddens, quod in radice perdiderat. . . . Laudo nuptias, laudo conjugium, sed quia mihi virgines generant.[11]

Professor Baldwin and other scholars have cited as a source for Sonnets 1-17 Erasmus' "Epistle to perswade a yong Gentleman to

[11] Epistle 22, secs. 19-20, in Migne's *Patrologia Latina,* vol. XXII, p. 406.

mariage," translated by Thomas Wilson in his *Arte of Rhetorique* and therefore easily available to Shakespeare. Since some of the most significant verbal parallels with Shakespeare have been overlooked, I quote portions of the "Epistle" below:[12]

301 *a* But I praie you, how little doe they swarue from this offence, which
binde them selues to liue barraine all the daies of their life? Doe they
b not seeme to *kill* as many men as were like to haue beene borne, if
they had bestowed their endeuours to haue got children? Now, I pray
c you, if a man had lande that were very fat and fertile, and suffered
the same for lack of mannering,[13] for euer to waxe barraine, should he
not, or were he not worthie to be punished by the Lawes, considering
it is for the common weales behoue, that euery man should well and
d truely *husband* his own. If that man be punished, who little heedeth
the maintenance of his *Tillage,* the which although it bee neuer so well
mannered, yet it yeeldeth nothing els but Wheate, Barley, Beanes, and
e Peason: what punishment is he worthie to suffer, that refuseth *to Plowe*
that land which being Tilled, yeeldeth children. And for plowing
lande it is nothing els, but paynful toyling from time to time: but in
getting children there is a pleasure, which being ordeined as a readie
reward for paines taking, asketh a short trauaile for all the
Tillage. . . . (p. 53)
f Old age commeth vpon vs al, will we, or nill we, and this way Nature
prouided for vs, that we should waxe yong again in our children &
nephews. For what man can be greeued that he is old when he seeth
g his owne countenance, which he had being a childe, to appeare liuely
in his sonne? Death is ordained for all mankind, & yet by this meanes
h only, Nature by her prouidence, mindeth vnto vs a certain immortal-
itie, while she encreaseth one thing vpon an other, euen as a yong
grasse buddeth out, when the old Tree is cut doune. *Neither can he*
seeme to dye, that when God calleth him, *leaueth a yong childe be-*
hind him. . . . (p. 56)
i Doe you yet esteeme this single life so greatly? Or doe wee praise so
much virginitie aboue all other? Why man, there will bee neither
single men, nor Virgines aliue, if men leaue to marrie, and minde not
procreation. Why doe you then preferre virginitie so much, why set
it you so hye, if it bee the vndoing of all the whole world? . . . you
j shalbe coumpted a *Parricide,* or a *murtherer of your stocke,* that
whereas you may by honest Mariage, encrease your *posteritie*: you suffer it to *decay* for euer through your wilfull single life. (pp. 60-61)

These passages have several close resemblances to Shakespeare's lines. The accusation against the celibate of self-murder or the murder of his "stock" is made definite by Erasmus, while it is only

[12] Ed. 1585, reprinted in Tudor & Stuart Library Series.

[13] *mannering.* Cultivating; manuring (in original sense).

hinted by the passages in the *Zodiake*. The first of the excerpts from Erasmus has not only the theme but also the actual language of Shakespeare's phrase "the *tillage of thy husbandry.*" Parolles' explicit attack on the preservation of virginity proceeds from Erasmus rather than from Palingenius, who does not use the term "virginity" in expressing a similar sentiment. We may therefore reasonably regard Erasmus' epistle as an important contributory source of the imagery discussed in this chapter.

Expressing the willingness to suffer his "stocke" to decay, Sonnet 10 attacks the celibate for "seeking that beauteous roof to ruinate" instead of repairing it. This clearly reflects the last excerpt from Erasmus, but the form of the phrase comes from Palingenius. The "beauteous roof" suggests a house. Palingenius has the image in a line from 243*a:*

302 The highest *houses* often *fall* and come to meere *decay*. (p. 92)

The author is using "houses" figuratively for noble families, stating that such Roman heroes as Pompey, Caesar, and Scipio Africanus have no living descendants. Who would have thought that such a "stately stock" as these could disappear? As he uses the image, the "houses" fall to decay through the failure to produce children. The image occurs a few lines before Q. 287, on Nature's restoring and renovating all things through new births. Shakespeare has borrowed the image, with the same figurative meaning. The word "stock" in both sources has apparently caused the association of the image with Erasmus' accusation that the celibate is guilty of self-murder and of the murder of his "stock" or family.

This image of the "house" occurs again in Sonnet 13:

O that you were yourself! but, love, you are
No longer yours than you yourself here live:
Against this coming end you should prepare,
And your sweet semblance to some other give.
So should that beauty which you hold in lease
Find no determination; then you were
Yourself again after yourself's decease,
When your *sweet issue* your sweet form should bear.
Who lets *so fair a house fall to decay,*

Which *husbandry* in honour might uphold
Against the stormy gusts of winter's day
And barren rage of death's eternal cold?
O, none but unthrifts! Dear my love, you know
You had a father: let your son say so.

Here again is the pun on "husband." The "decaying house" repeats Q. 302 and the "roof" of Sonnet 10. The "sweet issue" reflects the "*sweete* and goodly golpowlde Boy" (289*d*), which has combined with the "issue" of 288*d*; possibly the "sweet semblance" represents a similar combination with the "Image" of 289*f*. The "beauty which you hold in lease" again reflects the treasures lent us by Nature. Lines 3-6 echo the general theme of survival through one's children. The final couplet repeats the duty of those who have received life to give life to others.

The perpetual decline and renewal of Q. 287 are also evident in the first lines of Sonnet 11:

As fast as thou shalt wane, so fast thou grow'st,
In one of thine, from that which thou departest.

In lines 5-8, he praises the state of matrimony and parenthood:

Herein lives wisdom, beauty, and *increase;*
Without this, folly, age, and cold *decay.*
If all were minded so the *times should cease*
And threescore years would *make the world away.*

In other words, the youngest of those now living will probably live about sixty years, and if no more are born there will be no world of human beings. The last phrase reflects Erasmus' phrase "the vndoing of all the whole world," which occurs in conjunction with "decay." The "times should cease" may reflect 288*b,* on Venus (sexual love) without whom the use of the earth would "cease" and the "world" be given over to briers; the similar uses of "increase" strengthen the parallel. The meaning of "world" is the same in the three instances quoted: a world of men that would vanish with the failure to replenish the human race.

In Sonnet 16 there are several probable echoes of the *Zodiake.* The "happy hours" of line 5 seem indebted to the "happy tymes" of 297*b.* To "fortify yourself in your decay" by living in one's children is reminiscent of 289*b*. The final line's comparison of begetting children to drawing one's own picture has a kinship with the image used by King John, of himself as a figure drawn upon parchment (*supra,* p. 228).

This lengthy—and, I fear, tedious—enumeration of parallels serves to show how extensively the first seventeen sonnets are a result of adaptation. Not all of them are here discussed, and we should not suppose that this presentation has covered all the possible sources; in particular, Professor Baldwin cites a number which I have not used. Also, La Primaudaye's chapter "Of Marriage" (Pt. I, ch. 45) uses similar ideas and phraseology. Still, the instances here given are sufficient to illustrate Shakespeare's technique in handling such conventional themes as "Carpe diem," the ravages of Time, and self-preservation through one's children. The images as well as the themes used are very largely a reflection of his reading.

Sonnet 15 is part of this series and has the same general theme, but it employs an additional background of associated materials. It dwells upon the transiency of all things, in particular upon the fact that all things seem to have a natural limit of growth, on reaching which they begin to decline and finally perish. Shakespeare writes as follows:

When I consider everything that grows
Holds in *perfection* but a *little moment,*
That this huge stage presenteth nought but shows
Whereon the *stars in secret influence* comment;
When I perceive that *men as plants increase,*
Cheered and check'd even by the self-same *sky,*
Vaunt in their youthful *sap,* at height decrease,
And wear their brave state out of memory;
Then the conceit of this inconstant *stay*
Sets you most rich in youth before my sight,
Where wasteful *Time* debateth with *Decay*
To change your day of youth to sullied night;
And all in war with Time for love of you,
As he takes from you, I engraft you new.

Here the necessity of combating "Decay" is repeated, this time in connection with "Tempus edax." The "huge stage" of line 3 has already been discussed as a reference to the world-stage (*supra,* p.

26). In line 12, the "day" of life and the "night" of death may stem from the similar image in 132*l*.

Line 5 of Sonnet 15, "that men as plants increase," recalls a similar line from the *Zodiake:*

303 And all *the body doth increase, as plants* with showers of raine. (p. 122)

This line occurs in the omitted portion of Q. 56, describing the lamp or candle of life, a passage which influenced Shakespeare powerfully. In a related passage from *The French Academie* (Q. 60), there is described the "Radicall humour" which feeds the flame of life until it dries up. This may have suggested the "youthful sap" of line 7 in Shakespeare's sonnet. The opening lines of the passage state the theme of the whole sonnet:

304 For we haue already heard, how after the liuing body is growne vp to his full vigor and strength; it beginneth then by little and little to faile, and to tend vnto death, whereby in the end it falleth away altogether. (Pt. II, ch. 69)

Here is a statement of the same theme as that of Q. 56:

305 Now let vs seeke to know
How liuing things doe waxe so great, what causeth them to grow:
And why at certeine time they cease.

In these two sources there is a close parallelism of ideas which seemingly caused them to be recalled together. Since La Primaudaye refers to an earlier passage of his upon the same subject, we may turn back to find it:

306 We see likewise, that in the continuation of his workes, he [God] beginneth alwaies at the basest and least thing, and so goeth on *encreasing,* augmenting, and ascending vp vntill he hath placed them in their *perfection,* whereof we haue daily experience, principally in plants and liuing creatures. For the generation of plants commeth of their seedes, from which they take their beginning. And when the seed, which is the least part of the whole plant, is put into the ground, it taketh root therein and then commeth foorth, *encreasing* daily vntill it come to those bounds, that are allotted vnto it by the Creator, which it cannot passe: because it cannot attaine to greater *perfection* being of that kinde, but then daily *falleth to decay,* vntill it be wholly consumed and returned to the Elements from whence it was taken. The like is done in the generation of all liuing creatures, and namely in

> that of man. For what is his beginning? and what is his conception, natiuitie, childhood, adolescencie, youth, mans estate, and then old age? We see how small his beginning is, and how he groweth step by step, and from *age to age* vntill he commeth to the flower of his age, and to his full strength, *as plants doe:* and from thence the neerer he draweth to old age, the more he fadeth and *decaieth* vntill he come to death, whereby the body returneth to the Elements out of which it is taken. (Pt. II, ch. 32)

It should be noticed that La Primaudaye follows convention by listing seven "ages" of man but names conception and nativity as the first two. The "encreasing . . . as plants doe" and the "falling to decay" have obvious verbal links with the *Zodiake* and with Sonnet 15. (Cf. also "fall to decay" in Sonnet 13.) The one contribution of this passage not found in the other sources is the use of "perfection" to describe the brief period of one's maximum powers. This apparently has suggested its use in line 2 of Sonnet 15. In line 9, Shakespeare uses "inconstant *stay*" to describe the same period. This seems to result from another passage on the same subject by La Primaudaye:

307 This law was laide vpon nature by God the Creatour thereof that the things which it should bring forth in this inferiour world, should haue small beginnings at the first, and after grow by little and little, and when they were come to their full greatnesse should stand a while at a *stay,* and then fall by little and little, and returne to their originall and first beginning. (Pt. II, ch. 75)

The author continues the passage by illustrating this law from the ocean's tides, the body of man, and the rise and fall of kingdoms.

It seems highly probable that Shakespeare's "little moment" in which things are able to hold their perfection is recalled from La Primaudaye's "little moment of life," associated in a different context with other images borrowed by Shakespeare (*supra,* p. 157). This seems to me a more significant verbal parallel than Professor Baldwin's citation of Ovid's "momentaque cuncta novantur" from *Metamorphoses,* XV. 185 (*Literary Genetics,* p. 271), though the two phrases may have combined in Shakespeare's mind and one does not necessarily exclude the other as a source. The context of the Ovidian phrase is more relevant to the subject under discussion than is the context of La Primaudaye's "little moment"; it is therefore possible that the use of the image was suggested to Shakespeare by Ovid but that its precise form was recalled from La Primaudaye.

Sonnet 15 is perhaps the richest in meaning of the first seventeen. To the more conventional images of Time's ravages and his defeat by new births, Shakespeare has added a serious philosophic speculation upon the physical growth and decline of man. Tracing this speculation to its sources helps us to understand better Shakespeare's meaning and the workings of his mind.

Chapter 19

The Skyey Influences

In Sonnet 15, discussed at the end of the last chapter, Shakespeare attributes the changes of growth and decay in all things to the "influence" of the sky and the stars. The use of such a statement in this particular context was probably suggested by yet another passage from *The French Academie:*

308 As it is necessary that all things which haue a beginning should ende, and which increase should diminish and waxe olde, some sooner, others later, according to the disposition of that matter whereof they are compounded, and through the *influence of the heauenly bodies,* from which (nature working in them by her author) this continuall and mutual succession of generation and corruption proceedeth; so are publike estates first instituted, increased, maintained, lessened, changed, destroied, turned and returned one from another by the disposition of God. (Pt. I, ch. 63)

This passage states clearly the theme of growth and regression in all things, which is the subject of Sonnet 15 and would almost certainly have been associated with other sources in Shakespeare's mind. It therefore seems likely that the "secret influence" of the stars in the sonnet may echo La Primaudaye's reference to the "influence of the heauenly bodies." The phrase appears as "skyey influences" in the Duke's speech to Claudio:

A breath thou art,
Servile to all the *skyey influences*
That doth this habitation where thou keep'st
Hourly afflict. (*Measure for Measure,* III. i. 8-11)

Actually, both parts of this phrase appear in Sonnet 15, for line 6 reads: "Cheered and check'd even by the self-same *sky.*"

While the supposed power of the stars was a matter of common knowledge, it seems likely that the particular references to the "sky" and "stars" of Sonnet 15 result from the association of La Primaudaye's lines with several from the *Zodiake.* For example, the "secret" influence may well have resulted from this line:

309 Yet some that know the force of *Starres,* and *secretes* of the
skye. (p. 140)

Again, the "sky" that both "cheered and check'd" the state of man may draw a hint from these lines:

310 Of man the state alway (p. 92)
Can not endure. The *skyes* aboue *doe alter mortall things.*

A more specific application of such altering to the human body is found in these lines:

311 The body many things do chaunge: as Age, or Time, or Haps, (p. 120)
As also Meate, and Drinke sometimes, and Aire doth chaunge it quite,
And *Starres doth alteration make,* as learned men doe write.

From these several passages Shakespeare probably drew the elements of his image in the sonnet, which concerns alterations of the human body. The universal power of the sky and the stars appears in these lines from the *Zodiake:*

312 What vertue hath the Skye? (p. 213)
All force and vertues in the Starres and glistering planets lye.
The Starres do guide the compast world, and euery chaunge doth
bring[;]
The Starres create all things on earth and gouerne euery thing:
Thus teache the Astronomers, and thus the common fame doth flye.

The importance of one's horoscope, of the stars that reigned at one's nativity, is continually stressed by Palingenius. The conflicting Renaissance attitudes on this question have been studied extensively by Professor Allen,[1] and they are represented in the opposite views of Edmund and his father (*Lear,* I. ii. 112-149). Whatever Shakespeare's actual beliefs on the subject were, he used it frequently for literary purposes. Sonnets 25 and 26 are constructed about this concept:

Let those who are *in favour with their stars*
Of public honour and proud titles boast,
Whilst I, whom *fortune* of such triumph bars,
Unlook'd for joy in that I honour most. (Son. 25)

Till whatsoever *star that guides my moving*
Points on me graciously with fair aspect. (Son. 26)

The *Zodiake* reads as follows:

[1] Don Cameron Allen, *The Star-Crossed Renaissance,* 1941.

313 *a* I Seeke not here Th' Arabians wealth nor stones of value hye (p. 61)
That redde seas breede, ne golden sands in Tagus streames that lye.
b Nor people proude to gouerne here with sceptred hand and mace:
c Such things my *lucke* hath me denyd, nor once I waile the case,
That *destny* hath not giuen me such.

314 *a* O yong man voyd of blysse, and whom, such *destnies* dire do payne, (p. 41)
That spendst thy lyfe wyth bitter yeares, pull vp thy hart agayne . . .
b Doest thou not see, whome *fortune* oft, had fully once disdaynde,
The same wyth changed hand she ayds, and lyfteth vp on hye:
Now this, now that, nothing endures, beneath the hauty skye. . . .
c The tyme shall come *(the starres aboue, altring their course in skies)*
If death before, thee not destroy, when this thy present name (p. 42)
That now doth lye both drownde & hid, shall gayne immortall fame. . . .
d But scarce can I the Gods beleue such things of me,
Vnder so crabde aspect of starres, I know my byrth to be.
So sore the heauens do me vexe, but yet from thence I go:
e Wyth *ioyfull* heart I wander forth alone, and alwayes so,
These wordes in minde I muse.

In both of these passages, as in Sonnet 25, the man finds reason for joy in spite of being barred from great honors by his destiny, his fortune, and the stars that reigned at his birth. The transient nature of public honor (314*b*) may be reflected in lines 5-12 of the sonnet, on princes' favorites and great soldiers whose fame is quickly forgotten. The "public honour and proud titles" recall 313*b*, also. The possibility that unfavorable stars may alter their course and shine with fair aspect upon him (314*c*) is reflected in Sonnet 26, as quoted above. The sonnet implies that the star does not now shine upon him with fair aspect but that it may do so in the future.

We have already seen in Q. 243 that able men do not beget able sons "if skyes doe not agree" and if "starres agreeing be not founde." Palingenius repeats this theme in stating the requirements for wisdom:

315 Beginne and teach me in what sorte a wyse man should be wrought. (p. 183)
First vnderneath a *happy starre* he must to light be brought,
That after shalbe wise or blest. For greatly matter makes,
Vnder what signe or what aspect, a man his birthday takes:
As they affirme that knowe the names, and force, and motions hye
Of starres, and cast natiuities, and tel the *destinie*. . . .

> From whence proceedes all good on earth, therefore can no man liue
> As wise and blest, *whom starres in byrth an ill aspect do giue.* (p. 184)

While the phrase "happy star" was not uncommon, its use here as a good omen at one's birth may have suggested Shakespeare's use of it. Richard III hypocritically refuses the crown at first, saying that his nephew's birth entitles him to it:

> On him I lay that you would lay on me,
> The right and fortune of his *happy stars.* (III. vii. 171-172)

Later, he seeks to excuse the murder of his nephews thus:

> Lo, *at their birth good stars were opposite* . . .
> All unavoided is the doom of *destiny.* (IV. iv. 215-217)

Here we find the interpretation of the stars in terms of "destiny," a connection made in all three of the passages just quoted from the *Zodiake.*

Palingenius also affirms that marriage and matings are determined by destiny and the stars. Destiny sometimes causes the deformed slave to secure a fair lady, an old man to wed a young girl, another man to prefer a "ragged iade" to a fair and gentle wife. Beauty and wealth cannot prevail against the edict of destiny (*Zodiake,* p. 49). In *Love's Labour's Lost,* Biron may reflect these lines when he unwittingly falls in love with Rosaline, the least beautiful of the ladies attending the Princess:

> What! I love! I sue! I seek a wife! . . .
> And, among three, to love the worst of all . . .
> Well, I will love, write, sigh, pray, sue, groan:
> Some men must love my lady, and some Joan. (III. i. 191, 197, 206-207)

Joan is a stock name for a servant maid. As some men must love servant maids by destiny, so it is Biron's destiny to love a homely girl and he cannot help it, regardless of who she is or how she looks. This seems to echo the reference in the *Zodiake* to apparent misalliances which result from the unshunnable edicts of destiny. For comic relief, Armado is made to express the same sentiments when he confesses that he has unwillingly fallen in love "with a base wench" (I. ii. 62).

The stars are effectively used in *Romeo and Juliet,* for the young couple are "star-cross'd lovers" (Prol. 6). Romeo has a premonition of death, before going to Capulet's ball, from "some consequence yet hanging in the stars" (I. iv. 107). His fears are realized when he hears of Juliet's death and exclaims, "Is it even so? Then I defy you, *stars!*" (V. i. 24). He begins to plan suicide at that moment. Before drinking the poison, he says:

> O here
> Will I set up my everlasting rest,
> And shake the yoke of *inauspicious stars*
> From this world-wearied flesh. . . .
> Thou desperate pilot, now at once run on
> The dashing rocks thy sea-sick weary bark! (V. iii. 109-118)

The bark is his body, the pilot his mind. The image of the body as a bark had been used by Capulet (III. v. 134). It is perhaps recalled here from the merchant's ship "vnderneth vnhappy starre." The dashing rocks are the "rockes" which the star-crossed lover seeks to move, sometimes at the expense of his life (Q. 73).

The relations of destiny and the stars to each other are expressed by Palingenius when he is describing God as the founder of all things:

> 316 The chiefest cause that rowling ay the Globe where starres do
> shine, (p. 158)
> Doest guide by fixed law thappointed force of *destenie.*

Here "Globe" is used according to one meaning of the Latin. Some authors, e.g. Macrobius, apply it regularly to the starry spheres of the heavens. It is here applied to the circle of fixed stars and the other circles enclosed in that one; in other words, to the entire visible heavens. God is the cause that the spheres turn as they do, and they in turn indicate what is to happen in the lower world, what are the decrees of destiny. Destiny may be called the working out of divine decrees in the lower world; its scene of action is the earth. In *The Tempest,* Ariel addresses the guilty conspirators:

> You are three men of sin, whom *Destiny,*
> *That hath to instrument this lower world*
> *And what is in't,* the never-surfeited sea
> Hath caus'd to belch you up. (III. iii. 53-56)

This speech may also draw upon two other passages:

317 All mortal things, this *desteny* rules: she doth to all bestow (p. 49)
Conditions eke with fortune to, and ende of lyfe doth know.

On p. 133, Googe has a marginal note:

318 *Destenie* also is beleeued of som to haue the disposing and orderinge of all thinges, within the world contained.

This note accompanies Q. 18. The several passages from the *Zodiake* can account for Ariel's definition of destiny.

Palingenius also discusses the appearance of comets, which he calls "blasing starres," as omens:

319 The *blasing starres* do oft appeare, that *fall of Prince* doth showe. (p. 224)

Fearing the omens, Calpurnia says to Julius Caesar:

When beggars die, there are no comets seen.
The heavens themselves *blaze* forth the *death of princes*.
(II. ii. 30-31)

In *All's Well,* the Clown uses Palingenius' phrase for the comet, "blazing star." He jestingly comments on the lack of good women:

An we might have a good woman born but or every *blazing star* or at an earthquake, 'twould mend the lottery well. (I. iii. 90-92)

The point is that comets and earthquakes are rare, and that good women are even rarer. If one were born at each appearance of a comet or of an earthquake, there would be many more good women than there now are.

In *1 Henry VI,* the comets are thus addressed:

Comets, importing change of times and states,
Brandish your crystal tresses in the sky,
And with them scourge the *bad revolting stars*
That have consented unto Henry's death!
King Henry the Fifth, too famous to live long! (I. i. 2-6)

In *Hamlet,* the comet appearing before Caesar's death is mentioned by Horatio along with other phenomena, and their premonitory function is defined:[2]

[2] Cf. my article "On Ghosts," in *The Character of Hamlet*. For omens, cf. Polydore Vergil, *De Prodigiis et Sortibus,* Basle, 1553, pp. 258-260.

As *stars with trains of fire,* and dews of blood,
Disasters in the sun; and the moist star
Upon whose influence Neptune's empire stands
Was sick almost to doomsday with eclipse.
And even the like precurse of fierce events,
As harbingers preceding still the fates
And prologue to the omen coming on,
Have heaven and earth together demonstrated
Unto our climatures and countrymen. (I. i. 117-125)

The "trains of fire" identify the stars mentioned as comets. Horatio thinks of such phenomena as "portents" and thinks that the Ghost's appearance may also be of this nature.

Palingenius explains that the comet's tail is made by the reflection of light on vaporous clouds. Googe has a marginal note:

320 In the lowest region of the Aire appeares the *Blasing star.* (p. 224)

This suggests the phenomena elsewhere described by Palingenius as accompanying the plagues visited upon men:

321 *a* What should I tel the *woondrous flames that in the skyes appeere,* (p. 156)
More bright than day? & Locusts grim like cloudes the Sun to hide,
And tender corne with greedy iawes, to spoile on euerie side?
b How many *cities* wofull *plague,* and piteous famine sore,
Hath quite depriued of Citizens? how many places more,
Are almost spoiled and perished, with floodes which rage and rore?
c Alas *how iustly now doth God plague vs* in sundry case?
What mischief do we not commit? what iustice is in place?

The "woondrous flames" are another reference to the comets, here thought of as a portent accompanying the plagues of locusts and plagues of disease. In *King Lear,* the language of 321*c* is reflected in Edgar's comment on his father's suffering:

The gods are just, and of our pleasant vices,
Make instruments *to plague us.* (V. iii. 170-171)

Earlier, disguised as Mad Tom, he is addressed by his father:

Here, take this purse, thou whom *the heavens' plagues*
Have humbled to all strokes. (IV. i. 67-68)

Lear, at the mock trial, exclaims:

Now, all the *plagues* that in the pendulous air
Hang fated o'er men's faults light on thy daughters. (III. iv. 69-70)

The connection of the stars with "plagues" appears in *Love's Labour's Lost* in Biron's remark when his deception is detected: "Thus *pour the stars down plagues* for perjury" (V. ii. 394). Timon uses a similar image, attributing plagues of disease to the influence of the stars. He addresses Alcibiades, who is marching against Athens:

> Be as a *planetary plague* when Jove
> Will o'er some high-vic'd city hang his poison
> In the sick air. (IV. iii. 108-110)

The city and plague in conjunction may be indebted to 321*b*. The wicked or "high-vic'd" city is presumably punished for its vices by God (or Jove), reflecting the sentiment of 321*c*.

As Shakespeare uses the stars, the comets are omens of approaching disaster, while the planets and other stars are the actual instruments of good or ill fortune. This distinction is evident in the contrast between the comets and the "bad revolting stars" of the quotation already given from *1 Henry VI*. The image is the same as that in *Troilus and Cressida,* when Ulysses describes attendant plagues "when the planets In evil mixture to disorder wander" through a refusal to obey their chief, the Sun (I. iii. 95). The technical name for the planets, *stella erratica,* is explained by Palingenius in this line:

322 Seuen planets thus there are, that Grekes as Wandring starres do call. (p. 206)

The "wandring stars" appear again on p. 223, with Googe's note:

323 The seauen Planets or seauen *wandring stars.*

An understanding of this phrase serves to explain Hamlet's description of Laertes' ostentatious grief beside Ophelia's grave:

> What is he whose grief
> Bears such an emphasis, whose phrase of sorrow
> Conjures the *wand'ring stars* and makes them stand
> Like wonder-wounded hearers? (V. i. 277-280)

The phrase means that Laertes' outcry would make the planets stand still; and, since the Sun and the Moon were regarded as planets, there is a probable allusion to Joshua's making them stand still (Josh. 10:13). Hamlet's words are an ironic description of Laertes' voluble grief.

While I have chosen only such passages as seem indebted to the *Zodiake,* these instances will show how extensively Shakespeare used the stars as agents in human affairs. They strengthen the note of fate and destiny, which is evident in most of his work.

In *King John,* the plagues poured down from above are assigned a different origin by Faulconbridge:

Now, by my life, this day grows wondrous hot.
Some *airy devil* hovers in the sky
And pours down *mischief.* (III. ii. 1-3)

Here he puns on the word "hot," referring both to the heat of the sun and to the heat of battle. The image of the "airy devil" is drawn from Palingenius' description of Sarcotheus, or Lucifer, who dwells between the earth and the moon, having been imprisoned in a cloud by the archangel Michael:

324 *a* But now behold the middle parts, that *in the ayre* doth lye, (p. 167)
And there Sarcotheus see, aboue the rest a King most hie, (p. 168)
And of them all most *mischiefous.* The other Kinges that bee,
Doe feare and also worship him, the power and rule hath hee
b Of all the *deuils* in the world, *from whom the mischefs all*
Doe flow as from a poynt: and as the Beames from Phoebus fall. . . .
c And he that guide of light
Was once, and called Lucifer, loues now to walke by night,
And darknesse best of all esteemes, and leades with him his sprights,
And *bugges and goblins* grimme of hell and such deformed sights.
d Sometimes by day when as he ioynes a troupe of armed knaues,
And *strawes with bloudy corses fieldes,* or drowneth ships in waues,
Or when such *mischiefe* great he works: Then comes he forth by light
e But close, and sendes abroad his men in secret priuie plight,
Which moues the harts of wicked men, and them with furie fils,
And secretly with silent voice, persuades their mindes to yls.

The first line locates Sarcotheus' home "in the ayre." Two pages earlier, he and his fellows are described as "Aierie Kings." These instances sufficiently explain the sense of Faulconbridge's reference to an "airy devil," i.e., a devil whose home is in the air. One of the "mischiefs" that he works is to strew the field with bloody corpses

(324*d*), and all "mischiefs" flow from him. Again on p. 148 the devil is described as a purveyor of mischief. Both the words and the circumstances of their use suggest the *Zodiake* as the probable source.

The "bugges and goblins" of 324*c* may have provided Hamlet with his humorous phrase for the pompous style of the King's letter to England (V. ii. 22).

The influence of Lucifer's followers, as described in 324*e*, seems to be reflected in Lady Macbeth's speech upon receiving her husband's letter:

> Come, you spirits
> That tend on mortal thoughts, unsex me here,
> And fill me from the crown to the toe top-full
> Of direst cruelty. . . . Come to my woman's breasts,
> And take my milk for gall, you murd'ring ministers,
> Wherever in your sightless substances
> You wait on nature's *mischief!* Come, thick night,
> And pall thee in the dunnest smoke of hell. . . . (I. v. 41-52)

The "dunnest smoke of hell" seems to be a reminiscence of Rev. 9:2:

325 And he opened the bottomless pit, and there arose the smoke of the pit as the smoke of a great furnace: and the sun and the air were darkened by the reason of the smoke of the pit. (G)

In this chapter we have considered the influences that pour down upon men from the sky: influences from the stars, and influences from the spirits. So vast a subject cannot receive complete treatment in a small space, and we have been concerned primarily with that portion of it which Shakespeare derived from *The Zodiake of Life*. That portion was considerable, as shown by the phrases and images which he used.

Chapter 20

Manners Maketh Man

BESIDES EXPRESSING HIS views on philosophic and scientific subjects, Palingenius has much good advice to offer on manners and personal conduct. This kind of writing appears at times in Shakespeare, the most notable instance being Polonius' advice to Laertes, in *Hamlet,* I. iii. 58-80. Though it is difficult to assign platitudes to a definite source, certain of Polonius' lines are apparently echoed from Palingenius' longest passage of the kind, which follows:

326 *a* But here it comes in question, if by any meanes we can (p. 58)
Procure the loue of euere chone[1], the good and euill man.
b For loue in many partes disperste, is weaker euery howre:
In fewe of greater force it is, in two of greatest powre.
Deuided thus in many partes it vanisheth away:
Who byddes seeke not to many mates, doe therefore truely saye.
For harde it is to liue among so great a companie:
With them as it doth frendes become, eke conuersant to be.
c For fixed fayth denyes her selfe, with many for to dwell. . . .
Lyke as therefore, thou canst not loue so many feruently:
So, canst thou not of such a sort, be loued faithfully.
For who so loueth not for troth, is worthy of no loue.
d A ciuil common loue there is, wherewith it doth behoue,
The common sorte to loue, with which eche good, and euill man,
We ought assuredly to loue: which is perfourmed than,
When as we no mans hurt procure by wordes, or else by actes,
When as we leade our lyfe that none may wel controul our factes.[2]
When we to all men curteouse be, and eke with frendly face:
Doe them salute with honors due, and praysing them imbrace.
e But yet, at first it doth behoue with fewe to leade thy life,
If thou doste seeke in peace to liue, and flye from foolyshe strife. . . .
f But if, sometime it doth thee please the company to take
Of tag and rag, and neighbor John, let tongue in silence dwell:
g And take good heede what thing thou saist, and alwayes harken well. (p. 59)
And seldome speake, it is the signe of one, whose head is light
To much to prate, he eft offendes that so doth wordes recite.
h But such as rare and wysely speake, deserue the chiefest praise:
And in the prudent mouth it is a goodly gift alwayes.
i Speake yll of none behind their backe, ne yet before their face:

[1] *euere chone.* Every one.
[2] *controul our factes.* Reprove our deeds.

Let this thy chiefest warning bee, and rule of chiefest place.
j Nor prate not thou to no intent, nor ydle wordes let fall:
For then shall eche man laugh at thee, and eke a foole thee call.
k If thou shalt aunswere any man, or if thou question finde:
Before thou speakst in any case, determyn in thy minde.
l For when it once is fledde from thee, thou canst it not restraine:
The worde that once is flowne abrode cannot come home againe.
m A goodly thing also it is, in talke to tell sometime,
The pithy sense of aged sawes, and auncient poets rime.
And now and then examples founde in worthy stories olde,
Do giue the talke a greater grace, if they allude so tolde.
n Alwayes therefore, it needefull is on diuers bookes to reede:
And, as the Bees now there now here, on sondry floures to feede.
o Expell thou anger farre from thee, away with pride, that elfe:
Such kinde of men cannot be loud,[3] and alwayes shewe thy selfe
Of gentle minde, and lowly eke, so shalt thou all men please:
p If any man thy hurt procure, proue thou, hym to appease
Rather with Wit, than furious moode. To Wit doth Strength giue place. . . .
Wit all things rules with aide of force, to threaten much wyth crackes,[4]
Is cowardes gwise, & womens strength; to men belongeth factes.
q The wyse man doth dissemble hurt, the valeant prates no whitte,
But when he sees the time, then dare he doe that shall seeme fytte.
r First take good heede that none thee hurt, and if by iniury
Thou harmed art, when thou seest time reuenge it rightfully.
s If thou canst not, let griefe a while within thy heart remaine,
Least that by foolishe bosting wordes, thou maist more harm sustaine.
Tys naughty playing with edged tooles. The wyseman will refraine,
And spie hys time, and eke geue place his foe with wordes to traine[5] (p. 60)
That pleasant seme, and fawnings eke till he him bring to snare. . . .
t Wheresoeuer thou remainst, let not thy mouth be stretcht to wide,
With laughings loude, but when nede is then laugh thou moderatly:
It doth declare a simple wit to laugh excessiuely.
u And on the other side, it is not fyt for any man
Alwayes in dumps to be, therfore flie thou them now and than.
The middle kepe, there vertue sits, no Iester would I thee,
And yet, if that thou canst, I would that pleasant thou shouldst bee.

In Polonius' speech, the borrowings do not follow the order of the original. His first precept, "Give thy thoughts no tongue," seems to reflect 326*f*, "let tongue in silence dwell." The next line, "Nor any unproportion'd thought his act," has a general resem-

[3] *loud*. Loved.
[4] *crackes*. Boasts.
[5] *traine*. Entrap.

blance to *326q,* the advice to keep silent and act only in accordance with a careful plan. Polonius' next lines read:

> Be thou familiar but by no means vulgar.
> The friends thou hast, and their adoption tried,
> Grapple them to thy soul with hoops of steel;
> But do not dull thy palm with entertainment
> Of each new-hatch'd, unfledg'd comrade.

These lines repeat the advice of *326b, c* that one should not try to be close friends with all men, but rather with the few to whom "fixed fayth" is possible. One should choose his friends with care and not try to be on intimate terms too quickly with too many. This was essentially the error made by Timon in his choice of friends.

Polonius next says:

> Beware
> Of entrance to a quarrel; but being in,
> Bear't that the opposed may beware of thee.

This reflects *326r,* the advice to avoid injuries if possible and to avenge them if one cannot avoid them.

Again, Polonius says:

> Give every man thine ear, but few thy voice;
> Take each man's censure, but reserve thy judgment.

The first line reflects *326g:* "alwayes harken well. And seldome speake." The word "censure" is used to mean "opinion," and the line apparently reflects Palingenius' advice to avoid criticism of others (*326i*) and to speak only after due consideration (*326g,k*).

Professor Kittredge, in his edition of *Hamlet,* notes parallels to Polonius' speech in Lyly's *Euphues* and in Hoby's translation of Castiglione's *The Courtier*. He points out a particularly significant parallel to the line, "For the apparel oft proclaims the man." In Fynes Moryson's *Itinerary* (1599) occurs the sentence:[6]

327 The Wise man hath taught vs, that *the apparell* in some sort *shewes the man.*

Professor Baldwin (*Small Latine,* II. 611) adds a parallel for the lines:

[6] Pt. II, bk. i, ch. 1; p. 46 in 1617 ed.

Neither a borrower nor a lender be,
For loan oft loses both itself and friend.

He points out a proverb from Seneca to the same effect:

328 Amico mutuam roganti me pecuniam si dedero, & amicum, & pecuniam perdo.

Polonius' list of truisms concludes with one of the most striking utterances in Shakespeare:

To thine own self be true,
And it must follow, as the night the day,
Thou canst not then be false to any man.

Here again is shown the influence of adaptation in one of Shakespeare's finest phrases. The sentiment is not new, but it is here stated better than it had ever been stated before. Its essence is the belief that the highest form of truth to oneself will result in a standard of conduct which requires justice to all others. In Plato's *Gorgias* Socrates utters a similar sentiment, picturing the unjust man as discordant within himself and opposed to himself; he should be true to himself even if opposed by the whole world (482 C). A somewhat similar passage occurs in Marcus Aurelius' *Meditations,* IX. 1-4. The idea recurs in *The French Academie* (Pt. I, ch. 37):

329 Justice (saith Cicero) is a constant and perpetuall wil and desire to giue to euery one his right. Shee is the proper vertue of a noble minded man, because she is profitable to others, but to hir selfe fruitlesse, laborious, and perilous. Yea that man onely may be called iust, that profiteth as manie as he can, but hurteth none, *that is* alwaies *at agreement within himselfe,* and is *a friend* to God, to men, and *to himselfe.*

All these passages involve the idea that justice is the condition natural to the highest portion of man's nature, that injustice to others violates this highest portion of oneself, and that the unjust man is consequently false to himself. Shakespeare's contribution is aptness of expression, not originality of idea.

Other echoes of Q. 326 appear in *Hamlet.* At the beginning of the play within the play, the King addresses Hamlet:

King. How fares our cousin Hamlet?
Ham. Excellent, i'faith,—of the chameleon's dish. I eat the air, promise-cramm'd. You cannot feed capons so.

King. I have nothing with this answer, Hamlet; these words are not mine.
Ham. No, nor mine now. (III. ii. 97-103)

Hamlet's final line means that the words, once uttered, no longer belong to the speaker of them, for he cannot call them back. In this statement he reflects the sentiments of *326l.*

One of the clearest echoes of Q. 326 occurs in *As You Like It,* in Jaques' speech on the Seven Ages. The fifth age is represented by the Justice,

Full of wise saws and modern instances. (II. vii. 156)

To the Elizabethans "modern" meant trite or overused. The phrase is thus a close parallel to the "pithy sense of aged sawes" and the "examples founde in worthy stories olde" which are recommended as aids to speech-making (*326m*).

Q. 326 has also furnished some hints for the character of Gratiano in *The Merchant of Venice.* Bassanio's remark, "Gratiano speaks an infinite deal of nothing" (I. i. 114), reflects *326j,* "Nor prate not thou to no intent." The next words, that men will "laugh at thee, and eke a foole thee call," are perhaps recalled by Gratiano's own lines:

Let me play the fool!
With mirth and laughter let old wrinkles come. (I. i. 79-80)

In the remainder of his speech he mocks at those who keep silent to gain a reputation for wisdom:

With purpose to be dress'd in an opinion
Of wisdom, gravity, profound conceit,
As who should say, 'I am Sir Oracle,
And when I ope my lips let no dog bark!' (I. i. 91-94)

He is deriding the kind of advice found in the *Zodiake* (*326f-l*), with its emphasis upon gravity, silence, and the good opinions of others.

Gratiano's loud laughter recalls *326t,* which probably suggested Bassanio's words before the departure for Belmont:

But hear thee, Gratiano;
Thou art too wild, too rude and bold of voice;

> Parts that become thee happily enough
> And in such eyes as ours appear not faults;
> But where thou art not known, why, there they show
> Something too liberal. Pray thee, take pain
> To allay with some cold drops of modesty
> Thy skipping spirit, lest through thy wild behaviour
> I be misconster'd in the place I go to,
> And lose my hopes. (II. ii. 189-198)

The advice to observe moderation in mirth reflects 326*u*.

The same passages have provided some hints for the character of Falstaff. In banishing him, Henry V says:

> How ill white hairs become a *fool* and *jester* . . .
> Reply not to me with a *fool-born jest*. (*2 Henry IV*, V. v. 52, 59)

The "fool" comes from 326*j*, the "jester" from 326*u*. These last lines are also reflected in Prince John's words a moment later:

> I like this fair proceeding of the King's.
> He hath intent his wonted followers
> Shall all be very well provided for;
> But all are banish'd *till their conversations*
> *Appear more wise and modest to the world*. (V. v. 103-107)

The similarity of these lines to Bassanio's speech is quite evident. Apparently they are drawn from the same sources.

The advice to limit one's friends and not to seek intimate friendship with "the common sorte" appears in Henry IV's contrast of himself with Richard II:

> Had I so lavish of my presence been,
> So common-hackney'd in the eyes of men,
> So stale and cheap to vulgar company,
> Opinion, that did help me to the crown,
> Had still kept loyal to possession
> And left me in reputeless banishment,
> A fellow of no mark nor likelihood. . . .
> The skipping King, he ambled up and down
> With shallow jesters and rash bavin wits,
> Soon kindled and soon burnt; carded his state,
> Mingled his royalty with cap'ring fools . . .
> Grew a companion to the common streets,
> Enfeoff'd himself to popularity. (*1 Henry IV*, III. ii. 39-69)

This reflects the advice of 326 *a-f* and resembles Polonius' advice to the same effect. The King is warning his son against making a mistake like that of Richard.

In the earlier play *Richard II,* when Richard realizes that he is at Bolingbroke's mercy, he asks Aumerle whether he shall send defiance. Aumerle responds:

> No, good my lord; let's fight with gentle words
> Till time lend friends, and friends their helpful swords.
> (III. iii. 131-132)

This counsel is borrowed from *326s,* the advice to control one's grief, avoid rash words, pretend friendship until a chance comes for revenge. To "fight with gentle words" is borrowed from "his foe with words to traine That pleasant seme."

In this chapter we have seen how Palingenius' advice on personal conduct is used by Shakespeare. The dramatist is not so didactic as his model and uses some of Palingenius' recommendations for purposes of humor. In other instances they have contributed to the portrayal of character. They make yet more impressive the remarkable array of themes and phrases for which Shakespeare seems indebted to *The Zodiake of Life.*

Chapter 21

The Golden World

IN *As You Like It,* the life of the exiles in the Forest of Arden is pictured as one of idyllic simplicity. Charles the Wrestler is describing the exiled Duke and his followers:

> They say many young gentlemen flock to him every day, and fleet the time carelessly, as they did in *the golden world.* (I. i. 123-125)

This phrase is used parenthetically on p. 30 of the *Zodiake:*

330 When Saturne rulde *the golden world.*

A similar reference occurs at the end of a passage describing the joys of peace. Googe has a marginal note "The Golden Worlde" beside these lines:

331 Such times did flow when Saturn ruld his Empire here alone: (p. 52)
(O worthy *age* more worth than *Gold*).

These instances show where Shakespeare probably found his phrase—though the *Oxford English Dictionary* gives occasional earlier uses of it—and also show that he has in mind the Golden Age, as described in Ovid's *Metamorphoses,* I. 89-112, the age in which Saturn ruled before his dethronement by Jupiter. Professor Baldwin (*Literary Genetics,* pp. 68-69) quotes Ovid's description and adds Golding's translation. It is worth noting that Golding does not use the phrase "golden world" in this description but does use it in XV. 104, when Pythagoras refers back to the time known as the Golden Age.

Q. 331 is the conclusion of a description of peace and its joys, as contrasted with the terrors of war and violence. Charles' words "fleet the time carelessly" may have been suggested by these lines descriptive of "The Golden Worlde":

332 *a* Assured *Peace,* the worthiest is of all things here we see: (p. 51)
In time of *peace* do all things growe, and all things liuely be.
b Then liue men safe, in safety eke the trauayling wight he stands,
And takes his iourney voyde of harme, and scapes the robbers handes.
c Then buzzing Bees in hiues be kept by good aduise and care,

And beastes in pastures fat are fed, the ground is torne wyth share,
And yeldeth *fayre encrease* in tyme, then *plenty* beares the
sway: (p. 52)
d In bread, and mylke, and holsom oyles, then euery where they play,
The sounding shaume doth them prouoke to daunce, the Thyas round.

Googe's marginal note explains that the "Thyas round" is "a kinde of *stately* daunce in measure, dedicated to Bacchus." This passage may also be reflected in Edward IV's speech after his coronation:

Now I am seated as my soul delights,
Having my country's *peace* and brothers' loves. . . .
And now what rests but that we spend the time
With *stately* triumphs, mirthful comic shows,
Such as befits the pleasure of the court. (*3 Henry VI,* V. vii. 35-44)

The same passage is reflected more clearly in Richmond's speech at the end of *Richard III*:

Enrich the time to come with smooth-fac'd *Peace,*
With smiling *Plenty* and *fair* prosperous days! . . .
Let them not live to taste this land's *increase*
That would with treason wound this *fair* land's *peace.* (V. v. 33-39)

Again it is echoed, at the end of another war, in Burgundy's words in *Henry V:*

Why that the naked, poor, and mangled *Peace,*
Dear nurse of arts, *plenties,* and joyful births,
Should not in this best garden of the world,
Our fertile France, put up her lovely visage. (V. ii. 34-37)

The succeeding lines carry out the image of the "unweeded garden" (*supra,* p. 194). They also use the imagery of Q. 332 in reverse, stating what France has not had because she has not had peace. The untilled land is full of weeds, "while that the coulter rusts That should deracinate such savagery" (46-47). This seems to reflect 332*c,* "the ground is torne wyth share," and an associated passage on the "golden world" which provides the word "coulter":

333 For if the stepes of reason, all should treade in nerest wyse (p. 142)
Then peace on earth should alwaies dwell, and Mars his bloudy hand
Such slaughters nor such cryes should cause & townes & walles
should stand
And weapons framed first in hell by fiendish furyes wrought,
Should tille the field, with good exchange to *share and cultre*
brought.

> Then bees, and Cattell swarming thicke and riches of the fielde,
> Vnto the happy husbandman, a great *increase* should yelde.
> *The golden world* should then returne, and eke one place containe
> Bothe Man, & God, who would vouchsafe before our eyes to raine.

Here again the "golden world" is associated with the joys of peace. In his statement that weapons of war should be changed to "share and cultre" Palingenius echoes a passage from the Bible:

334 And he [God] shall judge many people . . . so that of their swords they shall make ploughshares, and scythes of their spears; one people shall not lift up a sword against another, yea they shall no more learn to fight. (Micah 4:3) (B)

The phrase also suggests that Burgundy has associated the two "golden world" passages from the *Zodiake* on the "share" and the "share and cultre," adopting "cultre" or "coulter" as better than "share" for the meter of his lines.

Palingenius' statement that in the "golden world" yet to come God will return to earth and rule in the presence of men is a reminiscence of the celebrated prophecy in Virgil's Fourth Eclogue:

335 Magnus ab integro saeclorum nascitur ordo.
Iam redit et Virgo; redeunt Saturnia regna;
Iam nova progenies caelo demittitur alto. (5-7)

Since it is the reign of Saturn, it is necessarily the Golden Age that will return. Throughout the medieval period, these lines were taken as an inspired prophecy of Christ's coming and of peace on earth during the period of the Millennium. Possibly some of this background was in Shakespeare's mind in his several passages on peace.

The Golden Age is used in *The Tempest* by Gonzalo, the wise and virtuous counselor, in explaining how he would rule:

> Had I plantation of this isle, my lord. . .
> And were the king on't, what would I do? . . .
> I' the commonwealth I would by contraries
> Execute all things; for no kind of traffic
> Would I admit; no name of magistrate;
> Letters should not be known; riches, poverty,
> And use of service, none; contract, succession,
> Bourn, bound of land, tilth, vineyard, none;
> No use of metal, corn, or wine, or oil;
> No occupation; all men idle, all;

And women too, but innocent and pure;
No sovereignty . . . . (II. i. 143-156)

It has long been recognized that this part of his speech is indebted to Montaigne's essay "Of the Caniballes," in Florio's translation. He is comparing the "natural" goodness of the Brazilian Indians with the ideal commonwealths of Lycurgus and Plato:

336 The lawes of nature doe yet command them. . . . For me seemeth that what in those nations we see by experience, doth not only *exceed* all the pictures wherewith licentious Poesie hath proudly imbellished *the golden age,* and all her quaint inventions to faine a happy condition of man, but also the conception and desire of Philosophy. . . . It is a nation, would I answer Plato, that hath *no kinde of traffike, no knowledge of Letters,* no intelligence of numbers, *no name of magistrate,* nor of politike superioritie; *no use of service, of riches or of povertie; no contracts, no successions,* no partitions, *no occupation but idle;* no respect of kinred, but common, no apparell but naturall, no manuring of lands, *no use of wine, corne, or mettle.* The very words that import lying, falshood, treason, dissimulations, covetousnes, envie, detraction, and pardon, were never heard of amongst them.
(*Essais,* I. xxx; p. 164)

The remainder of Gonzalo's speech reflects Ovid's description of the Golden Age in that there are no weapons of violence and no tilling of the soil, but an enjoyment of the natural fruits of the earth:

All things in common nature should produce
Without *sweat* or endeavour: treason, felony,
Sword, pike, knife, gun, or need of any engine,
Would I not have; but nature should bring forth,
Of it own kind, all foison, all abundance,
To feed my innocent people. . . .
I would with such perfection govern, sir,
T' *excel the golden age.* (II. i. 158-168)

It should be observed that the connection of the Indians with the Golden Age had already been made by Montaigne, and that Shakespeare's "excel the golden age" stems from Montaigne's "exceed. . . the golden age." The fact that Montaigne is comparing the "natural" condition of the Indians with the ideal states envisioned by the philosophers causes a certain confusion in Gonzalo's speech. Sebastian humorously notes the inconsistency: Gonzalo would allow "no sovereignty;—Yet he would be king on't" (156). It seems inconsistent to govern by abolishing government.

Shakespeare clearly recalls Ovid's account, but his use of "sweat" in line 159 seems to be a reminiscence of God's curse upon Adam:

337 In the *sweat* of thy face shalt thou eat bread. (Gen. 3:19) (G)

This may show an awareness of the identification of Ovid's Golden Age with the biblical description of life in the Garden of Eden. Arthur Golding makes this identification in line 470 of his *Epistle* prefixed to his translation of the *Metamorphoses.*

In Gonzalo's lines, Shakespeare does envision the probability that a wise ruler will bring about a happy people. This power of the wise ruler to produce a Golden Age is perhaps recalled from Palingenius' description of "wise and politike" men, who are discussed just after the contemplative men and just before the "Machiuales":

338 Discretest men, the seconde sorte, and good we them define, (p. 169)
Yet lene they some thing to the world, as fit to beare the sway
In cities and in common wealthes, and banners to display,
And faith and iustice eke they loue, and vertuous seeke to bee:
Yet from the pleasures of the worlde they are not fully free.
To whom if God at any time the rule and empire giue,
Then comes *the Golden times* againe, and Vertue here to liue, (p. 170)
And Iustice to the earth returnes, and Peace doth beare the sway,
And vice with punishment seuere is forced for to stay.

Here again is the prophecy of the return of justice and peace in the "Golden times" or the Saturnian reign. Palingenius feels that the men devoted wholly to contemplation are too unworldly to make good rulers. The ideal governors are men with some degree of worldliness but not enough to make them act from selfish motives. They are devoted to justice and virtue but know enough of the world to understand treachery and self-seeking. They might be called practical idealists. It seems that this account of the wise governor and the Golden Age which flourishes under his rule may have contributed something to Gonzalo's speech. It also emerges in Prospero's admission that his complete lack of the necessary worldliness had formerly made him an ineffective ruler (I. ii. 89-97).

On this note Shakespeare ended his period of creative activity. Whether or not it was his last play, *The Tempest* seems to have been the final word in the expression of his view of life. His weariness of strife and hypocrisy, his longing for peace and simplicity, reflect the perennial desire of all mankind found in an even greater message: "Peace on earth, good will toward men."

Chapter 22

Idea, Image, and Word

THE COMPLETION OF THIS study suggests certain tentative conclusions about poetic art in general and Shakespeare's art in particular. The use of imagery is only one of several factors in poetic art, but it is a highly important factor and is our especial concern in this book.

For purposes of analysis, we may name the stages in the coining of a poetic phrase as the *idea,* the *image,* and the *word,* though in practice it is scarcely possible to separate them. When a poet seeks to convey ideas to his readers, the ideas themselves are seldom original. His usual function is not to originate but to intensify, to realize more intensely the essence of an idea, to perceive its emotional significance, to bring it into sharper focus, to startle the reader from indifference into acceptance. Poetic "creation" is not creation *ex nihilo;* it is the act of reshaping materials already at hand.

In seeking to reshape an idea for his readers, the poet will use certain images. Some of these he may invent himself or draw from his own experience; others will be drawn from his reading. In the latter case he is likely to use some of the words in which his predecessor expressed the image. We may assume that this is often an unconscious process, not an intentional copying, that the image and the word have become identified in the poet's memory and naturally emerge together. Indeed, in the absence of a conscious attempt to avoid it, such repetition of significant words is almost inevitable.

This joint recollection of image and words appears in the technique of adaptation, whether from one or from several sources. The poet's art is shown in what he does with the words: stripping away nonessential verbiage, placing the words in fresh contexts, fitting them into a rhythmic pattern, clarifying and sharpening their emotional connotations. Like a convex lens, he gathers to himself diffused streams of light and centers them into one burning phrase.

This gift for arriving at the essential phrase reflects the clarity and depth of the poet's own mind and marks the highest reaches of the poetic art.

The most subtle elements in this transmission of words are the emotional connotations just mentioned. For full appreciation, these overtones of words require an emotional receptivity in the reader, a certain harmony of feeling between himself and the author, a perception of his own nebulous sentiments more clearly expressed in the words of another. As his emotions fluctuate, he may become less responsive to such connotations. On the other hand, a reader may be so attuned to the connotations which he receives that he feels them more deeply than the author did. They become more clearly and fully realized in the reader's consciousness; if he happens to be a poet himself, this fuller realization may appear in his own verse and be transmitted to his own readers. Something of this kind often happens through the technique of adaptation. I think it happened when Shakespeare read and used the work of Palingenius.

From the evidence in this book, it should be clear that much of Shakespeare's imagery was derived from earlier authors and that some of their words survive in his expression of the images. Almost invariably the Shakespearean phrase is more concise, more direct, and more intense than its sources. We have seen this process of recollection and transformation at work in the noblest passages of his verse; in fact, the more intense his emotion, the more active are his powers of recollective association. Like an electric transformer, he steps up the voltage on the currents of thought that reach him and sends them forth with increased intensity.

Perhaps this study will have suggested some revaluations of such words as *original* and *creative* when applied to poets. Clever inventiveness is not the sole measure of poetic genius. To clarify, sharpen, enrich, and transfer the thoughts of others is an achievement of equal value. Shakespeare had both abilities and used both for the production of profoundly emotional utterances as yet unsurpassed by man.

Index

(References, themes, and figurative expressions)